MW00636172

To David,

Here's to the Zebras!

See you at the ballpark,

Mark Cryon
7/16/08

CRADLE
OF THE
GAME

*Baseball & Ballparks
in North Carolina*

MARK CRYAN

a **August Publications**
Minneapolis, Minnesota

BASEBALL IN THE STATES
NORTH CAROLINA

Cradle of the Game

August Publications
527 Marquette Av., Suite 800
Minneapolis, MN 55402
612.343.5207
augustpublications.com

ISBN 978-0-9752706-3-9

9 8 7 6 5 4 3 2 1

Editor: Jim Robins
Designer (cover and interior): Natalie Nowytski

Table of Contents

Table of Contents (continued)

FOREWORD:

MILES WOLFF

Baseball — it's been woven into the fabric of North Carolina for well over a century. In that time the state has undergone a remarkable transition from a poor rural state with textile mills and tobacco farms to a modern economy of high-tech industry and growing cities. And yet, during this transformation, baseball has been a constant — part of the tapestry that makes this state unique.

Mark Cryan's book will give the reader a great picture of baseball in the Tar Heel State. He is well-equipped to paint this picture, having been part of the baseball scene as an operator of several minor-league and summer-college teams over many years. Other states in the United States have strong baseball traditions, but North Carolina's ties are unique, and Mark's volume points out North Carolina's special place in the baseball universe.

Of course, North Carolina has always been significant in the world of minor-league baseball. Currently, the state has every level of minor-league baseball, from Class AAA down to rookie ball. North Carolina had the most minor-league teams (45) in one year (1950) in the history of the game when it appeared as if every hamlet and crossroads in the state rooted for its hometown team. For a decade or so, North Carolina was the head office of minor-league baseball. Over the years some 73 cities in the state have been home to minor-league clubs, and over 20 leagues at one point have hosted teams from the state. The Tobacco State League and the Blue Ridge League are long gone, but the Carolina League has been in continuous operation for over 60 years.

College baseball is special in North Carolina, and some of the best college teams in the country play in the state. One of the earliest College World Series champions was the Wake Forest Demon Deacons back in 1951. But it is not just Division I baseball. Dozens of teams play great baseball at Division II or III, and junior-college baseball has a strong presence in the state. There are outstanding high-school programs in the state, and American Legion baseball has been a force with Gastonia winning the National Legion Championship back in 1948. One of the historic names in minor-league baseball, the Coastal Plain League, has been revived in recent years as one of the top summer college leagues in the country.

But baseball boils down to people, and great names in baseball have come from the Land of the Long Leaf Pine. Enos "Country" Slaughter and Jim "Catfish" Hunter learned their baseball growing up in the state, while "Trader Jack" McKeon and Grady Little came to play in the state, loved it, and never left. Mythical movie heroes Crash Davis and Moonlight Graham were real North Carolina people. Davis learned his baseball playing Legion ball in Gastonia, went to Duke under the legendary Jack Coombs, had his cup of coffee with the Philadelphia A's, and then became a local hero in the Carolina League. And Archie "Moonlight" Graham played his baseball at the University of North Carolina, went to the New York Giants, never got his at-bat, and became a doctor in Minnesota. Buck Leonard, Wee Willie Duke, Gaylord Perry, Jim Perry, Turkey Tyson, Bunn Hearn, Tony Cloninger—all names that make up the thousands of famous and not-so-famous North Carolinians who have played and influenced the game.

Travel the state and you will find ballparks in all sections. This book has pictures of many of the great old parks and modern new ones. Greensboro has a great new stadium, but proud, old World War I Memorial Stadium remains and is still in use. Travel to the eastern part of the state and discover a quant old park in Edenton or drive over to Tarboro and see the old Coastal Plain League park. From Asheville to Wilmington to Winston-Salem to Chapel Hill, baseball stadiums dot the landscape.

Baseball is meant to be enjoyed, so enjoy this book. And if you are not from North Carolina, come and visit and discover what makes baseball special in the state.

— *Miles Wolff*

INTRODUCTION:

The Cradle of the Game

"See you at the yard, Meat!"

— *Crash Davis (Kevin Costner) to Nuke LaLoosh (Tim Robbins)*
in the classic movie Bull Durham

I hope this book helps you enjoy the national treasure that is minor-league baseball in North Carolina. With a rich history that can be traced back to the turn of the century, sports fans in the Tar Heel State were watching organized professional baseball as early as 1901, less than 20 years after America's first professional baseball leagues were founded.

Today, crowds continue to gather to see history-rich teams like the Asheville Tourists and the Durham Bulls play in beautiful, modern facilities, and cheer on amateur teams like the Edenton Steamers and Wilson Tobs on home fields built before many of their fans were born.

Although North Carolina doesn't have a Major League team, the path to the big leagues has certainly carried many players down Tobacco Road. A quick listing of North Carolina's native and visiting ballplayers and their teams reads like a compilation of All-Star Game rosters: Jim "Catfish" Hunter (a native of Hertford); Manny Ramirez, Jim Thome, and Bartolo Colon (Burlington Indians, Kinston Indians); Luis Tiant (Alamance Indians); Andruw Jones and David Justice (Durham Bulls); Enos "Country" Slaughter (a native of Roxboro); Derek Jeter, Don Mattingly, and Bernie Williams (Greensboro Hornets/Bats); and Carl Yastrzemski (Raleigh Capitals). The list goes on and on.

From the beautiful beaches of the Atlantic Coast to the rugged Blue Ridge Mountains, North Carolina prides itself on "having it all," and surely the baseball fans of the region are blessed as well. With affiliated minor-league teams ranging from Rookie classification to Triple-A and with five different minor leagues overlapping, North Carolina has a total of 10 professional teams, nine collegiate-level Coastal Plain League teams, and over a dozen Division I college programs. That's more baseball per capita than just about any state in the nation, and maybe the most baseball-crazy place in the world outside of Latin America.

A traveling fan in North Carolina need never go a night without a cold drink and a scorecard in their hands between March and September.

Fans across the country were introduced to the charms of North Carolina's ballparks in 1987, the year Kevin Costner starred in the movie *Bull Durham* (*see The Movie*), written by a former minor-league ballplayer and filmed entirely in North Carolina. The film became a surprise box-office smash and made the Durham Bulls the country's most famous bush-league team. It also made Durham and North Carolina synonymous with minor-league baseball in the minds of baseball fans across the nation.

It is our hope this volume provides you with enjoyable reading, and the feel and atmosphere of baseball in North Carolina. While the focus is definitely on the minors, we know that a great ballpark is a special place, regardless of whether the baseball is professional or amateur. We also included information on the ballparks of North Carolina's summer-collegiate teams, many of which are former minor-league stadiums. There are also entries for many of the Division I college ballparks in the state, as well as a directory of the college programs.

Of course, we also hope that this book will serve as motivation to visit "the Old North State." It should also guide you in your travels if you are able to visit with us here in North Carolina — the Cradle of the Game.

CHARLOTTE &

1. Asheville

2. Charlotte

3. Gastonia

4. Hickory

5. Kannapolis

6. Salisbury

7. Forest City

SECTION 1

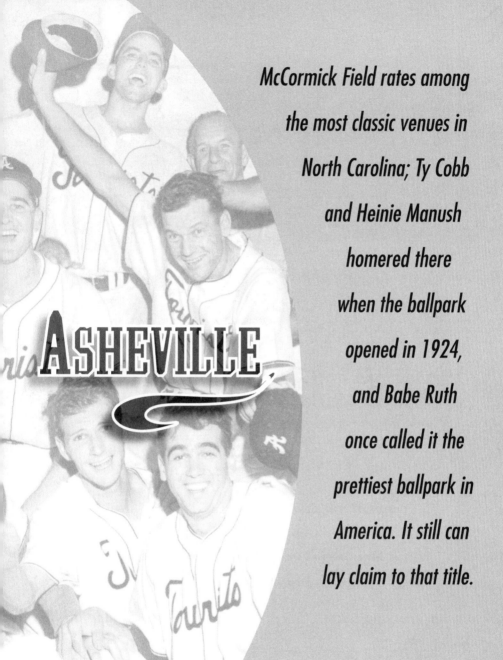

ASHEVILLE

McCormick Field rates among the most classic venues in North Carolina; Ty Cobb and Heinie Manush homered there when the ballpark opened in 1924, and Babe Ruth once called it the prettiest ballpark in America. It still can lay claim to that title.

CHAPTER 1

McCormick Field

Leading Off

Opened: 1924, rebuilt 1992 • **Dimensions:** 326L, 386LC, 320RC, 297R

Capacity: 4,000 • **Current Team:** Asheville Tourists, Class A South Atlantic League

Previous Minor League Teams: Moonshiners, Skylanders, Orioles, and Mountaineers.

Previous Leagues: Southeastern League (1910), Appalachian League (1911-12), North Carolina League (1913-17), original South Atlantic League (1924-30, 1959-63), Piedmont League (1931-32, 1934-42), Tri-States League (1946-55), Southern League (1964-66, 1968-75), Carolina League (1967), Western Carolina League (1976-79, became South Atlantic League)

A Great Place to be "Tourists"

As the nickname *Tourists* indicates, the Asheville area is a popular vacation destination. The largest city in western North Carolina boasts beautiful mountain scenery, fantastic attractions like the Biltmore Estate, and cool summer evenings that are the envy of the rest of the state. Asheville also boasts a rich minor-league baseball history dating back to 1897, when the hometown lads were known as the Moonshiners. Yet, to minor-league baseball fans around the nation, Asheville should best be known as the birthplace of "Thirsty Thursday."

Asheville also has a funky vibe that is equal parts college town, hippie refuge, retirement destination, and outdoor recreation mecca. You'll see all of this played out in microcosm at McCormick Field, a relatively modern ballpark that nonetheless has a classic feel. The current facility opened in 1992 on the same site hosting pro baseball since the opening of the original McCormick Field in 1924. The new grandstand is constructed primarily of brick and concrete, wedged onto a rocky hillside looming over the third-base concourse and the outfield. The surrounding hills encroach so closely and the park is so in tune with its surroundings that it almost seems McCormick Field sprang from the surrounding rocks. The Tourists certainly could not have a more appropriate parent club than their long-time partner, the Colorado Rockies.

The Tourists had new ownership as of the 2006 season, and some very prominent reminders of that transition are on display. One of McCormick Field's old-timey touches was an outfield wall made of thin steel, similar to the corrugated metal

McCormick Field — prior to the 2006 fence renovations

you'd see on tin-roof sheds throughout the country. The advertisements were painted right on this metal, giving the outfield a truly distinctive look. If you pay close attention to scenes in *Bull Durham* featuring Crash Davis "playing out the string" with the Tourists, you'll see the outfield wall was made of the same material back in the mid-1980s, too.

An entirely new outfield wall and scoreboard were constructed for the 2006 season, replacing upwards of 50 standard size signs with fewer than a dozen signs, many of them covering enormous sections of the wall. The rebuilding of the homerun fence, though, retained one of McCormick's quirks. Due to the uneven terrain, the right-field fence is very short (just shy of 300 feet), but its height keeps many balls from leaving the park. The old fence, though, had several gaps, including one on each side of the scoreboard that could turn a routine fly ball into a home run.

While the hill behind the right-field wall obviously couldn't be moved, the new wall offers a little more consistency. The new scoreboard, measuring 42 feet high by 94 feet wide, is estimated to have prevented at least 40 homers in its first year alone compared to the previous configuration. Still, many high fly balls wind up as home runs, suggesting this is good training for a pitcher who aspires to play at the launching pad known as Coors Field in Denver. While the air in Asheville is certainly not as thin as it is in the Mile High City, McCormick Field has some short porches and can be tough on pitchers.

Sponsored 1968 Tourists official program cover.
Image courtesy of the Notre Dame Rare Books collection.

In keeping with the smaller-than-life scenario, the parking at McCormick Field is an issue. The situation at McCormick Field brings to mind the joke told by Durham Bulls staffers from the team's return to the DAP in the early '80s. Asked about their "parking problem," they would respond, "What parking problem? No parking, no problem!" A game at McCormick Field is a wonderful experience, and whem combined with the other attractions the area has to offer it is a must-visit for any baseball trip through the region. Yet, parking remains a major challenge for everyone involved.

The original McCormick Field was built when parking wasn't much of a consideration. The actual stadium parking lots are reminiscent of the tiny lot at the DAP and, just like a tenant in any municipally owned facility, the team will need to rely on their landlord to help them alleviate the problem. It is hoped that the recent transfer of the ballpark's ownership from the county to the city will also contribute to some improvements in this area.

So, come early. Parking on the streets in the blocks below the stadium will be the best bet for most out-of-towners. Some brave souls park in the residential neighborhood behind the outfield wall, but be sure your parking brake is working and your nerve is strong. The streets are steep, and you'll often confront a tight squeeze if you can find a spot.

Majestic columns of McCormick Field

Once you're inside, you'll find a terrific ballpark experience featuring great selections of food and drink, as well the aforementioned "Thirsty Thursdays." On many nights, funnel cakes and a variety of other food items cooked up in the stands and tents on the concourse give the whole place a state-fair kind of smell. If school's in session at UNC-Asheville, you might think there's a fraternity mixer going on in the concourse. Live remotes from area radio stations are also common, and the atmosphere is generally festive.

As for stadium particulars, you'll find brick throughout, and a high concrete roof shelters the upper half of the seating bowl behind home plate. The mountains frame the backdrop on a very dramatic setting, and the unusual field dimensions provide the opportunity for offensive fireworks at any point in the game.

A walk-in souvenir shop located on the first-base side of the concourse has a vast array of souvenir merchandise. The main entrance and ticket offices are located at this end of the concourse, too, and the team offices are above. You'll climb a few stairs to get into the grandstand, although there is a handicapped ramp. Notable by their absence is the lack of luxury boxes. A small press box seems almost like an afterthought, perched at the top of the seating bowl right behind home plate. Other than that, there are simply seats running right up to the back wall of the grandstand. One can only imagine that owner Palace Sports & Entertainment is already studying the feasibility of adding suites to McCormick Field and, if done properly, they should only enhance the overall look of the place. (We should note there is nothing in the works at the present time.)

Of course, the most recent owners of the Tourists – the Michigan-based firm bought the team from longtime owner Woody Kern – represent the latest chapter

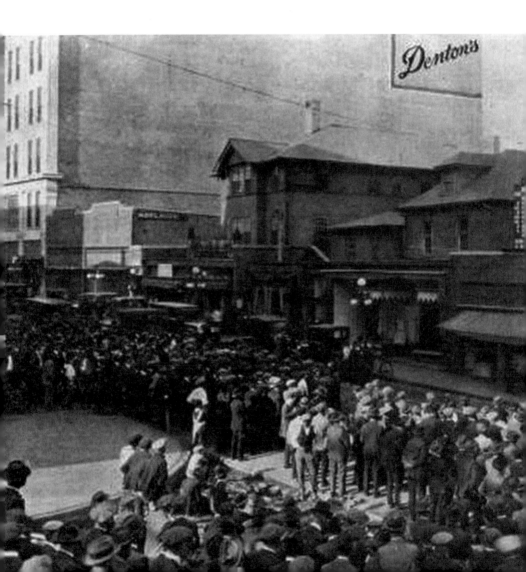

in an extremely long history. As previously mentioned, the earliest team in Asheville was a short-lived outfit named the Moonshiners, who played a few "professional" games as members of the Southeastern League in 1897. The city then went without a professional team for several years.

The Moonshiners called Riverside Park home. This ballpark shared the floodplain across from Riverside Cemetery with a small amusement park. This park hosted pro baseball off and on from 1905 until 1911 and eventually was destroyed by the Great Flood of 1916.

Next up was Oates Park, which served as Asheville's home park from 1911 through 1917. Located at the intersection of Choctaw and McDowell streets, this was said to be where author Thomas Wolfe (*You Can't Go Home Again; Look Homeward, Angel*) first followed the game of baseball. Oates Park is also said to have hosted several

Crowd gathers in 1923 to view the downtown scoreboard.

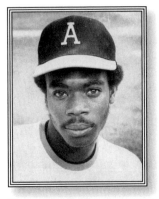

Eddie Murray played for the Tourists in 1975.
Photo courtesy of the Asheville Tourists.

major-league teams in exhibition games in the 'teens and '20s, when they used to barnstorm their way north from spring training. Oates Park, no longer standing, was replaced in 1924 when the original McCormick Field.

Over the early part of the century, Asheville's teams were known as the Skylanders, Mountaineers, and Tourists while competing as members of the reconstituted Southeastern League, as well as the Appalachian, North State, Piedmont, and Tri-States leagues.

An old-style wooden ballpark, McCormick Field opened with an exhibition game pitting the Asheville Skylanders against the Detroit Tigers. In those days, the major-league starters actually played extensively in exhibition games, and two future Hall of Famers — Ty Cobb and Heinie Manush — took advantage of the short fences at the new ballpark and hit homers. They weren't enough, as a crowd of 3,199 saw the local lads defeat the visiting American League power, 18-6. When originally opened, the park also featured a small covered grandstand in the outfield, but this was gone by the mid-1940s. Lights were added in 1940, and the park's first outfield wall wasn't built until several years after it opened.

The ballpark was named after Dr. L.M. McCormick, a pioneering bacteriologist from Asheville who sought to increase awareness about the disease risks associated with houseflies. His campaign, the "Swat That Fly" movement, spread across the nation.

Right field entrance to McCormick
Photo courtesy of the Asheville Tourists.

At the time it was replaced by the current brick and concrete grandstand, McCormick was the oldest wooden-grandstand park still in minor-league use.

The same beautiful setting and mountain air that makes Asheville such a great place to see a game today made the original McCormick a favorite among visitors. The legendary Branch Rickey is said to have been extremely fond of McCormick, and Babe Ruth called it the prettiest park in America.

Great baseball history, a wonderful, modern ballpark with a classic feel, and one of the nicest mountain vacation destinations you could ever want. What are you waiting for?

⏱ Insiders' Tip

Tickets to Tourists games are affordable, and the box seats boast waitress service. This is a great amenity: while food lines move relatively quickly here, where the concessions windows are all located in the concourse behind the grandstand, so you can't see the game while you're waiting in line. Unless you want to people watch on the concourse (which can be very entertaining, particularly on Thursday nights) then get the box seats and use the waitresses. I found them to be quick and friendly.

Thirsty Thursdays

Few minor-league promotions are as well-loved across the country as Thirsty Thursdays. By now, discounted beer is a standard minor-league promotion that nearly every team runs on Thursdays. But did you know the phrase was trademarked in Asheville? While there's no clear evidence who first offered dollar beers on Thursday, the Tourists hold the legal rights to the name.

With a healthy student population in town and a competitive entertainment scene, the Tourists tried selling beer for a dollar on Thursdays many years ago and hit the jackpot. When he realized local bars were trying to cash in his catchphrase, long-time Tourists GM Ron McKee, now retired, had the phrase trademarked. The team shares it freely with other minor-league teams and doesn't charge for its usage.

Umbrellas and the overhang protect the crowd on a rainy Asheville day.

Sports Around Town

While the Tourists have shown great staying power, several other recent minor-league franchises have shown Asheville can be a tough market. The NBA placed a D-League developmental franchise there in 2001. The Asheville Altitude struggled through several years of lackluster attendance despite some players with good local name recognition like former Wake Forest two-sport star Rusty LaRue and former

UNC star Joseph Forte. Despite a league championship in 2004, the Altitude never took flight with the fans, and David Stern and the NBA braintrust mercifully pulled

Your choice of beers.

the plug after the 2005 season. Asheville has also hosted two attempts at minor-league hockey: initially the Asheville Smoke from 1998-2002; and more recently, the Asheville Aces during the 2004-05 season. Both these failing clubs left the sports scene in Asheville dominated by the Tourists and UNC-Asheville, whose athletic offerings include Division I baseball and basketball as members of the Big South Conference competing with the likes of Winthrop, Charleston Southern, and Virginia Military Institute.

THINGS TO DO

See Another Ballgame

While Asheville is not particularly close to any of North Carolina's other ballparks, there are some other professional teams within a short drive. If you like the mountains and want to enjoy the many attractions Asheville has to offer during an extended stay, a number of easy day trips to these other ballparks would allow you to base yourself in Asheville.

Greeneville, Tenn., is home to the Houston Astros' entry in the Appalachian League. Pioneer Park, located on the campus of Tusculum College, is a beautiful facility and the class of the Appy League. Remember, they won't start playing until the third week in June and, despite playing on campus, they do sell beer. The trip from Asheville is about an hour over winding, scenic mountain roads. Oh, and don't forget the third E. It really ticks off the locals if you leave it out. That's why the G-Astros logo includes the emphasis in "GreenEville." **Pioneer Park, 135 Shiloh Rd.; Greeneville, TN; greenevilleastros.com; 423/638-0411.**

Once you've made it as far as Greeneville, you may want to travel the additional twenty minutes and visit the other area Appalachian League parks. The Johnson City Cardinals share Howard Johnson Field, a modest facility, with East Tennessee State University. It also backs up to a football facility known as Steve Spurrier Field. **Howard Johnson Field, 111 Legion St., Johnson City, TN; jccardinals.com; 423/461-4866.**

If you want to venture further into the heart of the Appalachian League, three more Appy League ballparks are less than a half-hour drive beyond Johnson City. Kingsport's modern, functional facility is Hunter Wright Stadium. This park opened in 1995, but the Mets have been sending their Appalachian level players to Kingsport since 1980. **Hunter Wright Stadium, 433 E Center St., Kingsport, TN; kmets.com; 423/224-2627.**

Bristol's homespun facility, Boyce Cox Field at DeVault Memorial Stadium, houses the White Sox Appy League team. Boyce Cox, for whom the field is named, was still running the show in Bristol at the time this book was printed. Boyce has personally witnessed practically all of the modern Appy League's history, so be sure to say hello to the Bristol Sox head man when you visit. **Boyce Cox Field, 1501 Euclid Av., Bristol, VA; bristolsox.com; 276/669-6859.**

The Minnesota Twins, renowned within the baseball business for their stability and commitment to patiently developing their own players, have their Appy League team at Elizabethton's scenic and quaint Joe O'Brien Stadium. With the primary seating area composed of a small concrete football-style grandstand down the first-base line, there's also room for

1954 Tourists clown around in the clubhouse.
Photo courtesy of the Asheville Tourists.

lawn chairs, and the ballpark has a spacious concourse. The facility sits right next to a river, making it even more scenic. A town with fewer than 10,000 residents, Elizabethton has made the E-Twins feel like a part of the family since 1974. **Joe O'Brien Stadium, 208 N. Holly Lane, Elizabethton, TN 97643; elizabethtontwins.com; 423/547-6441.**

If you're looking for a higher level of play, Sevierville, Tenn. (a suburb of Knoxville) is also about an hour away from Asheville, although that trip is entirely via interstate freeway. Located at what looks like a combination rest stop and tourist info center at an exit on I-40, Smokies Park is a modern facility housing the Tennessee Smokies of the Class AA Southern League. This franchise called Knoxville home for many years but moved when a replacement for aging (and since demolished) Bill Meyer Stadium wasn't forthcoming. Wooed a couple exits east along the highway by proximity to the Dollywood theme park and the shopping meccas of Gatlinburg and Pigeon Forge (and, of course, a spiffy new ballpark!), the Smokies began play here in 2000. **Smokies Park, 3540 Line Dr., Sevierville, TN; smokiesbaseball.com; 865/286-2300.**

Biltmore Estate

The Biltmore House is a French Renaissance-style mansion near Asheville, built by George Washington Vanderbilt II between 1896 and 1902. It is the largest privately owned home in the United States at 175,000 square feet. Although it is still owned by the family, it is operated as a museum. This is also a fairly pricey attraction (prices vary by season; more pricing information is below), but it's a once-in-a-lifetime chance to get a glimpse into the lives of American royalty.

While the Biltmore Estate occupies a huge swath of land, the Biltmore House itself covers an awe-inspiring four acres. It boasts 250 rooms, 65 fireplaces, an indoor pool, a bowling alley, and priceless art and antiques everywhere you look.

The following information was current as this book went to print and can serve as a guideline, but it is advisable to call or visit their website (**biltmoreestate.com**) for more up-to-date information.

Biltmore Estate, 1 Approach Rd.; biltmoreestate.com; 800/411-3812. *Tickets include daytime admission to Biltmore House, Gardens, Winery and Farm Village, and access to shopping and dining on site. Tickets prices range from $38-$44 dollars for adults; kids 10-16 are free during summer vacation and $20 other times.*

Thomas Wolfe Memorial

The boarding house that inspired the American literary classic, *Look Homeward, Angel*, is now a memorial to the life and works of Asheville native Thomas Wolfe. The building was severely damaged by fire in 2004 but has been beautifully restored. In fact, many details, including the paint color and much of the furniture, now more accurately represent how the house looked when Wolfe was growing up there in the early 1900s.

Thomas Wolfe Memorial State Historic Site, 52 N. Market St.; wolfememorial.com; 828/253-8304.

Grove Arcade

One of Asheville's signature buildings, the Grove Arcade is 269,000 square feet of locally owned businesses in a restored public market. This historic downtown building features a variety of shops including restaurants, crafts, and more.

Grove Arcade, 1 Page Av.; grovearcade.com; 828/252-7799.

The Asheville Urban Trail

The Asheville Urban Trail is a 1.7-mile walk that gives visitors a chance to explore the architecture, history, and neighborhoods of Asheville. Featuring public art and Asheville landmarks, this is a great way to get to know the core of Asheville.

The Biltmore House
Photo by E.M. Ball, courtesy of the U.S. Army

Guided tours are offered from April through October; regular tours will be scheduled every Saturday at 10:30 a.m. and 3 p.m. The charge is $5 per person ($2 for children) and the meeting place is at the front desk inside Pack Place. Those interested in self-guided tours can rent an audiocassette with a headset at Pack Place. Guided tours for special groups can be arranged by calling the Asheville Area Arts Council at 828/258-0710 or by e-mailing them at info@ashevillearts.com.

Urban Trail maps are available at the Arts Council office, **11 Biltmore Av., Pack Place, Asheville Art Museum, and the Chamber of Commerce.**

Blue Ridge Parkway

This is a beautiful, scenic drive with breathtaking views. There are a number of terrific short outings available nearby, including a quick jaunt south on the Parkway to the Graveyard Fields Trail, located at milepost 419. It's a comfortable hike (just under 2.5 miles) to Yellowstone Falls, a great picnic setting. Bring a lunch: since you're on vacation, make it sandwiches from one of downtown Asheville's many excellent restaurants.

In season, you can hike just a little farther along Yellowstone Prong and you'll find huge fields of blueberries.

On the way back, stop at Sliding Rock. This 60-foot natural rock formation serves as a refreshing water slide, so pack your suit and your aqua-socks. **Located about 7 miles south of the Blue Ridge Parkway along US 276.**

Where to Eat

Downtown Asheville features a restaurant on practically every corner. Featuring unique local eateries, there's something for everyone, including pizza, pub grub, comfort food, and a dizzying array of the funky and chic. With lots of live music, and a wide range of adult libations, you can't go wrong.

Barley's Taproom & Pizzeria is located in a renovated 1920s appliance store. The menu features fresh sourdough pizza, lasagna, and sandwiches. At night you'll find live bluegrass, jazz, and American music with no cover charge. Call for up-to-date information.

Barley's Taproom & Pizzeria
42 Biltmore Av.
828/255-0504
barleystaproom.com

Bier is German for beer, and the Bier Garden has more than 200 varieties to choose from. Yeah, you can order some standard bar food off the menu, but the beer is the star here. Enjoy!

Bier Garden
46 Hayward St.
828/285-0002
ashevillebiergarden.com

Located on busy Pack Square, Café on the Square offers some of the best people-watching in Asheville. Get a table at one of their large picture windows or, if the weather's right, grab an outdoor table. There's something for everyone, from high-quality meats and pasta to vegetarian meals.

Café on the Square
1 Biltmore Av.
828/251-5565
cafeonthesquare.com

One of Asheville's truly notable restaurants is the Flying Frog Café, located in the Battery Hill neighborhood. Run by the Shastri family, which was among the pioneers of Asheville's thriving restaurant scene, the café offers a widely varied international menu that defies categorization. From "Urban Indian" to "Continental Specialties" and a full bar including martinis and other specialty drinks, the cuisine draws from the Eastern European and Indian family heritage of the Shastris. This is one of Asheville's most talked-about restaurants and reservations are recommended, but beware this is a fine dining establishment, and it's not cheap.

If you are on a tight budget and you just want to check the place out, visit the Frog Bar and Sidewalk Cafe upstairs at street level for a drink or a cup of coffee.

The Flying Frog Café
1 Battery Park Av.
828/254-9411
flyingfrogcafe.com

Fresh seafood in the mountains? Why not. The Lobster Trap gets fresh deliveries from the mythical Captain Tom. Enjoy real Maine lobster and a variety of live music from local performers.

Lobster Trap
35 Patton Av.
828/350-0505
thelobstertrap.biz

Enjoy home-style cooking Oliver & Annabelle's in Asheville's historic Grove Arcade.

Oliver & Annabelle's
1 Page Av.
828/350-8366

Dig into huge, stuffed burritos, tacos and enchiladas at Rio Burrito. A good value, Rio Burrito's signature offering was voted the best burrito in western North Carolina by a local independent newspaper.

Rio Burrito
11 Broadway St.
828/253-2422

Enjoy sidewalk dining at Tupelo Honey Café in the heart of downtown; southern home cooking with an uptown twist, specializing in food prepared with local and organic ingredients. Located across from Pritchard Park.

Tupelo Honey Café
12 College St.
828/255-4404
tupelohoneycafe.com

Operating for over 15 years, Vincenzo's is known for northern Italian cuisine. Another venue for live local music, this restaurant prides itself on providing exceptional value.

Vincenzo's Ristorante & Bistro
10 N. Market St.
828/254-4698
vincenzos.com

Ah, Beer...

Mirroring the national growth in craft beers and specialty brewing, Asheville boasts a thriving microbrew scene.

If you want to visit Asheville's finest brewpubs without the worries of driving, ride with Asheville Brews Cruise. For a fixed price, they provide sample beers, a souvenir pint glass, snacks, and all the transportation and planning for their evening "cruises." You'll get an inside look at the business of craft brewing while tasting local products ranging from pale ales to porters, ESBs to IPAs. Prices at press time were $37 per person, or $70 for couples. Contact them at 828/545-5181 or visit their website at **brewscruise.com** for up-to-date schedule information. If you'd rather do your own thing, information on the breweries included in the tour are included below.

Known to locals as the Brew & View, Asheville Pizza and Brewing Company is a microbrewery combined with a $2 movie theater and, of course, a pizzeria. The Shiva IPA and Houdini ESP are their most popular beers. This is a unique experience and an ideal place to spend an off-night on the baseball schedule.

Asheville Pizza and Brewing Company
675 Merriman Av.
828/254-1281
ashevillepizza.com

Opened in 1999, the French Broad River Brewing Company features award-winning beers like the Marzen Amber Lager, a copper-colored, Oktoberfest-style beer, or the Wee Heavy-er Scotch-style ale. Brewery tours are offered on the first and third Saturdays of the month at 1 and 2 p.m. There is also a Tasting Room with music on Fridays, and they are licensed for retail sales.

French Broad River Brewing Company
101-D Fairview Rd.
828/277-0222
frenchbroadbrewery.com

Located in the basement of a historic downtown building, the Highland Brewing Company was Asheville's first brewing company when they rolled the first barrels off the line in 1994. While there's no tasting room or retail sales, the brewery is located just behind and below Barley's Taproom. Highland's best-known brew is Gaelic Ale, a malty, amber ale, while the Cold Mountain Ale is a seasonal specialty.

Highland Brewing Company
42 Biltmore Av.
828/255-8240
highlandbrewing.com

"Go Read a Book!"

While serving as the pitching coach for Houston Astros teams in the Appalachian League, former big-leaguer Jack Billingham would run his young charges through their pregame exertions. Then, with their workout finished and time to kill prior to the game, he would order them to "go read a book." It's hard to know how many of the Astros pitchers took his advice, but give him an "A" for effort.

If you're looking for something to read on your trip other than this fine volume, or if you're interested in author readings and such, drop by Malaprops Bookstore/ Café. This is Asheville's best-known independent bookstore, and it's a great place to browse, sip a cup of coffee, or grab a bite to eat while soaking up the hip literary ambience.

Malaprops Bookstore/Café
55 Haywood St.
828/254-6734
malaprops.com

Lodging

The ballpark is located about a mile south of downtown Asheville, so you can always stay downtown and walk to the game. (This approach also addresses the problem of parking at the ballpark.)

Located less than a half mile from downtown, this Colonial Revival home built in 1905 features spacious porches for talking baseball, as well as a full breakfast and afternoon social hours.

Chestnut Street Inn
176 E. Chestnut St.
828/285-0705
chestnutstreetinn.com

The location of the large Asheville Renaissance Hotel allows visitors to walk to downtown, but it also includes an array of amenities within the hotel, including a fitness club, restaurant, and bar.

Asheville Renaissance Hotel
31 Woodfin St.
828/252-8211
marriott.com/hotels/travel/avlbr-renaissance-asheville-hotel

This laid-back Lion & the Rose Bed & Breakfast is housed in a turn-of-the-century Georgian mansion in the Montford Historic District, within walking distance to downtown. Convenient to all the area attractions, the Lion & the Rose offers reasonably priced rooms with a wealth of art and antiques.

Lion & the Rose Bed & Breakfast
276 Montford Av.
828/255-7673
lion-rose.com

If your budget is little more generous, consider Crowne Plaza Resort Asheville, a 125-acre resort located just a few minutes from downtown and Biltmore Estate. It features full-service tennis and golf facilities and, if you really want privacy, there are even villas available.

Crowne Plaza Resort Asheville
One Resort Dr.
Phone: 828/254-3211
ashevillecp.com

Located in the hip Weaverville area, this Victorian Inn on Main Street is just minutes from downtown Asheville and historic Biltmore Estate. You can walk to a variety of art galleries, restaurants, and even a mountain lake. Whirlpool tubs, Jacuzzis, and fireplaces highlight selected rooms.

Inn on Main Street
88 S. Main St.
828/645-4935
innonmain.com

For more information on lodging & attractions, visit **exploreasheville.com**.

 **Directions**

From I-240:

Take I-240 to exit 5B Charlotte Street South exit, go south approximately one mile on Charlotte, and turn left on McCormick Place (AAMCO Transmission is on the corner). McCormick Field is on the left.

From I-40 Westbound:

Take I-40 to Exit 50 Biltmore Avenue, go right off the ramp and north on Biltmore Avenue past Mission St. Joe's Hospital, past the Ford dealer, through one traffic light and right at the next street, McCormick Place (a gas station is on the corner). McCormick Field is on the right.

From I-40 Eastbound:

Take I-40 to Exit 50 Biltmore Avenue, go left off the ramp and north on Biltmore Avenue past Mission St. Joe's Hospital, past the Ford dealership, through one traffic light and right at the next street, McCormick Place (agas station is on the corner). McCormick Field is on the right.

CHARLOTTE

At one time envisioned as a ballpark expandable should a Major League Baseball team move to Charlotte, Knights Stadium could become the former home of the Charlotte Knights if the team moves to a planned new Uptown ballpark.

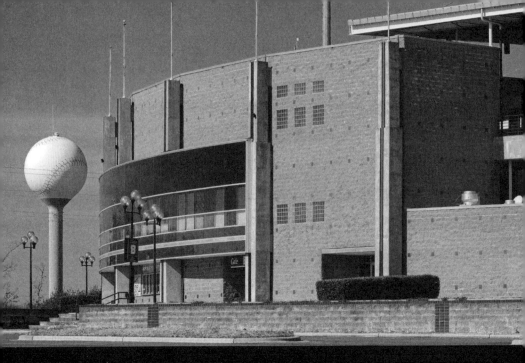

CHAPTER 2

KNIGHTS STADIUM

Leading Off

Opened: 1990

Capacity: 10,002

Dimensions: 325L, 400C, 325R

Current Team: Charlotte Knights, Class AAA International League (1993-present)

Former Team: Charlotte Knights, Class AA Southern League (1990-1993)

Architect: Matrix AEP

A Concrete Castle Across the Border

If a professional football team playing in the swamps of New Jersey can call themselves the New York Giants, why shouldn't the Triple-A franchise making its home in the former textile town of Fort Mill, S.C., be called the Charlotte Knights?

When teams plan ballparks these days it's all about location, location, location. Head south on I-77 from downtown Charlotte at the end of the workday and you can just about make it to the Knights Stadium for first pitch at 7 p.m. If you're lucky. Location, indeed.

After braving that 11-mile ordeal, you'll be rewarded with…Triple-A baseball. I promise you, you didn't come for the ballpark. If you like concrete, you'll love this ballpark. When you're through the traffic, you can park in the ocean of asphalt surrounding the stadium. When you get in the ballpark, you'll likely have plenty of seating choices, as the 10,000-plus seats of Knights Stadium are rarely filled to capacity anymore. You will then know why the Knights have been working so hard to build a new ballpark in Uptown Charlotte – and they want out of Knights Stadium so bad they're willing to build the ballpark on their own dime.

For a booming commercial center like Charlotte, the recent history of baseball in the Queen City area and the forces that led to the construction of Knights Stadium seem to be a classic case of poor timing and a little bad luck. For many years, the Charlotte Orioles were a successful member of the Double-A Southern League, drawing respectable crowds. Then, in March 1985, the O's longtime home, Crockett Park, burned to the ground. After the demise of the old wooden grandstand, temporary bleachers were erected, and the franchise made do in their makeshift home for another five seasons, changing their name to Knights in 1988 and their affiliation to the Cubs in 1989.

With no permanent home on the horizon in Charlotte, the Knights were wooed "south of the border" by a state-of-the-art facility, originally known as Knights Castle, that was the class of Double-A baseball when it was built. Much like Chicago's new Comiskey Park, which debuted around the same time, this ballpark was a victim of poor timing. Remember, this stadium was a product of the pre-Camden Yards era that produced ballparks like St. Pete's dreary Tropicana Field. People weren't building sports venues downtown, and a highway exit 11 miles away from downtown Charlotte seemed just fine. It's also worth noting that the Knights owner at the time was George Shinn, who has shown no hesitation in relocating his NBA team, the New Orleans Hornets — formerly the Charlotte Hornets — across state lines (North Carolina, Louisiana, Oklahoma).

It didn't take long, even as the Knights stepped up to Triple-A in 1993, for the luster to wear off. Charlotteans had became enamored of major-league sports with the arrival of the NBA in 1988 and the NFL in 1995, and the same growth and resulting commuter traffic that made Fort Mill seem so attractive began to keep fans away.

Ironically, a little over 20 years after Crockett Park burned down and just months after the opening of Charlotte's *second* new publicly financed NBA arena during that

Little was left of Crockett Park after the 1985 fire.
Photo by Mark B. Sluder / Charlotte Observer

same period, the return of minor-league baseball to downtown Charlotte seems inevitable.

In the meantime, Knights Stadium will certainly scratch the itch for baseball, and the current management team has brought some new life to the operation. Attendance has grown over the last few years despite the team's delicate balancing act of making the case for a new facility while still attempting to attract fans to the old one.

While a little short on charm, the park actually is very functional: a huge open concourse at the top of the lower seating bowl runs downhill to the field. A very large upper deck with freestanding luxury boxes above also includes another spacious concourse with plentiful concessions and restrooms.

The seating bowl carries one very distinctive feature: the seats themselves carry stripes of color from the field level all the way up to the top of the bowl, along with stripes running up through the upper-deck seats. These colored stripes vary in width, with some just a few seats wide and others covering half a section. This is the work of North Carolina's resident fashion designer, Alexander Julian, the same man who brought teal pinstripes to the NBA when the Charlotte Hornets debuted. The effect is a bit muted in a setting so drab; these stripes are the only real splash of color other than the outfield wall. There's just no getting away from the dominant concrete and cinderblock theme of this place; even the luxury boxes are simple cinderblock squares.

Knights Stadium was constructed with thoughts of expansion to a Major League facility.

A playground, located all the way at the end of the first-base side of the lower concourse, is less-than-ideally located out of view from the playing field. Some berm seating sprawls at the ends of the main seating bowl, and it's evident that this ballpark was built to be expandable to Major League seating capacity. In fact, when

team owner Don Beaver last made a public pitch for a big-league team in North Carolina, expanding Knights Stadium for use as an interim home field was the plan's lynchpin. (No stranger to sports ownership, Beaver also owns the Hickory Crawdads and the New Orleans Zephyrs.)

In a state with a lot of great baseball history, the Charlotte area can lay claim to a lot of great players passing through the city. The Charlotte Hornets, the property of Washington Senators owner Clark Griffith, was a long-time Senators and Minnesota Twins farm team, no matter whether the team played in the Class B Tri-State League, the original South Atlantic League, or the Southern League. Crockett Park was originally known as Clark Griffith Park (built in 1940 for $70,000), and many of the franchise's greats, including Harmon Killebrew, Tony Oliva, Minnie Mendoza, Graig Nettles, and Rick Dempsey, wore the Charlotte Hornets uniform during a long run as a Senators and Twins affiliate that covered parts of the 1950s, 1960s, and 1970s.

Surprisingly, Charlotte lost minor-league baseball in 1973, but in 1976 Jim Crockett brought back the Southern League in the form of the Charlotte O's, which had a 12-year run from 1976 to 1988 as a Baltimore farm team. These clubs were led by players like Cal Ripken, Jr., Eddie Murray, and Curt Schilling, and managed by future big-league skipper Grady Little and future major-league GM John Hart.

The previously mentioned fire at Crockett Park and the lack of a suitable facility in Charlotte prompted the move to Fort Mill. The early reviews were all raves, too, as "Charlotte" led Double-A in attendance for two years running. When the Knights stepped up to Triple-A in 1993, they set another franchise attendance record as an Indians affiliate.

Sadly, it didn't last, as increased competition for the fans' dollars and leisure time combined with some losing teams to take the bloom off the rose. Beginning in 1995, the Knights also faced competition within their own market when the Spartanburg Phillies moved to Kannapolis, a northern suburb of Charlotte. While

Charlotte-Griffith/Crockett Park

The Lost City of Atlantis, the Bermuda Triangle, Jimmy Hoffa's final resting place, and... Crockett Park. The common theme? They all exist only in memory and legend. Like Raleigh's Deveraux Meadow, Charlotte's Crockett Park — or Griffith Park, as it was originally known — was a major part of the area's baseball history, but there's nothing but memories left.

Charlotte had hosted organized professional baseball as early as 1901, and teams had played in a variety of parks until Griffith Park opened on the corner of Magnolia Avenue and McDonald in 1941. The ballfield in the Dilworth neighborhood would be the home to professional baseball in Charlotte for almost the next half century, although the original grandstand survived only into the mid-80s.

Firefighters at the scene March 16, 1985 had no chance to save Crockett Park.
Photo by Mark B. Sluder / Charlotte Observer

The Griffith family, which owned the Washington Senators, began operating a minor-league affiliate in Charlotte in 1937. In 1941, they built a state-of-the-art stadium with roughly 6,000 seats in a large covered grandstand. Like many other minor-league parks of the era, it was fatally flawed. Built primarily of wood, this park was consumed by fire in the spring of 1985.

The stadium, then named Crockett Park after the team's owners at the time, was quickly rebuilt, primarily with bleacher seating. But it was only five years before the city's unwillingness to build a new park would combine with the ambitions of a wealthy businessman named George Shinn and a bedroom community across the South Carolina border to begin baseball's exile from the Queen City.

A FAMILY AFFAIR

The Washington Senators/Minnesota Twins franchise put their stamp on baseball in Charlotte with a 33-season run from 1937 to 1972 (except for the World War II years of 1943-45). The Washington American League team was owned by a former big-league player and manager named Clark Griffith, who landed in the Hall of Fame for his ownership of the Senators. Childless, he and his wife adopted his Canadian-born nephew, Calvin Robertson, who would later take the name Calvin Griffith. Young Calvin, who came to Washington at age 11, grew up in the family business and eventually was dispatched to Charlotte to run the Hornets, a Senators minor-league affiliate. In 1940, the stadium named for the elder Griffith was built for $70,000. Shortly thereafter, Calvin was "called up" to Washington where he would begin a major-league front-office career with the Senators. He would become the principal owner of the franchise when his adoptive father died in 1955.

After twenty years in Griffith Park as a Senators affiliate, the Hornets' big-league team moved to Minnesota in 1961 and became the Twins. The Charlotte Hornets, still owned by the Griffith family, would remain affiliated with the Twins through the 1972 season.

Postcard of Clark Griffith Park (undated).

Frances Crockett took the helm in Charlotte — one of the earliest front office women in organized baseball.
Photo courtesy of the Charlotte Knights

Charlotte's baseball fans would be treated to the unusual spectacle of two minor-league teams sharing a stadium that season, as the Twins located both the Double-A Hornets and the Single-A Western Carolina League team, dubbed the Charlotte Twins, at Griffith Park. Just like the two-team arrangement in Nashville with the Triple-A Sounds and the Double-A Xpress in 1993-1994 (which, ironically, also involved a Twins affiliate), the move brought on baseball fatigue and proved to be a dismal failure. The two teams drew 25,000 fewer fans than the Hornets alone had drawn the year before and likely hastened baseball's departure from Charlotte.

Thankfully, this inauspicious ending was not the final chapter for Griffith Park.

FAMILY AFFAIR, TAKE TWO

The Griffith family tried to sell the park named in their honor for three years and finally announced plans to tear the place down. Before the 1976 season, Charlotte-based wrestling promoter Jim Crockett bought the park for $85,000. Crocket purchased the Asheville Orioles and re-christened them the Charlotte O's. The ballpark was painted Orioles blue and orange, and re-named Crockett Park.

And while one would expect that this ownership would install turnbuckles on the dugout roof and hold steel cage matches between games of a doubleheader, by all accounts, the baseball and wrestling operations were kept largely separate. While Klondike Bill served double duty as a wrestling headliner and O's groundskeeper, the stars of this show were players like Cal Ripken and Eddie Murray, and the Pepper Girls.

A team of goodwill ambassadors, the Pepper Girls name was a tribute to their sponsor, Dr Pepper, while also referencing the classic baseball warm-up game. They made off-season appearances, sold programs, tore tickets, ushered, and even served as bat girls during the games.

The Pepper Girls and promotions like the Money Roll, Ostrich Races, and the World's Longest Sub were the work of Frances Crockett, Jim's youngest daughter. After a short time in the hands of Crockett's sons David and Jimmy Jr., the team was handed off to Frances, who was one of the only women involved in a baseball front-office role at the time. With the help of her assistant Lib Shildt and one other full-time staffer, the O's rode a wave of success into the eighties.

This was something of a golden age for minor-league baseball in Charlotte. From 1978 to 1981, the team's attendance climbed from under 65,000 to over 200,000. Minor-league baseball was undergoing a resurgence throughout the nation. The O's also benefitted from having a fast-growing market almost to themselves. The Charlotte Checkers minor-league hockey team were the only other sports franchise in town, college sports was an afterthought, and the O's owned the summers.

The high-water mark for the Charlotte O's was probably the 1980 season, which culminated in a Southern League championship. Led by Cal Ripken Jr., who would lead Baltimore to the World Series just three years later, this team also included Charlotte fan favorite and long-time Charlotte Twins farmhand Minnie Mendoza (see Mendoza, page 43).

The O's captured another league championship in 1984, but sadly, the cheering stopped on March 16, 1985, when a fire (thought to have been arson) destroyed the Crockett Park grandstand. With the season only weeks away, the Crockett family quickly constructed a makeshift park of 5,000 bleacher seats.

The O's struggled on in their interim facility, and the team continued to feature future Orioles, such as Billy Ripken and Bob Milacki. Following the 1987 season, though, the Crocketts sold the team to George Shinn, who would go on to be better known as the carpetbagging owner of the NBA's Charlotte/New Orleans/Oklahoma City Hornets. The team was re-named the Knights as the Orioles were replaced as parent club by the Chicago Cubs.

The economics of the game had changed since 1941, or even 1976, and teams didn't build or own their own ballparks anymore. In the end, though, a new municipally financed baseball park was deemed a "want" by Charlotte's political leadership, while streets and schools were classified as "needs" for the fast-growing city. Plans were soon underway for the Knights Castle in Fort Mill, S.C. While that park's honeymoon would prove short-lived, in 1990 when the new stadium opened, it attracted rave reviews and record crowds.

Crockett Park is now long gone, replaced by condos, and there's not even a plaque to mark the spot. New life may be breathed into minor-league baseball in Charlotte when the Knights return to the city limits within a few years, but it's also fair to say that the heart of baseball in Charlotte effectively stopped beating that March day in 1985.

Under the lights at Crockett Park, circa 1949.
Photo courtesy of the University of North Carolina Charlotte – Sumner Collection

getting to Kannapolis from downtown Charlotte is no picnic at rush hour, the Knights were no longer the only game in town.

Today, the Knights continue to push for a new downtown stadium that would undoubtedly do for this franchise what similar downtown facilities have done for Greensboro or Greenville, S.C. In the

The ballpark in Fort Mill, S.C. was originally known as the Knights Castle.

meantime, the Knights staff is charged with the nearly impossible task of selling the public on how inadequate their current facility is while also enticing them to attend a game.

For the traveling baseball fan, there are nonetheless a few compelling arguments to be made for seeing a game here. Proximity to Gastonia, Kannapolis, and Hickory, or even Greenville, S.C., makes this a logical stop on your itinerary. The team's progress toward a new downtown ballpark also means that this facility's days are numbered, so it may be your last chance to see the place in action as a baseball facility. Short track to auto racing, anyone?

Concessions

Plenty of concession windows can be found on both the upper and lower concourses in this park, and the lower concourse is open to the field. The normal ballpark menu is offered, including Carolina Pride hot dogs, hamburgers, and brats.

You have your pick of sweets, too, with shaved ice, cotton candy, ice cream, and lemonade. There's a nice beer selection, including all the major domestic brands and a number of premium and import beers, including Labatt's, Red Stripe, and Sam Adams, and beer is easy to get from the many free-standing beer sales locations. A grill down the third-base line also has Sonny's BBQ sandwiches if you've had your fill of hot dogs and pizza.

Fans have plenty of room to sit and enjoy a snack or beverage along the concourse at Knights Stadium.

Promotions

The Knights run a solid promotional calendar with plenty of giveaways, fireworks shows, and the normal on-field fun and games. This is another of a growing number of teams that provide fans a free program as they enter the park. Called "First Pitch" by the Knights, it's called "Play Ball" in a number of other ballparks, as a play on the "Playbill" programs distributed at theatrical productions. It's a small format, about half the size of a sheet of paper, but it's loaded with information (including player bios) and lots of color.

The theory behind this is that program advertisers will pay significantly more to reach all the fans entering the park than they would to reach the smaller percentage that will actually buy a program. This increased advertising revenue should more than make up for the increased printing costs and loss of program sales revenue.

The Knights' mascot, Homer, is a dragon. He's very kid-friendly, and this is another case where smaller crowd sizes can make it a little easier for the little ones to get up close and personal.

Sports Around the Town

When the Charlotte O's were in their heyday, they were the only sports team in town. Charlotte was also the only major metropolitan area in the state without Atlantic Coast Conference basketball, which is among the most ardently supported spectator sports in the region.

Major Renovations
at UNC Charlotte

Major renovations have been completed at the University of North Carolina Charlotte ballpark where the Charlotte 49ers made the transition to Atlantic-10 in style, claiming the 2007 conference championship in only their second year of league play.

The renovation of Tom and Lib Phillips Field at Robert and Mariam Hayes Stadium amounted to a total transformation into a showcase collegiate facility. The $5.9 million in improvements include an inviting entrance plaza, seating accommodations for over 1,000 people — including more than 500 chair-back seats — a spacious press box with radio and TV booths, in-ground dugouts similar to the big-leagues style, hospitality suites, concessions, and restrooms. Charlotte-based Overcash Demmitt provided the architectural services. Equipped for television broadcasts, the surrounding orange brick columns and wrought iron fencing fit in closely with the modern style of the burgeoning north Charlotte campus.

The 2007 year of transition to the new ballpark will be memorable in several ways for UNCC baseball players and fans as substantial construction work continued well into the season. The Niners earned the nickname of Nomads as the first 13 "home" games were played quite a ways off campus at Fieldcrest Cannon Stadium in Kannapolis, Pfeiffer University's Ferebee Field in Misenheimer, and at Winthrop University's ballpark in Rock Hill, S.C.

Constant traveling must not have disrupted the squad much at all as the 49ers fashioned a 12-1 "home-away-from-home" record and then kept the momentum going in their new digs and throughout the rest of the season. The first game at Hayes Stadium moved along at a brisk pace, completed in only one hour, 36 minutes.

The 49ers defeated Massachusetts 3-1, with starting pitcher Adam Mills getting the complete-game victory, and slugger Chris Lane notching the first home run in the transformed ballpark. You won't see much in the way of cheapies at Hayes Stadium, with the fences measuring 335 feet down each line and reaching 390 in dead center.

After returning to campus, the team played those earliest games in an unfinished stadium. It would be a few more weeks until the chair-back seats were installed. Of course, the renovations kept some popular characteristics of the original field, including the hillside fan

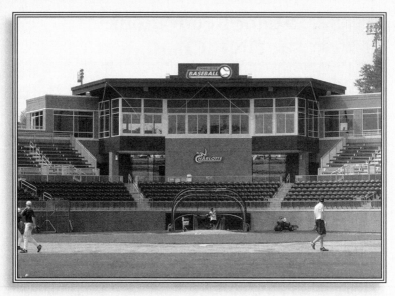

Major renovations were completed in 2007 at Hayes Stadium on the University of North Carolina Charlotte (UNCC) campus. *Photo courtesy of the UNCC Athletic Department.*

seating area near the first-base dugout and down the line — an area typically frequented by students. A picnic area farther down the right-field line also remains in place.

Not only did Charlotte claim its first A-10 crown in 2007, but the 49ers went on to earn a national ranking and picked up its first victories in NCAA postseason tournament play after getting blanked in its first two previous tourney appearances. So, any slight inconveniences experienced in making the transition to a new venue likely will be fondly remembered based on the 49ers' best-ever season record at 49-12.

The 49ers started play in 1979 at Crockett Park downtown and have played on campus at the current site since 1984. The naming of the playing field came at the time of resurfacing in 1994 with a large share of that cost funded by Tom and Lib Phillips.

One bittersweet note: Mariam Cannon Hayes donated $3.6 million to the latest renovation, but she didn't have an opportunity to see those final finishing touches. She died at age 91, less than three months before dedication ceremonies were held in October 2007.

Clearly, people in North Carolina love basketball, but the pro game had never gained a foothold in the state. The American Basketball Association's Carolina Cougars gave it a shot in 1969, but the franchise was positioned as a regional team, splitting "home" games between the original Charlotte Coliseum, Greensboro, Raleigh, and Winston-Salem. That approach worked to an extent, but the presence of former UNC stars Billy Cunningham and Doug Moe wasn't enough to keep the team from moving to St. Louis at the end of the 1974 season.

But the arrival of the NBA's Hornets in 1988 combined the love for hoops with Charlotte's hunger to be seen as a "big league" city, and area sports fans responded by filling the new 24,000-seat Charlotte Coliseum, nicknamed "The Hive," on a regular basis. For much of their history, the Hornets led the NBA in attendance, but during the franchise's last few years in town the team suffered a string of public-relations setbacks. These incidents involving alleged bad behavior by players, as well as by Shinn himself, began to erode the team's support. In the end, Shinn sought a new downtown arena as the solution to the club's woes, despite the fact that his current home was barely more than 10 years old.

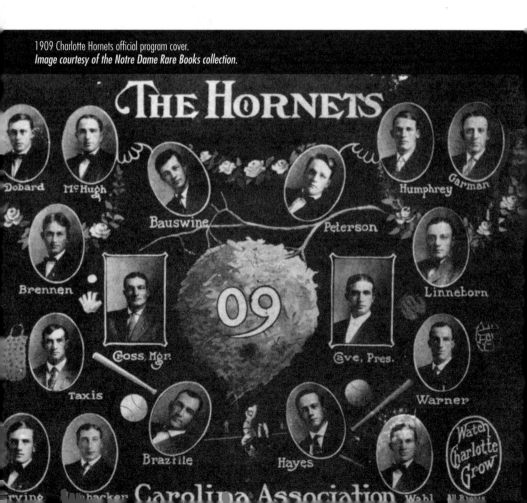

1909 Charlotte Hornets official program cover.
Image courtesy of the Notre Dame Rare Books collection.

Years later, Charlotte's leadership did pay for a new downtown arena, but it was increasingly clear during the Hornets' last years that there would not be an arena built for Shinn. Even the area's most fervent NBA fans seemed pleased to be rid of George Shinn. The Hornets, of course, moved to New Orleans prior to the 2002-2003 season, and have subsequently played home games in Baton Rouge and Oklahoma City in the aftermath of Hurricane Katrina.

The NBA is back in Charlotte, though, under the guidance of Black Entertainment Television founder Bob Johnson. The aptly named Bobcats began play in 2004 in the same arena that had hosted the Hornets, but moved to the new downtown Charlotte Bobcats Arena the following season. This building also serves as the home arena of the minor-league Charlotte Checkers of the ECHL.

Charlotte's "other" arena, originally known as the Charlotte Coliseum, is now known as Cricket Arena (for now; naming rights could have been sold after this book went to press), although many locals continue to refer to it by its previous name,

Playing for the Charlotte Hornets in 1962, Tony Oliva demonstrates the swing the swing that earned him three American League batting championships (1964, '65 and '71). *Photo courtesy of the Charlotte Observer.*

Independence Arena, or simply as "the old Coliseum." Considered an engineering marvel when it opened in the 1950s, the "Big I" featured the largest freestanding steel-dome roof in the world when it opened, and it served as the long-time home of minor league hockey, as well as a variety of other events, including ACC basketball. It also was home to the aforementioned Carolina Cougars of the ABA.

ⓘ *Insiders' Tip*

Any account of Charlotte's baseball history wouldn't be complete without mentioning Minnie Mendoza, a career baseball man from Cuba who can bridge any cultural gap with his smile and personality. Minnie spent 10 years playing for Charlotte when the team was in the Southern League and is said to have turned down promotions to Triple A due to his reluctance to leave behind his ties in the community.

He finally did make it to the big leagues as a 36-year-old rookie in 1970, when he played in 16 games for the Minnesota Twins. Minnie, born Cristobal Rigoberto Mendoza in Ceiba Del Agua, Cuba, is still in uniform today, more than 30 years after his playing days in Charlotte ended.

Originally signed as an amateur free agent by the Cincinnati Reds in 1954, he was picked up by the Senators in 1958, logging 12 years in their minor-league system before his first big-league appearance. He has managed and coached at nearly every level of the minors, including stints as the Burlington Indians skipper, where he is regarded as the hardcore fans' favorite manager in franchise history. He currently works as a roving minor-league instructor for the Cleveland Indians.

Charlotte has become quite a sports town between Bank of America Stadium (the home of the NFL's Panthers), Bobcats Arena, and the planned NASCAR Museum and Hall of Fame scheduled to open in 2009. Just north and east of town along I-85 is Lowe's Motor Speedway in Concord, but nonetheless includes Charlotte in its name. (*For more on Lowe's Motor Speedway, see our chapter on Kannapolis.*)

Bank of America Stadium (formerly Ericsson Stadium) is visible from I-77 as you come into town, and plentiful signs guide you there. The stadium is clad in Panthers' team colors black, silver, and Carolina blue. Despite an overall losing record since joining the NFL in 1995 (the first league expansion since 1976), the

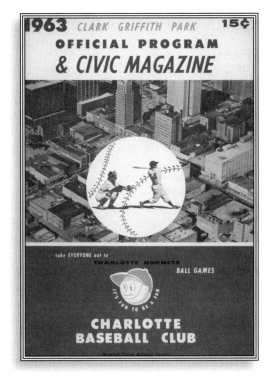

1963 Charlotte Hornets official program cover.
Image courtesy of the Notre Dame Rare Books collection.

Panthers achieved glory in the 2003 season when they reached the Super Bowl, as well as the 1996 and 2005 seasons when they reached the NFC championship games. Tours are offered each Wednesday at 10 a.m. from in front of the ticket office located between the East and South gates on Mint Street. The tour is free for children under age five, $2 for children under 16, $4 for adults, and $3 for seniors. Group tours are given Monday through Friday, based on availability, and must be reserved in advance. A flat fee of $60 is charged per group of 25 people. Call 704/358-7538 or visit **panthers.com** for more information.

Bobcats Arena is also located in the middle of Charlotte's city center (known as Uptown) at **333 E. Trade St.** Tours are offered on non-event days, but must be arranged well in advance. Contact the Bobcats at 704/688-8687 or visit **charlottebobcatsarena.com** for more information.

Even years before its completion, people in Charlotte were already talking about the planned NASCAR Hall of Fame. Scheduled to open in 2010, this facility will boast a striking exterior and memorabilia, with exhibits showcasing the sport born in the Carolinas. The region is still home to the majority of the race teams and their drivers. For more information, visit **belongshere.com.**

Attractions

Charlotte once closed down after five, but in recent years Uptown Charlotte has developed a genuine nightlife and offers a number of great restaurants.

For family entertainment, the area boasts a wealth of activities. If you like roller coasters and amusement parks, you'll probably enjoy Paramount's Carowinds. Located right on the North Carolina/South Carolina border on I-77 (just a few miles from the ballpark), this park is open from March until early fall. It also features a 16-acre water park and a Nickelodeon-themed kids' area.

Paramount's Carowinds
I-77 & 14523 Carowinds Blvd.
800/888-4386
paramountparks.com/carowinds

If you're an outdoor sports enthusiast, you'll want to check out the U.S. National Whitewater Center. USNWC is a 300-acre campus just 10 minutes from downtown Charlotte featuring kayaking, rafting, low ropes, and climbing. Designed as a training location for Olympic and international competitors, they welcome weekend warriors and couch potatoes, too. Amenities include a restaurant, lockers, and equipment rental. Even if you don't want to paddle, you can walk the trails that crisscross the park alongside the Catawba River for free.

U.S. National Whitewater Center
820 Hawfield Rd. (the intersection of I-85S & I-485)
704/391-3900
usnwc.org

You can also see another baseball game. UNC-Charlotte's Tom and Lib Phillips Field has been extensively renovated in recent years (see page 39 for more information). Gastonia (page 47) and Kannapolis (page 67) are both very convenient to Charlotte, and if a day game is scheduled in any of the three cities, one could easily hit two games. Hickory (page 57) is less than two hours away.

Lodging

While you're visiting Charlotte, you'll want to carefully consider your lodging choice. Staying in the city center will make getting to the ballpark, particularly for weekday games, a real hassle. On the other hand, staying in Fort Mill doesn't offer much in the way of atmosphere. For convenience, I'd recommend staying close to the ballpark. But if you decide you want to enjoy downtown (or, rather, Uptown) Charlotte, make sure you're heading south on I-77 well before rush hour.

There is no hotel within walking distance of the ballpark. If you want to stay as close as possible, Plaza Hotel Carowinds in Fort Mill is a good choice, although it is two miles from Knights Stadium. For families interested in visiting Paramount's Carowinds Theme Park during the trip, the Plaza is a convenient full-service lodging choice right across the road.

225 Carowinds Blvd.
803/548-2400
plazahoteloncarowinds.com

The other three properties are located less than 10 miles from the ballpark, including the hotel listed in Charlotte. Additional hotels choices in the heart of Charlotte will be high-end and typically priced accordingly.

Courtyard by Marriott
1300 River Run Court
Rock Hill, SC 29732
803/324-1400
marriott.com

Wingate by Wyndham
760 Galleria Blvd. (I-77 and Dave Lyle Blvd.)
Rock Hill, SC 29732
803/324-9000
wingateinns.com

Although the Four Points by Sheraton Charlotte is located in what's not considered to be a prime neighborhood south of downtown just off of I-77, this location works well if you plan to spend some time in the city center but still want reasonable proximity to the ballpark.

Four Points by Sheraton Charlotte
315 E Woodlawn Rd.
Charlotte, NC 28217
704/522-0852
starwoodhotels.com/fourpoints

N W E S **Directions**

Coming from Charlotte and points north:

Take I-77 South to Exit 88 (Gold Hill Road). Make a left at the top of the ramp. The stadium will be on your right-hand side.

Coming from Fort Mill/Rock Hill and points south:

Take I-77 North to Exit 88 (Gold Hill Road). Make a right at the top of the ramp. The stadium will be on your right-hand side.

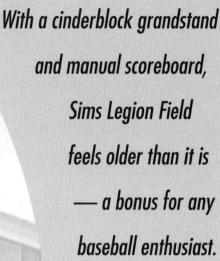

With a cinderblock grandstand and manual scoreboard, Sims Legion Field feels older than it is — a bonus for any baseball enthusiast.

GASTONIA

CHAPTER 3

Sims Legion Park

Opened: Baseball has been played at the site since the 1930s, while the current grandstand dates back to 1977 • **Capacity:** 3,500 • **Dimensions:** 335L, 360LC, 380C, 360RC, 335R
Current Team: Gastonia Grizzlies, summer-collegiate Coastal Plain League (2001-present)
Former Leagues: original South Atlantic League (1923, 1959), North Carolina State League (1938), Tar Heel League (1939-40), Western Carolina League (1950, 1960, 1963-70, 1972-74, 1977-79), Tri-State League (1952-53), South Atlantic League (1980-92), independent Atlantic Coast League (1995). Team names included Gastonia Cardinals (1938-1940, 1977-1982), Gastonia Expos (1983-1984), Gastonia Jets (1985), Gastonia Pirates (1963-1972), Gastonia Rangers (1973-1974, 1987-1992), Gastonia Rippers (1960), Gastonia Tigers (1986), and King Cougars (1995)

Address: 1001 N. Marietta St., Gastonia
Website: gastonia-grizzlies.com
Phone: 704/866-8622
Ticket Prices: $4-$7

Where Future Latino Legends Roamed the Outfield

As you approach Sims Legion Park, the back of the grandstand presents a stark, plain wall from the roof right down to the asphalt of the parking lot. Yet, once you're inside, this ballpark has the feel of a classic old-time minor-league park. In fact, the site has hosted baseball in this area for over fifty years, but many fans will be surprised to learn that the current cinderblock grandstand at Sims Legion Park dates only to the 1970s (see the plaque mounted on the third-base end of the grandstand).

This cozy seating bowl, viewable from I-85/40, holds about 1,500 fans and is almost entirely covered by a roof. Four rows of box seats are located below the walkway, and about a dozen rows of aluminum bench seats sit above. Like many of the older parks in the Southeast, Sims features a large press box perched on the front edge of the roof rather than at the top of the seating bowl, providing a fantastic vantage point if you're lucky enough to get up there. The roof and press box are accessed by a set of stairs at the top of the grandstand's seating area. Lockers, restrooms, and concessions are all underneath the grandstand. You'll notice that the players emerge from the same door leading to the public bathrooms — the locker rooms are just a little way down the hall from the restrooms located at the third-base end of the grandstand.

The ticket windows and main (and only) entrance to Sims Legion are also located on the third-base end of the grandstand, adjacent to the team offices, which face into the park behind the third-base bleachers.

An eight-foot-tall cinderblock wall encloses the entire park. Starting from either end of the grandstand, the wall climbs uphill as it marches toward the foul poles. Across the outfield, this wall sits a good 30 feet up a bank above the playing field, dominating the view. Unlike most parks where the outfield fence signs are located on the home-run fence, at this ballpark the signs are painted on the cinderblock wall, while the home-run fence is a simple chain link structure with green windscreen attached.

The bank behind the outfield wall is open to spectators. Some fans venture out to chat with the scoreboard operator in left field as he sits in his lawn chair and periodically hangs a new number with a long pole reminiscent of a shepherd's crook. This is the other feature dominating the view at this park: a huge, non-functioning electronic scoreboard, which was converted into a manual scoreboard with the addition of hooks and wooden numbers when the Coastal Plain League (CPL) arrived. A small working electronic scoreboard in right field displays the score and inning.

A pair of very tall bleacher stands, each with capacity of close to 1,000, flank the grandstand. Just a few years ago the team faced the very real danger of not having their use for an entire season. In light of the accidental death of a toddler who fell through a set of bleachers in Cary, the City of Gastonia threatened to close the bleachers for the entire summer. In the end, chain link was added underneath the foot treads, attached to the underside of the bleachers. For good measure, the city also had chain link wrapped around the back and sides of the bleachers to prevent kids from crawling underneath the seats. It's hard to fault the operator of any public facility for erring on the side of safety, but this arrangement is certainly not

The grandstand canopy at Sims Legion Park offers plenty of protection from the elements.

visually appealing and is indicative of the overall need for a significant investment in this ballpark.

Beyond the third-base bleachers there is a "beer deck" area with an old milk-truck box converted to use as a walk-in beer cooler (a recurrent theme throughout many CPL ballparks). On your way to the beer deck, you'll also pass an auxiliary concession stand selling drinks, candy, and peanuts.

The main concession stand is hidden away on the first-base end of the grandstand; it features standard ballpark fare, including hot dogs, pizza, and such. In previous years, a local hamburger restaurant's products also have been available. Unfortunately, the main stand can only be reached by walking up several steps into the grandstand. The auxiliary concession stand behind the third-base bleachers may be easier to reach for some patrons, although no hot food is served there.

As the name implies, this park was originally built to house the local American Legion team, which still plays its home games here. Tucked into an older residential neighborhood, the stadium shares a parking lot with a Little League field, while a BMX track can be found just beyond the centerfield wall.

Organized baseball has had a long on-again, off-again relationship with Gastonia. This former textile town just west of Charlotte fielded entries in the Tar Heel League, the Western Carolina League, the Carolina League, and both incarnations of the South Atlantic League, and has carried nicknames ranging from Spinners to Rockets to Jets.

Gastonia's association with affiliated baseball ended, probably for good, after the 1992 season when Walt "No Neck" Williams managed the Gastonia Rangers through their final season in the South Atlantic League. Owner George Shinn, who also owned the then-Charlotte Hornets of the NBA, didn't cultivate many fans in Gastonia. In 1990 though, the Rangers featured one of the more notable promotions in Sally League history. Hornets stars Dell Curry and Muggsy Bogues actually played for the G-Rangers for one game, with Curry taking the mound to favorable reviews while the diminutive Bogues took two futile turns at bat. Despite these efforts, the team languished at the bottom of the Sally League in attendance. Shinn sold the club to nursing-home magnate Don Beaver, as the team packed up shop and headed about 35 miles north up Route 321 to move into a sparkling new ballpark and became the Hickory Crawdads.

The Rangers can't be faulted for the level of talent they brought to town, though. During one of that franchise's last years in Gastonia, two of the everyday outfielders were a couple of young, skinny Latinos named Sammy Sosa and Juan Gonzalez.

Many point to the lack of beer sales at the ballpark as a key reason that Gastonia had generally struggled to draw fans over the years. Local legend has it that longtime owner Jack Farnsworth set the precedent, refusing to sell beer for fear of damaging his primary occupation as one of the leading Bible wholesalers in the region. Gastonia was also effectively locked out of affiliated baseball when the Rangers left, as the expansion of home territories put Gastonia squarely in the protected turf of the Triple-A Charlotte Knights.

Gastonia has had two subsequent episodes with pro ball. In 1995, the ill-fated Atlantic Coast League placed a team at Sims Legion Park. This independent league was hastily organized and poorly funded and, along with Gastonia, included teams in Spartanburg, Greenwood, and Florence, all in South Carolina. The ACL went belly up after less than three weeks of play. In 1997, Gastonia was home to a team in another short-lived venture, this time featuring professional softball. To the horror of ballpark purists, the Women's Professional Fastpitch League placed teams in a half-dozen former minor-league ballparks in the Southeast, including the venerable Durham Athletic Park. The WPF was better funded than the ACL, but after two seasons of modest crowds and a name change to the Women's Pro Softball League, Sims Legion was once again without a major tenant.

The failure or departure of three teams in less than 10 years left officials in Gastonia understandably wary when the summer-collegiate Coastal Plain League came calling in 1998. It took almost three years to convince the city's leadership that this wouldn't be another embarrassment for the community. When a lease was finally secured, the CPL's Grizzlies began what has been a successful tenure. After being owned by the league during their start-up season, the Grizzlies were purchased by former Savannah Sand Gnats owner Ken Silver and his son Michael, a local doctor. Ken has retired to North Carolina and is frequently in attendance when the Grizzlies play at home.

The game experience in Gastonia will give you the feeling of attending a '70s-era Single-A contest. While the atmosphere is somewhat spare, this is another example of the Coastal Plain League restoring high-level baseball to a great little ballpark. The Grizzlies offer local fans an affordable, quality night at the park. For the visiting fan, it's convenient to Charlotte, within sight of I-85. And don't be discouraged if there's not a Grizzlies game on the schedule: Sims Legion is a very busy ballpark hosting over 100 events a year, including high-school games, Belmont Abbey College home games, and other events, such as a revival conducted in 2006 by Billy Graham's grandson, Will.

⚾ Insider's Tip

Go for the General Admission seats at Sims Legion. This is definitely a good park for wandering, so a few innings in the beer garden, a walk out to the outfield bank, and a few innings each in the bleachers and the upper reaches of the grandstand are all possible with just a GA ticket. Also, depending on the weather, the grandstand, which is completely roofed and closed-in at the top, can be oppressively hot. On a typical summer night in North Carolina, you'll likely be more comfortable near the top of the third-base bleachers or sitting at a table in the beer garden. (Yes, they run beer specials on Thursdays!)

THINGS TO DO

See Another Baseball Game

Seeing a game in Gastonia is easily combined with a game in Charlotte (page 25), Kannapolis (page 67), or even Greenville, S.C. But a historic facility you won't want to miss is just 45 minutes away in Spartanburg, S.C., Duncan Park Stadium. A 1920s-era ballpark that housed the Phillies Class A team for over 20 years and saw the likes of Mike Schmidt pass through, the ballpark is still standing, though its last tenant, the Spartanburg Stingers of the

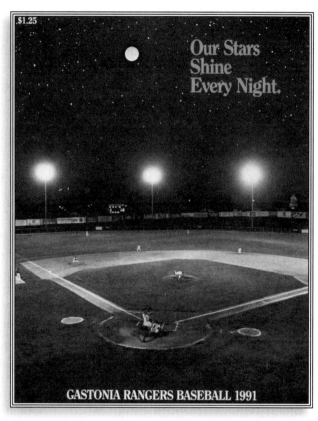

GASTONIA RANGERS BASEBALL 1991

1991 Gastonia Rangers official program cover. *Image courtesy of the Notre Dame Rare Books collection.*

Coastal Plain League, moved after the 2006 season. A group is working to renovate the facility; we can only hope they succeed. It's likely one of the five oldest standing parks in America; when the Phillies left town, it was the oldest active park in minor-league baseball. The park is worth a visit (it's located in Duncan Park, hence the name, and is easily found), but you'll want to visit during daylight hours. And don't delay; there's no telling how long this one will survive.

To Spartanburg's Duncan Park Stadium from Gastonia: Take I-85 south to Business I-85. Take the exit for I-585 (Pine Street). Stay on I-585 through downtown (approximately two miles) until it becomes N. Pine Street (also US-176). Turn right on St. Andrews Street. Going one block, turn left onto Union Street. After going approximately a half mile, turn right onto Duncan Park Drive. The stadium is directly ahead.

We discuss baseball in Charlotte (page 25) and Kannapolis (page 67) in separate chapters — as well as things to do in those cities.

Stop and Smell the Roses

One of Gaston County's top attractions, the still-under-development Daniel Stowe Botanical Garden, will eventually include over 400 acres of various flowers and foliage. Lots of events are offered all year long; check out their website for up-to-date information. The Garden is open seven days a week, 9 a.m.-5 p.m. Admission: $8 for adults, $6.50 for seniors 60+, $4 for children 4-12. Remember your camera, sunscreen and insect repellant; and picnic baskets are welcome.

Daniel Stowe Botanical Garden
6500 S. New Hope Rd.
Belmont, NC
dsbg.org/events.php

Directions: From Charlotte, take I-85 South to Exit 26 (Belmont-Belmont Abbey); turn right onto Highway 7 (Main Street); travel five miles through Belmont; turn left onto NC Highway 279 (South New Hope Road). The Garden will be three miles on your right. From the ballpark, take I-85 North to Exit 20 in Gastonia. Follow New Hope Road (NC Hwy. 279) south 10 miles. Garden is on the right.

Soothe the Soul

The church at Belmont Abbey, completed in 1893, is located on the 650-acre campus of Belmont Abbey College. The abbey features beautiful painted-glass windows, and the college's central campus has been designated a historic district on the National Register of Historic Places.

Belmont Abbey College is a private, coeducational Catholic liberal arts college offering undergraduate degrees in 17 major areas of study. The campus is shared with college founder Belmont Abbey, a Benedictine monastery started in 1876 that now includes about 20 monks. Bus tours and other large groups are not permitted, but individuals are permitted to visit the abbey and campus. For information on arranging a tour, call 704/461-6686.

Directions: Take exit 26 off I-85, and you'll see the campus just north of the highway.

For additional information on these or other attractions and accommodations in Gastonia and Gaston County, visit the Gaston County Department of Tourism at **gastontourism.com**.

Dining

If you come into Gastonia from the Charlotte side, you will see a sprawling string of shopping centers, big box stores, and chain restaurants just south of I-85 along Highway 74/29, also known as Franklin Avenue. If you long for the comfort of the chains, you'll have plenty of choices along here. Just get off the interstate at exit 20 or 21 and you'll see the usual suspects — Applebee's, Cracker Barrel, IHOP, etc.

If you want something more local, there are a few good choices. A true Gastonia institution, R.O.'s Barbeque has been slicing up delicious BBQ and serving their signature slaw since 1946. Founded by Robert O. (R.O.) Black and still run by the same family, R.O.'s is one of the few places you can still get curbside service from a car hop. Try a "Slaw Burger." I know, it sounds crazy, but this is a burger bun filled with slaw, and it's delicious. That's because this isn't any ordinary slaw. In fact, it's so popular that you can buy it in many area grocery stores. With tomatoes, unique spices and of course, mayonnaise and cabbage, it's like nothing you've ever tasted. If you've had enough of sitting in your car, though, you can go inside.

R.O.'s Barbecue
1318 Gaston Av.
704/866-8143
rosbbq.com

Directions: Take exit 17 off I-85, head south on 321 toward downtown, turn right on Airline Avenue (which turns into Gaston Avenue). Restaurant is on right.

Lodging

Both of the motels listed below are modern properties located right off the interstate on the Charlotte side of town, convenient to plenty of places to eat and shop. They are right next to each other as well, so if you're just showing up, you've got two shots at getting a room without driving around in the dark. Both have all the standard amenities.

Fairfield Inn by Marriott
1860 Remount Rd.
Gastonia, NC 28054
704/867-5073
fairfieldinn.com

Hampton Inn
1859 Remount Rd.
Gastonia, NC 28054
704/866-9090
hilton.com

Three hotels at Exit 17 are located very close to the ballpark. You can't walk to the ballpark from any of them, though, and there's not much else to recommend the neighborhood. But, if you really want convenience, the Holiday Inn is the best of the three.

Holiday Inn Express
1911 Broadcast Dr.
Gastonia, NC 28052
704/884-3300
holiday-inn.com

The Robin's Nest Bed and Breakfast is in Mt. Holly, a picturesque little town 2.5 miles north of I-85 at exit 27. Midway between Charlotte and Gastonia, on the Gaston County side of the Catawba River, this B&B is a 15- or 20-minute drive from the ballpark in Gastonia, but could provide a convenient base for a multiple-day stay with visits to both Charlotte and Gastonia, or even Hickory.

Robin's Nest Bed & Breakfast
156 N. Main Street
Mt. Holly, NC 28120
888/711-NEST or 704/827-2420
robinsnestbb.com

Directions: From Exit 27, head north on Highway 273, then turn left onto Main Street at the Eckerd Drug Store. Follow Main Street through downtown Mt. Holly until it crosses over Hwy. 27 (Charlotte Avenue). After crossing Hwy. 27, the house can be found one block up on your right.

See also the Charlotte chapter (page 25) for more information on the area lodgings.

 Directions

From I-85 North or South:

Take Exit 17 (Lincolnton, Gastonia) and go left at the light (Highway 321). Take a right at next light (Rankin Lake Road), and then a right onto N. Marietta Street. Sims Legion Park is on the right. Distance from exit is 0.6 mi.

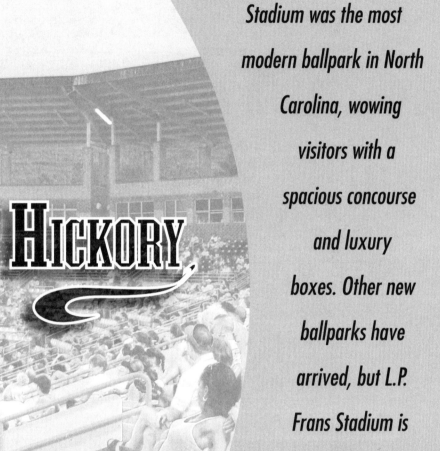

HICKORY

When it opened, L.P. Frans Stadium was the most modern ballpark in North Carolina, wowing visitors with a spacious concourse and luxury boxes. Other new ballparks have arrived, but L.P. Frans Stadium is a modern pioneer and still a great place to take in a game.

CHAPTER 4

L.P. FRANS STADIUM

Leading Off

Opened: 1993 • **Capacity:** 5,092

Dimensions: 330L, 400C, 330R

Current Team: Hickory Crawdads, Class A South Atlantic League (1993-present)

Former Hickory Teams (All Known as the Hickory Rebels): Western Carolina League (1952, 1960), Tar Heel League (1939-1940, 1953-54), North Carolina State League (1942, 1945-50), Carolina League (Independent) (1936-38) **Architect:** Matrix AEP

ESSENTIALS

Address: 2500 Clement Blvd., Hickory, NC 28601
Website: hickorycrawdads.com
Radio: 92.1 WMNC-FM
Phone: 828/322-3000
Ticket Prices: $6-$8

L.P. Frans Stadium: Beginning of a Fine Ballpark Trend

Hickory's ballpark, L.P. Frans Stadium, was one of the first of a new wave of facilities to sweep the South Atlantic League starting in the early '90s. Leaving behind a basic '70s-era facility (which still stands; see our Gastonia chapter on page 47), the Gastonia Rangers franchise was purchased by nursing-home magnate Don Beaver and moved to his hometown, bringing professional baseball to Hickory for the first time since 1960. Complete with a restaurant, walk-in souvenir stand, and tons of seating and parking, all constructed with tasteful concrete and brick, this park was just as significant for the Sally League when it opened in 1993 as Oriole Park at Camden Yards was for the majors.

Newer facilities in Lexington, Lakewood, and Greenville have supplanted L.P. Frans Stadium as the Sally League's premier facility. Nonetheless, anyone who can remember visiting this park for the 1994 SAL All-Star Game can tell you that the amenities and atmosphere were awe-inspiring at the time.

This ballpark remains one of the nicest places you'll find to see a game. The grounds are nicely manicured, with parking adjacent to the stadium costing just $2. The complex also includes a historical site with a museum and a rustic farmhouse that you can peek inside, thanks to Plexiglas doors, even when it's closed.

A row of luxury suites rings the top of the seating bowl, shielding most of the seating bowl from the evening sun. Two primary concession windows, one on each side of the grandstand, are positioned in a partially covered concourse behind the suites. A small grandstand roof provides more much-needed shade and some rain protection for the last few rows in the seating bowl.

The bottom half of the grandstand sports about a dozen rows of red box seats, while the upper half of the seating bowl features blue box seats in the center section and backless aluminum benches down the foul lines. The grandstand seats about 5,000 people, which is plenty for Hickory's relatively small market area (40,212 estimated city population in 2006).

Head all the way down the third-base line and you'll find a real carousel, complete with carved horses and a pink canopy. (Surprisingly, this isn't the state's only ballpark carousel, as the Winston-Salem Warthogs also offer this amenity.) There's also a nicely terraced picnic area at this end of the ballpark, another new addition since the park's construction.

At the top of the seating bowl above the first-base side you'll also find an in-stadium restaurant where you can take refuge from the heat and enjoy a hamburger or some chicken fingers, along with a cold draft beer. This is another amenity that was simply unheard of in a Single-A ballpark when the place opened; it remains fairly rare at that level.

The other concessions are good and reasonably priced, with standard fare like hot dogs, pizza, and popcorn; as a bonus, the draft beer is very cold. The team's game program is a winner, too. The Crawdads Chronicle, a big, tabloid-sized publication, is a welcome change from the trend toward the small freebie program found in most minor-league ballparks. Loaded with player information and statistics, this program is also updated during the season and features an easy-to-use scorecard page and baseball bingo. It's a great souvenir for just $2.

Twilight brings out the detail in the grandstand at L.P. Frans Stadium in Hickory.

The Crawdads play under the lights at L.P. Frans Stadium.

In front of the restaurant you'll find a small elevated seating area providing a little extra breeze for the fans sitting there. Below the elevation and beyond the end of the seating bowl there's a large, covered wooden party deck.

Plenty of space allows for milling around at the top of the grandstand, and the walk-in souvenir store located behind home plate is a good place to cool off for a few minutes on a hot summer night. A broad selection of merchandise is offered, and Hickory does a great job capitalizing on one of minor-league baseball's best logos.

The Crawdads were a merchandising sensation when the name and logo were unveiled. A unique, new name was a terrific choice for Hickory, especially since using the city's historic name, as the Durham Bulls had done in 1980, was simply not an option. Hickory's prior minor-league teams had all been named the Rebels, and while that may have been acceptable in 1960, it would not have been warmly received by baseball's powers that be in 1993.

General Manager David Haas has been running things in Hickory since the team's inception. Don Beaver and his ownership group at one time had aspirations to bring major-league ball to the Charlotte area and felt that establishing their own "farm system" would be a good step in that direction. At one point Beaver owned the Triple-A Charlotte Knights, the Double-A Tennessee Smokies, the high Class-A Winston-Salem Warthogs, and the Crawdads. Beaver's "system" lacked only a couple short-season teams and, of course, a big-league team.

This dream fizzled back in the 1990s as a flirtation with the Minnesota Twins led to nothing, and area voters refused to approve public funding for a big-league ballpark. Beaver eventually sold off the Smokies and the Warthogs, but still retains ownership of the Crawdads and the Knights, while also adding the Triple-A New Orleans Zephyrs in the Triple-A Pacific Coast League. Beaver also owns a share of the Pittsburgh Pirates, the team's parent club.

Hickory was originally affiliated with the White Sox when they joined the Sally League, and Chicago provided some very bad teams (like their first, a 52-88 squad) and some very good teams (like the 86-54 club the following year). There were some notable players, such as Magglio Ordonez and Aaron Rowand, during Hickory's years with the ChiSox, but the Pirates have boasted a virtual pipeline from Hickory in recent years. Much of the Pirates corps of young pitchers, including Zach Duke and Bryan Bullington, as well as position players like Brad Eldred, have come through Hickory.

Despite Beaver's inability to leverage his big-league credentials into a major-league team for North Carolina, the Hickory community embraces this team. This is Beaver's hometown, and the strength of the team's sponsorship support is evident in the towering right-field wall with four levels of fence sign advertising adjacent to the scoreboard and video board, accompanied by two levels of signs in left field.

L.P. Frans Stadium changed the way people looked at minor league ballparks when it opened in 1993 — the same year play started in Oriole Park at Camden Yards.

Hickory is a charming city with a revitalized downtown, including lots of unique restaurants, coffeehouses, and shops. For the less adventurous there is, of course, the typical collection of chain restaurants near the freeway, including Hooters, Longhorn, and Buffalo Wild Wings, and chain hotels south of downtown along the interstate, and near the intersection of U.S. highways 321 and 70.

Hickory is another club located so close to the Triad and Charlotte area teams that it is a must-visit on any multi-day trip to this part of the state. You'll find a clean, comfortable ballpark and an operation run with a tremendously friendly hometown feel. And when you visit the dazzling new ballparks around the South Atlantic League, remember that Hickory is where it all began.

Sports Around Town

In 2006 the Crawdads played a "throwback" game in nearby Granite Falls. M.S. Deal Stadium, a tidy concrete ballpark with a beautiful playing surface, was home to professional baseball for one season, 1951. Granite Falls had fielded successful teams in the textile leagues and moved into organized baseball as a member of the Class D Western Carolina League. While the team posted a dismal 14-96 record, the worst in pro baseball history, the Rocks hold the distinction of signing the first black players in North Carolina professional baseball history. A total of five blacks wore the Granite Falls uniform as the season mercifully wound down, but due to shoddy record keeping, this historic first went largely unreported.

Deal Stadium consists of a semi-circular concrete seating bowl with capacity for about 2,000 fans, and a small press box and concessions building above. Located on the grounds of Granite Falls Middle School, this is a great little side trip if you're a serious ballpark "collector," as it's less than 10 miles from Hickory.

To get to Deal Stadium, leave L.P. Frans Stadium and turn left on US-321 N. In no time you'll cross the Catawba River. About a mile after crossing the river, you'll turn off 321 N to the left onto 321 N Alt. Continue on 321 N. Alt into downtown Granite Falls and watch for Granite Falls Middle School.

Address: **90 N. Main St., Granite Falls, NC 28630.**

⚾ Insider's Tip

As you approach the entrance to the L.P. Frans parking lots, you will see a church housed in a large, modern building overlooking the ballpark. When the stadium first opened, this building was a convention center, built with the idea of sharing parking and other infrastructure with the ballpark. The convention center apparently didn't attract adequate traffic, so it was closed and the church took over the building. You can pay to park at the church for the ballgames, too, and some folks will come early and tailgate; the view of the game is pretty good from the front rows of this lot. If you're looking for a place to play some catch and watch batting practice before the gates open, this perch high above right field should be just the ticket.

Who is L.P. Frans?

The ballpark was named after L.P. Frans, a local businessman who donated the land for the ballpark. He owned the local Pepsi bottling operation, which can be seen prominently past the center-field fence.

Local Attractions

For the golf enthusiast, there's another Beaver operation worth checking out: Rock Barn Golf Club & Spa in nearby Conover. This course is best known as the home of the Greater Hickory Classic, a Champions (formerly known as the Seniors) Tour event. Rock Barn features an 18-hole, 7,033 yard layout created by legendary golf course designer Robert Trent Jones, Jr., and was selected by *Golf Digest* as the fourth-best new upscale public golf course in the country in 2003. For more information on the course, visit **rockbarn.com** or **greaterhickoryclassic.com**, or call 866/ROCK-BARN.

Hickory is known as a furniture shopper's mecca with two huge furniture malls, each boasting furnishings from over 100 different manufacturers in acre-upon-acre of retail space. The Hickory Furniture Mart (**2220 Hwy 70 SE., Hickory**; 800/462-MART) presents a complete selection of domestic and imported furniture and furnishings in 100 factory outlets. In addition to the four-level main building, the complex includes a hotel, restaurant, coffeeshop, shipping service, lounge, and tearoom. The Catawba Furniture Mall (**377 US Hwy. 70 SW., I-40 Exit 123b, Hickory**; 800/789-0686, 828/324-9701) offers over eight acres of discount sale furniture.

There's hands-on fun for kids as they learn about the natural and physical sciences through participatory exhibits at Catawba Science Center (**243 Third Av. NE., Hickory**; 828/322-8169; **catawbascience.org**).

The Hickory Motor Speedway (**Hwy. 70 E., Newton**; 828/464-3655; **hickorymotorspeedway.com**) is hailed as the birthplace of the NASCAR careers of Dale Earnhardt, Junior Johnson, Ned and Dale Jarrett and Harry Gant. The season runs March through October.

Dining

Serving the best beers from North Carolina, the Olde Hickory Tap Room also serves a very fine selection of food, fine handcrafted and imported beers and a large selection of fine single malts and liquors. Open daily for lunch and dinner.

Olde Hickory Tap Room
222 Union Square
828/322-1965
oldehickorybrewery.com

Head to downtown Hickory for coffeehouse atmosphere, live music, desserts, food and, of course, coffee at Drips Coffeehouse.

Drips Coffeehouse
256 First Av. NW.
828/324-1644

Lodging

Hickory isn't the largest of cities, so there are not a large number of lodging choices. Here's a sampling.

Councill House Bed and Breakfast
118 3rd Av. NE.
Hickory, NC 28601
828-322-3900
councillhouse.com

Courtyard By Marriott
1946 13th Av. Dr. SE.
Hickory, NC 28602
828/267-2100
marriott.com

Fairfield Inn
1950 13th Av. Dr. SE.
Hickory, NC 28602
828/431-3000
marriott.com

Hampton Inn
1520 13th Av. Dr. SE.
Hickory, NC 28602
828/323-1150
hilton.com

Directions

L. P. Frans Stadium is located near Hwy. 321 on Clement Boulevard.

From I-40:

Take Hwy. 321 north to the fifth traffic light. Turn left onto Clement Boulevard.
The ballpark is across from Hickory Regional Airport on the right.

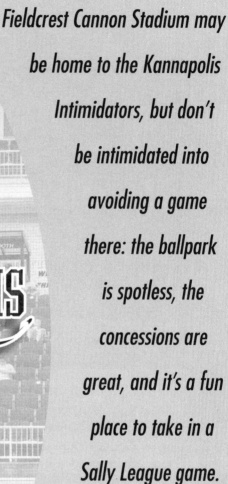

Fieldcrest Cannon Stadium may be home to the Kannapolis Intimidators, but don't be intimidated into avoiding a game there: the ballpark is spotless, the concessions are great, and it's a fun place to take in a Sally League game.

CHAPTER 5

FIELDCREST CANNON STADIUM

Leading Off

Opened: 1995

Capacity: 4,700

Dimensions: 330L, 410C, 310R

Current Team: Kannapolis Intimidators, Sally League (formerly Piedmont Phillies 1995, Piedmont Boll Weevils 1996-2000)

Overcoming Tragedy, Intimidators Find Ways to Celebrate

The Kannapolis Intimidators have been through a variety of identities since the team pulled up stakes and left Spartanburg, S.C. after the 1994 season. Upon arrival at Fieldcrest Cannon Stadium, the franchise was known as the Piedmont Phillies. The following season, they became the Piedmont Boll Weevils, which seemed like a sure bet to join the Mudcats and Muckdogs as a perennial merchandise leader among minor-league teams.

But one more change was in store for this franchise when an ownership group that included local hero and NASCAR legend Dale Earnhardt purchased the team in 2000. The name and logo were reworked by Sam Bass, who had done artwork and color schemes for a number of race teams. The ballclub's new identity gave proper tribute to the "Man in Black," his hometown, and the hard-charging driver's personal style. The Kannapolis Intimidators were born.

Sadly, the team didn't get long to bask in the limelight of the new association after Earnhardt's untimely death following a crash on the final lap of the Daytona 500 in 2001. His death lent a somber tone to the subsequent baseball season, and the Intimidators chose to honor Dale Sr. by retiring team jersey number 3, Earnhardt's car number. The team owners retained the Intimidators name, though, and the fans seem to acknowledge their local baseball team as a celebration of their favorite native son's life.

The ballpark experience in Kannapolis is certainly celebratory, as a spotless ballpark, a fantastic playground, and lots of concession windows create a great night of entertainment. Built for just $4 million in time for the 1995 season, this is an attractive but relatively simple ballpark. The seating bowl, with room for 4,700, lies below the entrance-level concourse, and the concessions face the field at the back of this plaza (although they are too far back to see much of the game while you're in line). The concourse is roomy, though, and there's plenty of space to stand and watch. There is no roof at this park, but the structure that houses the main entrance to the park holds six luxury boxes overlooking the concourse on the first-base side, as well as team offices and the souvenir shop.

The crowds are good in Kannapolis, and the demographics just keep getting better. This is the neighboring town to Concord, part of greater Charlotte that houses Lowe's Motor Speedway. A new $1 billion biotech campus on the site of the former Pillowtex plant is expected to completely change the face of this community. Like Kannapolis, the entire suburban area north of Charlotte area is growing like a weed, and the Intimidators are well positioned to reap the benefits.

Speaking of weed, one of the franchise's most notable players was former Texas Longhorn running back Ricky Williams. Williams, who played for the NFL's New Orleans Saints and Miami Dolphins (as well as the CFL's Toronto Argonauts while sitting out a drug suspension), also played four years of minor-league baseball during his college years. Drafted by the Phillies in 1995, Williams played for the

Kannapolis
Fieldcrest
Cannon Stadium

Piedmont Boll Weevils and foreshadowed his Heisman Trophy win with a much sought-after trading card that shows him striking the football statue's famous pose.

But football isn't the theme here – it's all about NASCAR. In addition to the team name, the kids' area is the "Pit Stop Playground." Since the Charlotte area, especially the northern suburbs, is the home base of most the big-time race teams, you may also find a driver and his team holding a picnic or a promotional night at any given ballgame.

You'll also notice some whimsical touches at this ballpark, but the best one is now gone. At one time the scoreboard read "Good Guys" for the home team and "Bad Guys" for the visitors. This is a nice gag, but Tim Mueller, the K-Dators Vice President, is no dummy. The gag made it possible not to change a scoreboard panel for years!

You don't have to go to Hollywood to play the Wheel of Fortune. Just walk the concourse at Fieldcrest Cannon Stadium and, as the song says, "pay your money and take your chances." For just a dollar, you can pull the wheel. There's no Vanna White, and the prizes don't include any vacations or cars, but you could win a hot dog, a drink, or free round of speedpitch. It's not to be missed.

The K-Dators have been a White Sox affiliate since 2001 and is part of a grouping of three Chisox affiliates in the area, including Triple-A Charlotte, High Class-A Winston-Salem, and Low Class-A Kannapolis. Jimmy Rollins and Dave Coggin are among the big-league alumni from the Phillies years.

This is a simple, clean, and attractive ballpark. It's not the most impressive facility in the state, nor does Kannapolis boast the baseball history or even the retro ballpark look found in many North Carolina cities. Yet, the brickwork, immaculate landscaping, bustling crowds, and well-run operation will make you glad you came to see Dale's team. The proximity to Charlotte, Hickory, and Greensboro make it a logical addition to any baseball trip through North Carolina.

⚾ Insider's Tip

You'll want to come early to Fieldcrest Cannon Stadium, or "The Cannon," as the team would like you to call it. While there are plenty of parking spaces, the entire complex is fed by one lane in and one lane out. Additional lanes are supposed to be in the works, but getting in can be tough close to game time, and getting out is even harder, so have that last beer and linger a little. Shop for some souvenirs or maybe try to get some autographs.

You'll also want to bear in mind that this ballpark has no covered seats, so bring your sunscreen and a hat. If you don't want to work on your tan, ask for seats immediately in front of the press box, which provides some shade.

Unless you have an umbrella or hat, little shade is available at Fieldcrest Cannon.

Sports Around Town

While the sports scene in the Kannapolis/Concord area is dominated by NASCAR (see "Things to Do," below) and, of course, the K-Dators, there is another minor-league team in town, at least as of this writing. Concord is home to a nice little modern arena complex known as the Cabarrus Arena & Events Center, which hosts the Carolina Speed, a team in the American Indoor Football Association. Given the shaky history of minor-

Dale Earnhardt Jr. (left) with Dan Hughes on QVC's For Race Fans Only, filmed outside the ballpark in 2001 with many fascinated young women in the audience.
Photo courtesy of the Kannapolis Intimidators

league indoor pro football, there's no telling how long this operation will last, but scheduled home dates run until late May, so one could conceivably catch a game during baseball season. And, if the Speed fold, there may be another team of some kind to take its place, so the best bet is to visit the arena site at **cabarrusarena.com**. Heading from Kannapolis, the arena is located **south of I-85; take US 601 south, and turn left on NC 49.**

A rich baseball history exists in the area, although the arrival of the current franchise marked the end of a 44-year drought. After many years competing in the area textile leagues, Concord fielded a team in the Carolina League from 1936-38. This is known as the "outlaw" period in the Carolina League's history when the teams, including the Concord Weavers, were openly paying all their players, with no salary cap, but outside the jurisdiction of the National Association. It's said that the generous salaries attracted a level of talent rarely seen outside of the major leagues, but in the end, it proved to be too great a burden, and the league disbanded.

A stint in the Class D North Carolina State League followed, which included the debut of a minor-league pitcher named Tommy Lasorda, who went 3-12 in 1945. The final season of professional baseball in Concord came in 1951.

Kannapolis' baseball history follows roughly the same path, from textile teams to a membership in the "outlaw" Carolina League to the North Carolina State League. The Kannapolis Towelers only made it until 1941, leaving the community without pro ball until the current franchise arrived prior to the '95 season.

Lodging

If you decide to stay in the Kannapolis area you will want to decide whether staying close to the ballpark is your highest priority, or whether to opt for the bustling Concord area 14 miles closer to Charlotte near the Concord Mills Mall and Lowe's Motor Speedway. Either way, you are not likely to find the accommodations inexpensive; spending a few dollars more can significantly upgrade the quality of your stay here.

Among the small handful of Kannapolis properties near I-85 exit 63, Fairfield Inn enjoys a particularly strong reputation.

Fairfield Inn Kannapolis
3033 Cloverleaf Pkwy.
Kannapolis, NC 28083
704/795-4888
marriott.com

Any number of hotel chains are represented near I-85 exit 49, but Embassy Suites distinguishes itself for its resort atmosphere as the manager of the adjacent Rocky River Golf Club. Both the Embassy Suites and Wingate Inn consistently rate highly for their level of service. The Wingate décor features a NASCAR theme.

Embassy Suites
5400 John Q. Hammons Dr. NW
Concord, NC 28023
704/455-8200
embassysuitesconcord.com

Wingate Inn
7841 Gateway Lane NW
Concord, NC 28027
704/979-1300
wingateinnconcord.com

THINGS TO DO

Lowe's Motor Speedway

This may have been dumb luck, but the last time I visited Lowe's Motor Speedway I was able to drive right into the facility down a service road and park directly behind the grandstand on the concourse at Turn 1. For anyone who is a ballpark buff, Lowe's Motor Speedway is an awesome sight; over 100,000 seats in one venue, and all of them sold every time the big guys roll into town. Another striking thing about this track is the patchwork quality of the place; some sections are sparkling and new with smoked glass and all the bells and whistles. At the opposite extreme, in at least one of the older sections the seats actually consist of metal folding chairs, legs removed, bolted to the concrete.

A smaller dirt track is located across the street, and a wealth of activities is offered at this complex, so your chances of seeing some racing or a car show are good. If you are a serious race fan, it is possible to combine a visit to see games in Kannapolis and Charlotte with a NEXTEL Cup race, as LMS hosts both the All-Star Challenge (formerly known as the Winston) and the Coca Cola 500 on consecutive weekends in May. The track also hosts an October Cup date, making it the only track in the business with what amounts to three NEXTEL Cup races. Visit the official website at **lowesmotorspeedway.com** for up-to-date race information.

Of course, if you can't make it on a race weekend or get your hands on tickets, there are very good tours. The "Feel The Thrill" tour is just $5 and includes several stops that aren't open to the public on race days, like the NEXTEL Cup garage, pit road, and Victory Circle. The highlight of the half-hour tour is a van ride around the track. The tour runs on non-event days, Monday through Saturday, on the half hour from 9:30 a.m to 3:30 p.m. with a break for lunch, and Sundays from 1:30 p.m. to 3:30 p.m. Call 704/455-3204 for more details.

You can also get your hands on a souvenir at the Lowe's Motor Speedway Gift Shop, located on the second floor of the Smith Tower. It's open Monday through Saturday from 9 a.m. to 5 p.m., and Sundays from 1 to 5 p.m.

Bass Pro Shops

For a person who cherishes the peace and tranquility of the outdoors, what could be better than a huge, crowded, indoor retail store overlooking an interstate highway? Nothing, judging by the traffic at the Bass Pro Shop at Concord Mills. With an unmatched selection of fishing, hunting, and camping gear, this place draws a crowd. Take I-85 toward Charlotte and get off at exit 49, the same exit as the racetrack. There's a huge cluster of retail there, everything from Chuck E. Cheese's to a Starbucks. Visit Bass Pro Shops online at **basspro.com** or call 704/979-2200.

For additional information on attractions, lodging and dining, visit **visitcabarrus.com**.

Also, see our Charlotte chapter (page 25); many of you will want to stay there and travel out to Kannapolis for a game. It's only 27 miles away.

 **Directions**

From I-85 South:

Take exit 63, turn right on Lane Street. From I-85 North, take exit 63, turn left on Lane Street. Stadium Drive will be 0.4 miles on your right.

SALISBURY

You just don't see many wood-roof ballparks anymore, so a visit to Salisbury's Newman Park, home to the Catawba College team, is a must for anyone wanting to see what ballparks were like in the 1920s and 1930s.

CHAPTER 6

NEWMAN PARK

Leading Off

Opened: 1926, grandstand constructed 1934 • **Current Team:** Catawba College (1926), NCAA Division II, member of South Atlantic Conference

Former Teams: Salisbury Bees (1937-38), North Carolina State League; Salisbury Giants (1939-1942), North Carolina State League; Salisbury Pirates (1945-1952), North Carolina State League; Salisbury Rocots (1953), Tar Heel League; Salisbury Braves (1960-62), Western Carolina League; Salisbury Dodgers (1963-64), Carolina League; Salisbury Astros (1965-66), Western Carolina League; Salisbury Senators (1967), Western Carolina League (future SAL)

ESSENTIALS

Capacity: 2,500
Website: gocatawbaindians.com
Phone: 704/637-4474
Ticket Prices: Free

A Rare Wooden Gem

Located on the campus of Catawba College, Newman Park is one of the finest examples of a roofed wood grandstand in use anywhere in the country. The Catawba College Indians because playing baseball on this site in 1926. After construction of the grandstand in 1934, Newman Park also hosted more than 25 years of monor-league baseball from 1937 through 1968. In North Carolina, only Edenton's park is in the same category, but Newman Park has been continuously maintained, whereas Edenton's ballpark required a major renovation the late '90s.

This ballpark still hosts the Catawba College baseball team, as well as the local American Legion team. To look at the ballpark, with its pristine outfield wall adorned with billboards advertising local businesses, you would think it was still hosting a minor-league team. A modern press box and concession building is of more recent vintage, part of a 1994 renovation.

A more recent renovation added fold-down stadium seats to the front rows of the grandstand. But until this upgrade, box-seat holders sat in straight back chairs like you'd find in your country grandmother's kitchen.

The park is named for Dr. H. H. Newman, who served as the Catawba team doctor for over 20 years from the mid-1920s through the late 1940s.

This park has hosted North Carolina State League, Tar Heel League, and Western Carolina League (precursor to today's South Atlantic League) teams, and saw affiliations with the Senators, Pirates, Giants, Colt .45s, Mets, Dodgers, and Astros.

Newman Park shows its age, yet still serves at home field for Catawba College.
Photo courtesy of Dennis Bastien.

Salisbury's last minor-league team, the Salisbury Senators, struggled to a 34-87 record during the 1968 Western Carolina League season.

PLAY BALL

Don
PADGETT

....12 YEARS IN MAJOR LEAGUES....
(CARDINALS, DODGERS,
PHILS AND BRAVES)
....HIT .399 SECOND
YEAR IN MAJORS....
POWER HITTER WITH
ALL CLUBS......
....PLAYED WITH OAK-
LAND PACIFIC
COAST LEAGUE IN
1949)....HIT 28
HOME RUNS IN
1950....BATTED
.363 FOR RUNNER-
UP HONORS....
NEVER PLAYED
BELOW 'A' BALL....
FIRST YEAR AS
MANAGER... 6'-2"...
WT. 250....HAILS
FROM HIGH POINT.

MANAGER
SALISBURY
ROCOTS....

SALISBURY ROCOTS
SCORE CARD

1952   10c

1952 Salisbury Rocots score card features manager Don Padgett.
Image courtesy of the Notre Dame Rare Books collection.

Notable players to call Newman Park home include pitcher Jack Billingham, who played for the Salisbury Dodgers in 1963 and later pitched for Cincinnati's "Big Red Machine" Reds teams. Bob Watson, who would go on to big-league success as an outfielder for Houston and later as general manager of the New York Yankees, played for the Salisbury Astros in 1965.

If you have a fondness for the old parks, you won't want to miss this one. Visit the Catawba College athletics website to check the schedule and take in a game for free. Salisbury is convenient to Kannapolis, Greensboro, and Winston-Salem, so it's an easy park to visit even if there's not a game. The wooden ballparks are a vanishing breed, so don't delay.

WHAT TO DO

See our chapters on Kannapolis (page 67), Greensboro (page 95), and Winston-Salem (page 161), as those are the largest cities near Salisbury.

Salisbury is a picturesque community with a compact downtown dominated by two-story stone and brick buildings. It's also the hometown of U.S. Senator Elizabeth Dole, although she hasn't lived there regularly in decades.

Grab a meal at Hap's Grill, a local institution featuring hot dogs and hamburgers. Located in a long, narrow building at 116½ N. Main Street that used to be an alley, you'll need to stand while you eat, but it's the fastest lunch in town. Plan ahead; Hap's Grill is only open from 10 a.m. to 3 p.m.

For train buffs, the N.C. Transportation Museum in nearby Spencer features an extensive train yard and shop. Admission is free, although there are some small charges for rides and other special attractions. *From I-85, take exit 79, head north on Andrews Street, turn left on S. Salisbury Avenue; the museum will be on the left.*

For more information on area lodging and attractions, see **visitsalisburync.com**.

 Directions

Take exit 76 off I-85, head north on E. Innes Street through downtown Salisbury. E. Innes will become W. Innes and pass onto Catawba College campus. Turn left on Summit Avenue; the ballpark is straight ahead.

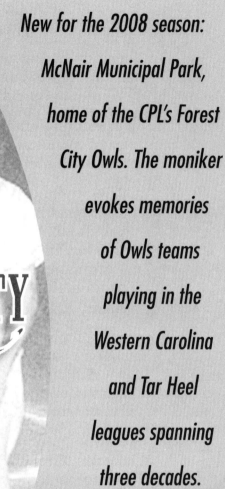

FOREST CITY

New for the 2008 season: McNair Municipal Park, home of the CPL's Forest City Owls. The moniker evokes memories of Owls teams playing in the Western Carolina and Tar Heel leagues spanning three decades.

CHAPTER 7

MᴄNᴀɪʀ Mᴜɴɪᴄɪᴘᴀʟ Pᴀʀᴋ

Leading Off

Opened: 2008

Capacity: 2,500

Dimensions: 315L, 380C, 330R

Current Team: Forest City Owls, Coastal Plain League (2008-present)

Former Teams: Forest City Owls, Western Carolina League (1948-1952, 1960); Forest City Owls, Tar Heel State League (1953-1954)

ESSENTIALS

Website: forestcitybaseball.com
Phone Number: 828/245-0000
Ticket Prices: Box $7, General Admission $5 Adult, $4 Kids & Seniors

The Owls Come Home to Roost

"Small Town Friendly" is the motto of this bucolic hamlet, and that's what you'll find in Forest City, the newest entry in the summer-collegiate Coastal Plain League. With beautiful mountain views and a team of its own, this community of 8,000 will serve as a kind of book end opposite the CPL's other small town, Edenton. The Owls complete the CPL's journey from the Triangle to the Coast, and now west to the foothills of the Blue Ridge Mountains.

Of course, the new Coastal Plain League began by providing minor-league-style baseball for many communities in eastern and central North Carolina still sporting great old ballparks. Communities like Wilson, Edenton, and Asheboro have charming baseball facilities but had left behind by pro baseball. Putting CPL baseball into some of these old ballparks involved major renovations, but facilities built specifically for the CPL were practically unheard of during the league's first nine years. The "new ballpark" in Petersburg was really a rec complex field with no grandstand.

Thomasville was the first, although the Hi-Toms' wonderful new ballpark is really the third incarnation of Finch Field, complete with the same historic playing field, lights, and outfield wall. And Thomasville's ballpark was an upgrade for an existing franchise. But a new ballpark, built just to attract a Coastal Plain League team, is uncharted territory. In fairness, it should be noted that this stadium is being built on the site of an existing ballfield, the city's old Legion field. This will be a completely new facility, though, including a new playing surface, grandstand, and lights.

But that's just what the erstwhile Spartanburg Stingers are headed for in Forest City, which has rolled out the red carpet for baseball. After years of struggles at historic Duncan Park Stadium in Spartanburg, S.C., the Stingers were pushed out following the 2006 season and spent 2007 at Wofford College's Russell C. King Field. This was an attractive new college park, but the team had no assurances regarding their future, and they knew they would always play second fiddle to Wofford's own team.

For baseball fans in Spartanburg, this must have been déjà vu all over again. In the fall of 1994, Spartanburg watched their South Atlantic League team make a much-anticipated move up the road to a North Carolina city offering a brand new home. That time, it was Kannapolis, just north of Charlotte, dangling a new $5 million facility for the Class-A team now known as the Kannapolis Intimidators.

This time around it was the town of Forest City, located about 30 miles directly north across the North Carolina state line from Spartanburg, casting the lure. And, once again, while the city of Spartanburg watches their treasure of a ballpark deteriorate, a new facility is being constructed in a nearby community. While there are plans to renovate Duncan Park Stadium, one of the country's great old minor-league parks, it didn't happen soon enough for the Stingers.

Forest City's new park is McNair Municipal Stadium, named after Bob McNair, owner of the NFL's Houston Texans. McNair grew up in Forest City but made his fortune in the electricity business in Houston. In addition to his NFL team, McNair is involved in horse racing and recently donated $100 million to Baylor University's school of medicine, where he serves as a trustee. McNair, who operates a charitable foundation in Houston and in Forest City, donated $850,000 toward the building

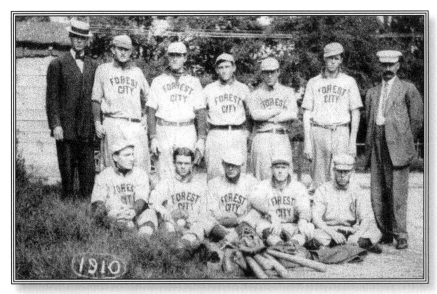

1910 Forest City ball club. *Photo courtesy of the Forest City Owls.*

of the new park. Clearly McNair, who hasn't lived in Forest City for decades, retains a sense of pride in his old hometown. And that spirit is just the beginning, as the business community and baseball fans of Forest City have come out of the woodwork in a display of support that Owls staff has termed "stunning."

Oh, yes, the name. Owls. Fantastic. Sometimes the simplest answer is the best and, like the Durham Bulls, Wilson Tobs, and the Asheville Tourists, the team owners chose a simple, classy name synonymous with minor-league baseball in the community.

Never mind that Forest City hasn't fielded a team since 1960. Their teams in the Western Carolina League (the forerunner of today's South Atlantic League) and the Tar Heel League were all known as the Owls. Local legend says that the team was originally named after the nocturnal birds when they began play in the forties because Forest City was one of the only teams in the league with lights, allowing them to play night games. Regardless, it's a simple, original name with a solid place in local history, and team owner Ken Silver and his boys came up with a classic understated logo sure to be a big hit.

On the approach to the park, wrought iron and brick fencing surrounding the park will greet fans. The ballpark itself will feature a playing surface four feet lower than it was when the park was known as Legion Field. There will be about 500 box seats and 1,000 general admission seats in the grandstand, with room for about 1,000 more combined in the beer garden and a grass-berm seating area.

The main grandstand will have some similarities to Thomasville's Finch Field, including a steel girder structure with a roof and a press box at the top of the grandstand. There will be brick standalone buildings for tickets, souvenirs, bathrooms, and concessions, but the sunken field should give this park a very distinctive feel.

The concessions stand will offer a full range of offerings, including pizza, soda, fries, hamburgers, hot dogs, chicken tenders, pop corn, ice cream, and candy bars, to name just some of the planned items. For fans who love a little local flavor, try a barbeque sandwich from City Table BBQ, a well-known take-out restaurant in Forest City.

It won't make you forget the Green Monster, but McNair Municipal Ballpark will have a 30-foot high outfield wall in left. Call it "The Multi-Colored Monster," since it will likely be loaded with advertisers. The plans as of press time also called for a scoreboard with a video screen.

Parking will be available in a lot beyond center field, behind the Cool Spings Gym across the street from the park, as well as another lot behind the third-base side of the stadium. Other parking can be found in several adjacent bank and business parking lots behind right field.

1949 Rutherford County Owls

Front Row (l to r) Buren Jolley, Willie Lovett, James Caddy, Lefty Haynes, Richard Rizario, Paul Sisco
Second Row (l to r) Rube Wilson (manager), Roy Lamb, Charles "Buddy" Morrow, Jack Gilbert, Richard Pottketter, Grady Millwood
Third Row (l to r) Ralph Padgett, Bill McKenny, Dean Padgett, Charlie Timm, Jess Hill(business manager)

1949 Rutherford County Owls. *Photo courtesy of the Forest City Owls.*

For the first year, the team's offices and locker rooms will be at Cool Springs Gym, which is about a quarter mile from the park. Long-term plans call for team offices and locker rooms in the ballpark, as well some other amenities that include a playground.

The Owls will play in traditional home whites with "Owls" stitched across the chest. The road uniforms will be traditional road gray with lettering spelling out "Forest City." Keep an eye out for a Forest Green alternate jersey, as well as throwback uniforms honoring the Owls teams of the '40s and '50.

There is little doubt that this team will be successful. Take the excitement of a new team and a new ballpark, combine it with healthy dose of the history of baseball in Rutherford County, add summer college baseball, and you have a winning combination. In a small community, the host family relationships unique to summer-college baseball are a team's best marketing tools. Host families get to know the kids and care for them like they are their own children. And the players generally treat their hosts like gold, often staying in touch well beyond the end of their playing days.

Ken Silver's history as a well-regarded owner in both minor-league and

Did You Know?

Smoky Burgess, who was a Major League catcher and noted pinch hitter from 1949 to 1967, was originally known as Forrest Harrill when growing up in Forest City. He played for the Cubs, Phillies, Reds, Pirates, and White Sox, and was an All-Star six times, coaching in the Braves farm system in the '80s.

A current Braves minor-league manager, Randy Ingle is from Forest City, as is Chad Flack, who is the third baseman for the UNC Tar Heels.

summer college baseball also tells you that this team will do things right. Look for a long, successful roost for the Owls in Forest City.

⏰ Insider's Tip

You can have your hot dog or barbecue sandwich with a beer, but you'll need to carry it to the beer garden down the third-base line. As is the case in several of the CPL's smaller communities, beer is a relatively sensitive topic. As a result, the Owls will err on the side of caution and restrict beer to the as-yet-unnamed beer garden (we're voting for The Nest). And if that strikes you as a bit inconvenient, remember that the alternative is likely having no beer sales. Now, that would be inconvenient! And let's face it, don't you always wind up in the beer garden anyway? After all, that's where the beer and all the fun people are.

Food & Lodging & Attractions

For a travelling fan, McNair Municipal Stadium's proximity to downtown should make for a pleasant game-day experience. Drive over the ballpark early and pick up your box seats; if you want reserved seats, buy them early, since most of the box seats sold out as season tickets. If you're timing is right, you can probably check out batting practice. Then, stroll over to the Old Mill Tavern. You'll find several TVs playing all the games, a good selection of food including burgers, pizza, sandwiches, and steaks. Several beers are offered on tap and in a wide selection of bottles.

If you have a little more time to kill, take a walk around downtown. It will remind you a bit of Mayberry, yet you'll find modern conveniences like a specialty coffee shop called the Daily Grind, and a retro movie theater currently under construction.

When you've taken in a pregame meal and a drink, walk back over to the park. Enjoy the game, including a barbecue sandwich from City Table BBQ — just to make sure you don't leave hungry.

Forest City could make for a nice day trip if you are staying in the Charlotte or Hickory areas. If you decide to stay in Forest City, there are a number of lodging choices, but I recommend the Holiday Inn Express, the area's newest hotel, or if your budget is little tighter, the Jameson Inn. The Holiday Inn Express is relatively new, but both have all the standard amenities including free breakfast, a fitness center, and Internet access.

In addition to City Table BBQ, which you can get at the park, you'll want to try Hickory Log BBQ. There also are several other restaurants in town, including chains like Zaxby's, Bojangles, Chili's, and Fatz.

Jameson Inn
164 Jameson Inn Dr.
Forest City, NC 28043
828/287-8788
jamesoninns.com

Holiday Inn Express
200 Holiday Inn Dr.
Forest City, NC 28043
828/755-2000
holiday-inn.com

Author's Disclaimer

Unlike the other chapters in this book, this section is a preview of a ballpark not built as of press time, covering a team that hasn't yet played a game. The information included reflects the best information available.

⊕ Directions

From Charlotte, take I-85 toward Gastonia. Take exit 10B for US-74 West toward Kings Mountain and Shelby. Take exit 182 for 221-Alternate toward Forest City/ Alexander Mills. Turn left onto US-221 Alt. / S. Broadway. Turn left onto US-221 Alt N / US-74 BR W / E. Main Street. E. Main becomes W. Main, turn right on Wingo Street, ballpark is on right.

Greensboro -

PIEDMONT

SECTION 2

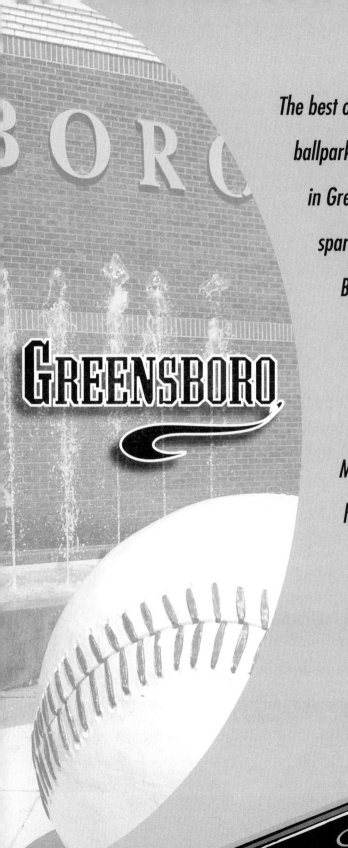

The best of new and old
ballparks can be found
in Greensboro, where
sparkling NewBridge
Bank Park hosts
professional
baseball, and
venerable War
Memorial Stadium
hosts college and
amateur ball.

CHAPTER 8

NewBridge Bank Park

Leading Off

Opened: 2005

Capacity: 7,499, including 5,300 chair back seats

Dimensions: 315L, 365LC, 400C, 392RC, 312R

Current Team: Greensboro Grasshoppers,

Class A South Atlantic League

Architect: Ken Mayer, Moser Mayer

Phoenix Associates

Construction: Barton Malow

Company

ESSENTIALS

Address: 408 Bellemeade St., Greensboro
Website: gsohoppers.com
Phone: 336/268-BALL (2255)
Online Broadcast: gsohoppers.com

State of the Art in Classic Style – And Quite the View

The Greensboro Bats, traditionally among the leaders in the South Atlantic (Sally) League attendance race, had fallen on tough times in recent years. An occasional fireworks show or weekend promotion still packed the place, but War Memorial Stadium was really starting to show its age. First opened in the 1920s as a football facility, War Memorial had been reconfigured to host baseball and served that task admirably for over 50 years. But Greensboro needed a new facility, and after several failed referendums where voters were asked to approve a publicly financed ballpark, the Bats' ownership (a local group with strong ties in the community) teamed up with the Bryan Foundation, a well-funded Greensboro nonprofit, to foot the bill. The result is a beautiful new facility that adds momentum to the city's revitalized urban core, which features a thriving nightlife scene, local theater, a children's museum, and more.

As the 2005 season got underway, the Bats became the Grasshoppers, and the then-named First Horizon Park opened up with an exhibition game pitting the Hoppers, a Florida Marlins Single-A affiliate, against their big-league parent. (The name changed in 2007 when First Horizon National pulled the plug on the naming-rights deal.) With the Marlins just a year removed from their World Series win in 2003, the place was sold out months in advance. The Marlins lineup included Mike Lowell, Dontrelle Willis, Carlos Delgado, and Paul LoDuca, and they were led by manager Jack McKeon — an area resident. The Marlins pounded the Grasshoppers, but it was a walk-off home run of a debut for this fantastic new ballpark.

Most of the structure in this retro facility is built of brick. You enter the park at the top of the seating bowl, filled with fold-down stadium chairs in classic dark green. The 30-foot-wide concourse is open to the seating bowl, with 16 luxury boxes overhead. Although the seating bowl lacks a real roof to protect against the elements, the open concourse provides a sheltered feel and plenty of room for a crowd to take refuge. A hint of a roof arches over the luxury boxes, and

Fans enjoy plentiful shade on a hot Greensboro day at NewBridge Bank Park.

it's got a scalloped facing evoking the famous arched façade of the original Yankee Stadium. Intentional or not, the association with New York is historically appropriate, as the Bronx Bombers served several stints as Greensboro's parent club, including one run throughout the 1980s and 1990s. A parade of future stars, including Don Mattingly, Derek Jeter, and Curt Schilling passed through the Gate City on their way to the big leagues.

Overall, the basic design of the ballpark is fairly standard when compared to other recently opened facilities.

Then again, why reinvent the wheel?

A number of the finishing touches manage to bring this ballpark into its own. Ultimately, this is an extremely well-designed, well-executed, state-of-the-art ballpark that blends with its cityscape and exhibits a classic feel. Construction was completed by Georgia-based Barton Malow Company.

The new park does have some unique features, like the "Grandstand" sports bar area down the left-field line replicating the feel of the wooden-roofed open-air sports bar in the old park. This is a hugely popular area, particularly on Thursday nights when the Grasshoppers, like nearly every minor-league team in the country, sell $1 beer. The scene on Thursdays features masses of young singles milling around the Grandstand and Natty's Hill, many of whom barely notice there's a game going on. It doesn't matter, though, because the 'Hoppers have become the place to be seen on Thursday nights, whether you care about baseball or not.

The design team also effectively re-creates the open seating boxes in the bar area at the old park. These boxes feature a wide variety of sizes and shapes divided by wooden half-walls, and plastic patio chairs and tables filling them. The new boxes are sectioned off with pipe railings and are filled with tall silver chairs and tall bar-style tables. Located at the end of the third-base side of the seating bowl, they are a little more symmetrical and uniform than anything in the old park, but they are a very comfortable way to watch a game and even feature waitress service. This option also allows the 'Hoppers to offer a corporate seating option less expensive than their luxury suites.

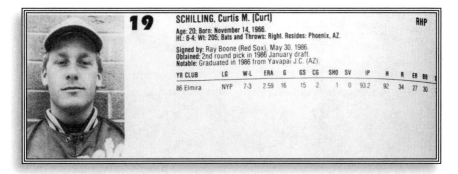

19	SCHILLING, Curtis M. (Curt)													RHP

Age: 20; Born: November 14, 1966.
HL: 6-4; Wt: 205; Bats and Throws: Right. Resides: Phoenix, AZ.

Signed by: Ray Boone (Red Sox), May 30, 1986.
Obtained: 2nd round pick in 1986 January draft.
Notable: Graduated in 1986 from Yavapai J.C. (AZ).

YR CLUB	LG	W-L	ERA	G	GS	CG	SHO	SV	IP	H	R	ER	BB
86 Elmira	NYP	7-3	2.59	16	15	2	1	0	93.2	92	34	27	30

1987 Hornets program entry for future star pitcher Curt Schilling.

If you are fortunate enough to visit the luxury-box area, you'll see more of the little details that make this park special. Both stairs and elevators lead to an open-air concourse serving the suites. The support posts holding up the roof over this walkway have the look of carved porch posts on an antebellum mansion; they also bring to mind the Old Well on the Chapel Hill campus, a Piedmont touchstone. Even the use of a yellow clapboard-type material in the exterior of the luxury suites brings to mind a rural North Carolina farmhouse.

There's a huge playground down the first-base side of the concourse, and the kids love Guilford the Grasshopper (Greensboro is in Guilford County). Guilford, though, is just one of a large cast of game-day characters. Miss Babe Ruth is a well-trained golden lab who retrieves bats from home plate and brings baseballs to the umpires. But this is no show dog; Babe is GM Donald Moore's pet, and she can often be seen roaming the ballpark with him before games.

The park has tons of classy bathrooms (everything's automatic: flush, sinks, paper towels). Take note of the main ballpark gates next to the souvenir shop: they are a unique piece of baseball sculpture. It's almost a shame they're open during the games, since they are best admired closed. There is a neat little architectural touch at the first-base entrance, too, where the uprights of the gates are full-size metal bats. These are just a few of the many small architectural details that make this park something special.

Several entrances bring you onto the concourse extending all the way around the park. In right field, you can walk right up underneath the second-largest video board in minor-league baseball.

Many concessions stands throughout the main concourse feature names referencing local history. The menu is varied, including hot dogs, chicken fingers, pizza, and much more. A variety of excellent beers are offered, including several selections from local brewer Natty Greene's.

The previously referenced Natty's Hill is an expanded berm area next to the Grandstand bar. Originally a small grassy area oriented toward the family crowd,

View from down the right field line at NewBridge Bank Park.

the berm proved surprisingly popular during the 2005 season, and on Thursday nights it became an overflow location for the dollar-beer crowd. Prior to the 2006 season, the team more than tripled the size of the berm, adding a concrete concourse with café-style seating at the top of the hill. Through the use of portable beer boxes and hot-dog cookers, this is now an extension of the Grandstand bar on Thursdays, with plenty of taps and lots of mingling space. The hill also provides a wonderful roomy area for a family to lay out their blanket every other night of the week. Sponsored by local brewpub Natty Greene's (*more on this in Dining*), this area also hosts live music on non-game days and some corporate functions on game nights, as well.

Grasshoppers?!? Huh?

Although the name has now become synonymous with big crowds and a beautiful ballpark, the name *Grasshoppers* was not well received by everyone in the community when it was announced prior to the 2005 season. The team's arguments were reasonable: they had wanted something starting with "G" to go with Greensboro, grass is green, baseball is played on grass, etc. One argument the team couldn't advance publicly was also likely a factor: it's very difficult these days to find a name

that isn't already trademarked. Despite this criticism, the name grows on you, the logo and the mascot have proven to be kid-friendly, and the merchandise has sold briskly. These are the real tests, after all.

The 'Hoppers uniforms have a nice old-timey look, and the color scheme, with cream, green, and a muted orange, is very attractive. A wide range of reasonably priced souvenirs is displayed in the roomy walk-in souvenir stand behind home plate next to the main entrance. This area has the advantage of being air conditioned, which is a great way to draw people in during North Carolina's hot summers. This space is also cleverly arranged, as the souvenir shop serves as the lobby for the Grasshoppers offices when there's not a game going on and can be used for press conferences, receptions, and other functions.

The Grasshoppers' record-breaking crowds have certainly validated the construction of this new facility. It's worth keeping in mind the park was built to Double-A specifications. It certainly seems Greensboro could support that level of baseball, and they are well within the geography of the Double-A Southern League, which has several franchises that would be delighted to have the crowds the Grasshoppers draw. It also seems like the same type of civic boosterism that led to a privately financed downtown ballpark may lead the 'Hoppers to pursue a higher level of play.

WAR MEMORIAL STADIUM

Leading Off

Opened: 1926
Capacity: 8,000
Dimensions: 327L, 401C, 307R
Current Team: North Carolina A&T Aggies,
Mid-Eastern Athletic Conference
Greensboro College Pride,
USA South Conference

"Classic," according to the Merriam-Webster dictionary; historically memorable, or noted because of special literary or historical associations.

Greensboro's former home to minor-league baseball, War Memorial Stadium, is truly a classic. The name says it all. It was named simply "War Memorial" because at the time of this park's construction, there had only been one great "War" with a capital W — World War One. War Memorial was built in 1926 and for many years was the oldest active ballpark in all of Minor League Baseball.

Ironically, this facility, considered by many to be the epitome of old-time North Carolina ballparks, was originally built for tennis and track. If you walk along the small gravel parking lot outside the first-base side of the ballpark, you'll notice a stream running under right field. Much of right field sits over a babbling brook, which was eventually covered over with a sort of concrete bridge complete with several feet of topsoil and sod on top. This is the clearest testament to this ballpark's original purpose and configuration.

Fans flocking into War Memorial Stadium were featured on the front of the 1980 Greensboro Hornets Souvenir Program.

The flowing water below right field also provided current General Manager Donald Moore with the signature moment in his first season in charge of the franchise. An admitted baseball novice at the time, Moore was several innings into the team's opener when the opposing team's right fielder chased a ball to wall and suddenly disappeared from sight. The aging plywood wall had given way when he hit it, and by the time Donald and some of the team's other staffers reached him, he was struggling out of the creek as his hat floated downstream. The player's hat was retrieved, plywood was located to patch up the outfield wall, and Donald realized he had been officially initiated.

Often described as an inverted J, War Memorial's main structure is a roofed grandstand overlooking the infield, with the long stem of the J consisting of a long football-style set of concrete bleachers running down the third-base line. Where the stem meets the left-field corner is the location of the original Grandstand sports bar, built in the early 1990s. Billed as having the longest bar in the state at the time of its opening, the Grandstand became an attraction in its own right and often stayed open for hours past the conclusion of the night's contest. This made Greensboro a favorite of visiting players, who enjoyed this tremendously convenient post-game night spot, but the neighbors were not nearly as happy about this new arrangement and the late-night activities eventually were curtailed.

The dramatic entrance to this park features a massive triple archway leading between two stout towers. Concessions were crammed underneath the grandstand in the enclosed concourse. A small walk-in souvenir shop sat to the right of the main entryway, and the team offices were to the left. The team was so desperate for additional concessions space that when a renovation was undertaken to add a walkway around the front of the grandstand and install new dugouts closer to the field, the old dugouts were converted into concessions stands.

If you've been to Asheboro, you'll see familiar-looking yellow seats in this park: War Memorial and McCrary Park feature used seats sold during the 1994 renovation of the Greensboro Coliseum, which were reportedly being sold for $1 apiece provided you carried them away yourself.

When War Memorial Stadium was built the configuration was more oriented to football and track than baseball. When the Greensboro Patriots of the old Piedmont League became the park's first baseball tenant, the dimensions were reminiscent of the Polo Grounds in New York, with extremely short home-run distances in both right and left and the distance to the right-field foul pole barely 250 feet. Prior to the 1930 season, the playing field was rotated clockwise, trading a smaller foul territory behind home plate for a more traditional set of outfield dimensions.

Lights were also reportedly introduced to the facility in 1930, and that year's team also saw Hank Greenberg and Johnny Mize make their Greensboro debuts. Johnny Vander Meer played here as a member of the Durham Bulls, while Ted Williams

War Memorial Stadium had its share of oddities, including a grandstand in the left field corner. The ballpark was full on this day when the Asheville Tourists came to town.

made an appearance when he was attending flight school at Chapel Hill. Williams is said to have hit a towering home run over the right-field fence.

This park hosted several major-league exhibition games, including an appearance by the Brooklyn Dodgers led by Jackie Robinson, Carl Erskine, Duke Snyder, and Pee Wee Reese that drew a crowd of nearly 9,000 people. Mickey Mantle's Yankees also visited War Memorial when the Yankees were Greensboro's parent club, a relationship that began in 1958 with the birth of the Greensboro Yankees. The New York Yankees sent some of their best talent to town, including Yankee standouts like Mel Stottlemyre (1962), Roy White (1963), and Bobby Murcer (1965). Murcer was the '65 Carolina League Most Valuable Player and was called up to New York that September.

The 1981 souvenir program cover is a map of the South Atlantic League cities featuring 1980 champion Greensboro at the top.

The Yankees gave way to the Houston Astros in 1968 (with the team switching back to the Greensboro Patriots moniker), but by 1969 Greensboro was without minor-league baseball and did not get back into the game until 1979. Interestingly, this drought (1969-1978) virtually coincided with the same period that Durham was also without minor-league baseball (1972-1979). This is a clear illustration of the sad

Night game at War Memorial Stadium.

state of minor-league baseball in the 1970s, when the Western Carolina League (now the South Atlantic League) and the Carolina League were reduced to just four teams each, playing an interlocking schedule as a means of survival. If minor-league baseball couldn't survive in Durham and Greensboro, it's a miracle it survived anywhere.

It's hard to comprehend those struggles today as the minor-league baseball continues the boom began in the late 1970s in Columbus, Ohio, and Nashville, Tenn. The Greensboro Hornets of the Class A Western Carolina League were also one of the early success stories, as they led all of Class A with attendance of 165,635 in their 1979 inaugural season.

1997 Greensboro
Official Program

Former Greensboro player Derek Jeter and the 1996 Yankee championship trophy are prominently featured on the 1997 Bats' program cover.

Greensboro's future Yankees had great success on the field, too, as the 1980 team won the championship of the newly renamed South Atlantic League with star players including Don Mattingly, former Louisburg College standout Otis Nixon, Greg Gagne (who later won two World Series rings as shortstop for the Minnesota Twins), and Rex Hudler.

In 1993, the team's last year as the Hornets, the roster featured a shortstop named Derek Jeter, who led the team to a playoff appearance.

The Bats name and logo were unveiled in 1994, and outfielder Ruben Rivera won the Sally League's Most Valuable Player award with 28 home runs, an almost unheard-of total in Single-A ball.

When the Bats were renamed the Grasshoppers in October 2004 and moved their operations to then-First Horizon Park in February 2005, it was the end of more than an era. In nearly 80 years as the city's premier baseball facility, War Memorial saw several eras come and go — from baseball's preeminence in the 1930s and 1940s to the decline of the sport in the 1960s and 1970s. And War Memorial was still there, ready to play host to the beginnings of minor-league baseball's boom. Ironically, the old stadium was ultimately a victim of the game's success.

There's no debating the community's need for NewBridge Bank Park, but it's also worth remembering that there are those who fought the new ballpark, although they are rarely heard from these days. Many of these well-intentioned folks simply worried that the incredible history of War Memorial Stadium would be lost. It seems, though, that those fears were unfounded. War Memorial will continue to serve as the home to the baseball teams of both North Carolina A&T University and Greensboro College baseball teams, and when combined with some high-school and adult baseball, this should remain a very active ballpark.

For North Carolina A&T schedule information, visit **ncataggies.com/baseball/home.htm**. For Greensboro College schedule information, visit **gborocolllege.edu/athletics/sports/ baseball.htm**.

Derek Jeter at Greensboro War Memorial Stadium

It's impossible to talk about Greensboro's baseball history at War Memorial Stadium without talking about the city's long relationship with the New York Yankees. Mel Stottlemyre, Bobby Murcer, and Don Mattingly were just a few of the future Yankees to pass through the Gate City on their way to the Bronx.

Among active Yankee players, though, there's no more notable Greensboro alum than Derek Jeter, the Yankee shortstop and team captain. And Greensboro fans remember him well, too. He was in the South Atlantic League for almost two full seasons; he consistently batted around .300 but also struggled with the glove. Like a lot of the best middle-infield prospects, he could make plays that took your breath away and then boot a routine grounder in the next inning. He also got to more balls than any shortstop in the league, giving him more chances to bobble a ball or throw one away.

Jeter's stint in the Sally League coincided with my time working for the Fayetteville Generals, the Low Class-A affiliate of the Detroit Tigers. (The South Atlantic League was already a far-flung league at that point, and Greensboro was our nearest rival, about 2.5 hours away.) The Hornets would occasionally eat at the Fayetteville ballpark to save time and money, since they commuted back and forth from Greensboro rather than staying in a hotel.

Since the Generals were too tight with a dollar to keep a couple concessions workers around, the front-office staff would get to serve the Hornets their dollar hot dogs and drinks. There wasn't much memorable about manning the concession-stand cash register at 11 p.m. in an empty ballpark. But Jeter stood out among this group of young aspiring Yankees, both because of those icy blue eyes, and the way he carried himself: precise, upright, and in control.

Even today 15 years later when I see the Yankees play on television, I can see him in my mind's eye like it was yesterday, ranging into the hole to make an impossible play and then waiting calmly for his hot dog.

ⓘ Insider's Tip

With the crowds enjoying Grasshoppers games, a fan would be wise to order tickets in advance. This is particularly true for a weekend game or a Thirsty Thursday tilt. Most of the available parking is on the city streets and in the decks to the east of the ballpark, closest to the right-field corner. This is where Will Call is located. There's rarely any line, although you'll need to pay attention to find it. Surprising in this brand-new, multimillion-dollar ballpark, Will Call is run from a portable table on the sidewalk. Nonetheless, picking up your tickets from this location is also much more convenient than battling what can sometimes be very long lines at the ticket office behind home plate. (Our advice: pay for the lot parking directly south of the ballpark, near the ticket windows. Proceeds go to charity, and you'll have great access to the game.) Order online at **gsohoppers.com** or call the Hoppers at 336-268-BALL (2255).

Sports Around the Town

Greensboro markets itself as a "Tournament Town," and it certainly has rung true in recent years. Home to the Greensboro Coliseum and the offices of the Atlantic Coast Conference, this community has become the de facto home of the ACC men's basketball tournament and the official home of the women's tournament. With a central location and proximity to North Carolina's four ACC schools (Duke, North Carolina, N.C. State, and Wake Forest), Greensboro has a long history of hosting the men's tournament, with first-round games played there in 2006. A massive renovation in 1994 brought the seating capacity in the arena to 23,000 for basketball. The men played their championship in Greensboro in 2006, and while the event will visit Atlanta, Charlotte, and Tampa in the coming years, it will return, as it always does, in 2010. The women's tournament is played in Greensboro year after year and certainly contributes to the venue's strong relationship with the ACC.

The Coliseum also had a recent stint as a "big league" arena. The NHL's Hartford Whalers relocated from Connecticut and became the Carolina Hurricanes, playing their first two seasons (1997-99) in front of sparse crowds in Greensboro while awaiting construction of the RBC Center in Raleigh.

Historically, Greensboro has a long record of solid support for minor-league hockey with many area fans having memories of the old Greensboro Generals at the smaller, pre-renovation Coliseum. The East Coast Hockey League's Greensboro Monarchs successfully returned the sport to the arena in the late '80s, but it's been all downhill since.

The Monarchs ownership made a move from the ECHL (roughly "Double A" hockey) to the AHL ("Triple A" hockey). Despite playing a higher level of the game, the team didn't connect with Greensboro's fans. The loss of traditional rivalries was a big factor, as was the loss of the rougher style of play and more colorful personalities offered by the ECHL. It was into this shrinking pool of hockey fans that the Hurricanes dropped in 1997, offering big-league ticket prices and inaccessible athletes to a town that was accustomed to having a couple beers after the game with their team's players. The result was a largely empty arena.

An ECHL team named the Generals brought hockey back to the Coliseum following the 'Canes departure, but the hastily put together operation lasted only a few seasons. Despite periodic flirtations, Greensboro is still left without a hockey team of any level as of this writing.

For more information on the Greensboro Coliseum, **greensborocoliseum.com**.

Lodging

Good choices near NewBridge Bank Park are relatively limited, but the first two selections below are consistently considered among the favorites near the downtown area. If you are looking for low-cost chain options, numerous choices are offered along High Point Road at I-40 (Exit 217) about three miles southwest of the ballpark.

O. Henry Hotel
624 Green Valley Rd.
Greensboro, NC 27408
336/854-2000
ohenryhotel.com

Widely considered the top pick among the classic and boutique hotels, you probably will spend a little more for the pampering and amenities offered. Located beyond comfortable walking distance to NewBridge Bank Park.

Greensboro Marriott Downtown
304 N. Greene St.
Greensboro, NC 27401
336/379-8000
marriott.com

Although this property could use some updating, rates are lower than you would expect for a downtown Marriott, and no other full-service hotel is more conveniently located close to the ballpark.

Double Oaks Inn Bed & Breakfast
204 N. Mendenhall St.
Greensboro, NC 27401
336/379-8000
doubleoaksinn.com

If you want to stay just outside downtown in a cozy place, Double Oaks Inn is a good choice. Although the ballpark is a brisk walk away, you will be close to two college campuses — UNC-Greensboro and Greensboro College.

Park Lane Hotel at Four Seasons
3005 High Point Rd.
Greensboro, NC 27403
336/294-4565
800/942-6556
park-lane-hotel.com

Typically for only a few dollars more than the various national chain motels located nearby, the Park Lane provides full service and is managed by locally based Koury Corp. Lodging in this area is convenient to the Greensboro Coliseum, Koury Convention Center, and the airport.

 **Directions**

From I-85 South/I-40 West, Burlington

Take I-40 West to Greensboro: take Exit 218-B, Freeman Mill Road. Freeman Mill Road will turn into Edgeworth Street: NewBridge Bank Park is located on the corner of Edgeworth and Bellemeade Street.

From I-85 North, Charlotte

Take I-85 North toward Greensboro: Take the I-85 Bus. exit toward I-40 West. Take exit 122B onto US-220 North toward Coliseum Area: US-220 North becomes Freeman Mill Road, Freeman Mill Road becomes Edgeworth Street: NewBridge Bank Park is located on the corner of Edgeworth and Bellemeade Street.

From I-40 East, Winston Salem

Take I-40 East to Greensboro: Take exit 218-B, Freeman Mill Road. Freeman Mill Road will turn into Edgeworth Street: NewBridge Bank Park is located on the corner of Edgeworth and Bellemeade Street.

Highway 220 North, Asheboro

Highway 220 North to Greensboro turns into Freeman Mill Road: Stay on Freeman Mill Road. After crossing I-85, Freeman Mill Road will turn into Edgeworth Street: NewBridge Bank Park is located on the corner of Edgeworth and Bellemeade Street.

Highway 220 South, Virginia

Highway 220 South will change in to Battleground Avenue in the city of Greensboro. After crossing Cornwallis, stay left on Battleground and continue straight. Battleground will become one way and turn into Smith Street. Take a right on Eugene Street. NewBridge Bank Park will located on your right.

ASHEBORO

Minor-league baseball has never been played at Asheboro's McCrary Park, but that doesn't keep it from being one of the state's ballpark gems. Just don't poke around too much beyond the home-run fence.

CHAPTER 9

McCrary Park

Leading Off

Opened: 1946

Capacity: 800 seats, plus room for 500 in lawn chairs

Dimensions: 323L, 400C, 336R

Current Team: Asheboro Copperheads, Coastal Plain League (1999-present)

Former Industrial League Teams: McCrary Eagles, 1946-1957

ESSENTIALS

Website: teamcopperhead.com
Phone: 336/460-7018
Ticket Prices: $6 reserved; $5 general; $3 senior/child; under 5, free

Home to the Copperheads — Literally

McCrary Park is one of the hidden jewels of North Carolina's baseball landscape. Originally built by the Acme-McCrary hosiery mill, it hosted industrial league teams that were among the class of the region. The Acme-McCrary Eagles were legendary in the textile leagues, and it's said this success left the locals uninterested when opportunities to join organized baseball (in other words, the minor leagues) came along. After all, smaller communities the size of Eden and Mayodan were home to professional baseball, but Asheboro declined the invitations. The fact that Asheboro never appears in the official records of minor-league baseball is one of the reasons this park had remained such a well-kept secret outside of Randolph County.

The grandstand holds slightly fewer than 400 yellow fold-down stadium chairs salvaged from the Greensboro Coliseum during its last major renovation. These seats were purchased for $1 each and installed only in every other row. This choice to skip every other row makes the box seats at McCrary Field some of the most comfortable you'll find. The legroom is incredible, and you barely even have to move to let someone pass in front of you.

With its dark green paint and exposed steel girders, this grandstand has a truly classic feel. Flanking the grandstand are a pair of large bleacher sections, also painted dark green. The third-base bleachers sit just beyond a small field-level dugout, while the first-base bleachers sits up on a bank, allowing you to look right over the first-base dugout. This is also the preferred area for the lawn-chair crowd.

A small electronic scoreboard tallies the runs and tells you what inning it is. For a full inning-by-inning count, you'll need to check out the old-fashioned manual board built into the left-field outfield wall, complete with a young "scoreboard operator" sitting on a stool on the warning track, waiting to hang the next number.

Pat Brown, who was the original general manager and part owner, dubbed the team the Copperheads. "Before our first season, the city was installing new lights and poles," he says. "There's a wooded bank behind the outfield wall where the original poles stood, and when the work crews went back there to take down the old poles, they found a bunch of copperhead nests. We didn't want to scare people, but we thought it was a neat name, and had some basis in reality." Needless to say, when you visit Asheboro, you may want to discourage your youngsters from going behind the outfield wall after a home-run ball.

Go hungry to McCrary Park. The food is simple, but good: pizza, chili dogs, bottled soda, candy, and shaved ice. But don't go to McCrary thirsty for a "golden soda." The whole town is dry, and the ballpark is no exception. If you like a beer at the end of a hard day of traveling, you'll want to plan ahead and fill your cooler before you get to town.

The souvenir selection has expanded quite a bit in recent years, and the team sports a relatively new logo reminiscent of the early American flags featuring the "Don't Tread On Me" slogan. As befits a small-town operation, the souvenir "shop" is

The grandstand offers plenty of protection from the weather at McCrary Park.

a little stand tucked up under the grandstand, right behind home plate. Oh, and don't forget to buy your 50/50 ticket when you arrive: the jackpots can get pretty sizable.

While the Copperheads don't have the long history touted by many of the state's minor-league teams, they already boast a budding major-league star. Local product Dallas McPherson, who was a standout pitcher and third baseman for the Copperheads in their first year in the league, broke into the big leagues with the Angels in 2004. While the CPL has had number of alumni make the big leagues in its relatively brief history, McPherson is the first to be widely recognized as a likely major-league star in the making.

Asheboro went from hosting an industrial league team to a summer collegiate squad — with a four-decade break in between.

⚾ Insider's Tip

Despite the fact that the concessions stand in Asheboro is modern and kept extremely clean, the hot dogs at McCrary Park are cooked offsite due to some oddities in local health regulations. The dogs are good, but you want to eat early while they're fresh and hot, and before there's any chance they'll run out.

Sports Around Town

Most of the notable teams in Asheboro's baseball history were industrial-league teams, sponsored by the Acme-McCrary Mill. Probably the most talked-about sports event in the town's history, though, involved the mill's basketball team. The Acme-McCrary Eagles fielded some excellent squads over the years, including one that had a true brush with greatness. According to local legend, the University of North Carolina Tar Heels visited Asheboro for a 1956 preseason exhibition game.

Led by legendary coach Frank McGuire and star player Lennie Rosenbluth, the
Tar Heels faced a spirited battle that night and barely squeezed by the Eagles. The
Acme-McCrary team felt good about their effort, but the game eventually achieved
mythical status. Rosenbluth was named the national Player of the Year that season
as the Heels went on to win the 1957 NCAA championship in a triple-overtime
thriller over a Kansas team led by Wilt Chamberlain.

Author's Note

*Although McCrary Park was a surprise to me, it's no secret to the locals. When I was working
for the Coastal Plain League and searching for possible expansion cities following the 1998
season, I passed through Asheboro on my way to see a ballpark in another city. Just taking a shot
in the dark, I stopped at the municipal building in the middle of town and asked the elderly lady
at the front desk, "Where's the ballpark?" She responded without missing a beat, "You must
mean McCrary Park," and began writing me very neat, very accurate directions.*

The back of the
McCrary Park
grandstand
lists team
and ballpark
sponsors.

When I drove into the parking lot at the field, I felt like Columbus getting his first glimpse of the New World. I knew I was looking at the home of the CPL's next franchise. The entire facility, then, as it is now, was lovingly cared for, with an excellent playing surface, and a simple steel and concrete roofed grandstand.

Enter the Eagles

The McCrary Eagles were known as one of the perennial powers in the industrial leagues in the area during the 1930s, '40s, and '50s. The truly outstanding players, or "ringers," were set up with token jobs in the mill, a sprawling brick complex that completely dominates downtown. The Acme-McCrary mill was serious about athletics. The mill also sponsored basketball teams, and locals of a certain age still recall with pride the night in 1956 when the Eagles put a scare into the UNC Tar Heel basketball team that went on to win the national championship that season (*see Sports Around Town*).

The lawn chair crowd has plenty of room to spread out in Asheboro.

The mill had sponsored baseball teams since the 1930s, but in 1946 the mill owners finally decided to build a ballpark. It was built on land the mill already owned: you may notice that the small frame houses behind the right and center field wall have the distinct look of "mill housing." While textiles manufacturing is fading throughout the state, in Asheboro textiles is still the number-one employer. Although Sara Lee Brands is a major Copperheads sponsor and Acme-McCrary doesn't dominate like it once did, the company still holds the deed to the ballpark and leases it for $1 per year to the city. In fact, the McCrary family's approval was sought when the city wanted to enter into an agreement to host a CPL team.

This is a busy ballpark. In addition to the Copperheads, McCrary hosts American Legion baseball, the Blue Comets of Asheboro High, and Colt League baseball. So, even if the Copperheads are out of town when you're passing through, or if it's too early in the season, you might still want to ride by. There may be a game and in this setting any brand of baseball is worth watching.

Where to Sleep, Eat, and Pass the Time Until the First Pitch

Downtown Asheboro is charming and gives the visitor a good idea of what a typical North Carolina mill town looks like. Not much has changed since the Eagles ruled the textile leagues and, like most small towns in the region, much of the retail activity has migrated to the highways. A hometown eatery is worth seeking out: Jed's BBQ is a favorite of the locals and features a wide variety of food, drinks, soups, salads, vegetables and, of course, Jed's famous BBQ.

Jed's BBQ
1213 N. Fayetteville St.
336/626-2465

South of downtown on Route 64 there is significant retail, including the ubiquitous Wal-Mart shopping center, grocery stores, and numerous eateries, including a number of national chains. More importantly, this area also houses several new, comfortable hotels, listed below.

Much of this recent development has been aided by the presence of the North Carolina Zoo. This is a terrific zoo: the polar bears are a particular highlight. Race fans will want to check out the Richard Petty Museum in nearby Randleman. You'll learn about the many generations of racers in this legendary NASCAR family, and see some of the team's retired cars and a variety of other memorabilia. There's a gift shop, and if you get real lucky, you might even meet the King himself. Most of the family lives just down the road. More information on the sights is below.

ATTRACTIONS

The aforementioned North Carolina Zoo is a great zoo, but be prepared to walk. The animals here are in their natural habitats, and that means they have lots of room to roam. You will need to wear comfortable shoes, so plan on spending some time here. The zoo boasts everything from bison to polar bears to kangaroos.

North Carolina Zoo
4401 Zoo Parkway
800/488-0444
nczoo.org

The Richard Petty Museum is a magical place for race fans: the home base of the King. The Richard Petty Museum showcases cars, trophies, and other memorabilia from the career of NASCAR's 7-time champ.

142 W. Academy St.
Randleman, NC
336/495-1143
pettyracing.com

If you love minor-league baseball, maybe you'll like minor-league stock-car racing as practiced at Caraway Speedway. This track features NASCAR's minor league, the weekly racing series, on Saturday nights.

2518 Racetrack Rd. Ext.
Sophia, NC
336/629-5803
carawayspeedway.com

If you're traveling with someone whose interests include things that don't involve a ball, bat, stick, puck or gearshift, you'll probably want to visit Seagrove. Visitors to this rural town can choose from over 100 potteries in the area and view the 200-year-old heritage and craft of traditional North Carolina pottery making.

122 E. Main St.
Seagrove, NC
800/626-2672 or 336/626-0364
visitrandolphcounty.com

For additional information on these and other accommodations and attractions, surf to **visitrandolphcounty.com.**

Lodgings

Hampton Inn is one of the newer hotels in town and is convenient to the main shopping area along Highway 64.

Hampton Inn
1137 E. Dixie Dr.
Asheboro, NC 27203
800/HAMPTON or 336/625-9000
hilton.com

Holiday Inn Express Hotel & Suites is another nice, modern hotel right in the midst of the main shopping area.

Holiday Inn Express Hotel & Suites
1113 E Dixie Dr.
Asheboro, NC 27203
800/HOLIDAY or 336/636-5222
holiday-inn.com

The local Super 8 doesn't have quite as convenient a location as the other hotels, but it is a good option if you're on a tight budget.

Super 8
1020 Albemarle Rd.
Asheboro, NC 27205
800/800-8000 or 336/625-1880
super8motel.com

 **Directions**

From East and West:

Take Route 64 to Route 220 North. Exit at Presnell Street and turn left (westbound) onto Presnell. Take next left onto McCrary Street for approximately two miles. Ballpark will be on your right.

From North and South:

Take Route 220 to Asheboro and exit at Presnell Street. Turn onto Presnell heading westbound. Take next left onto McCrary Street for approximately two miles. Ballpark will be on your right.

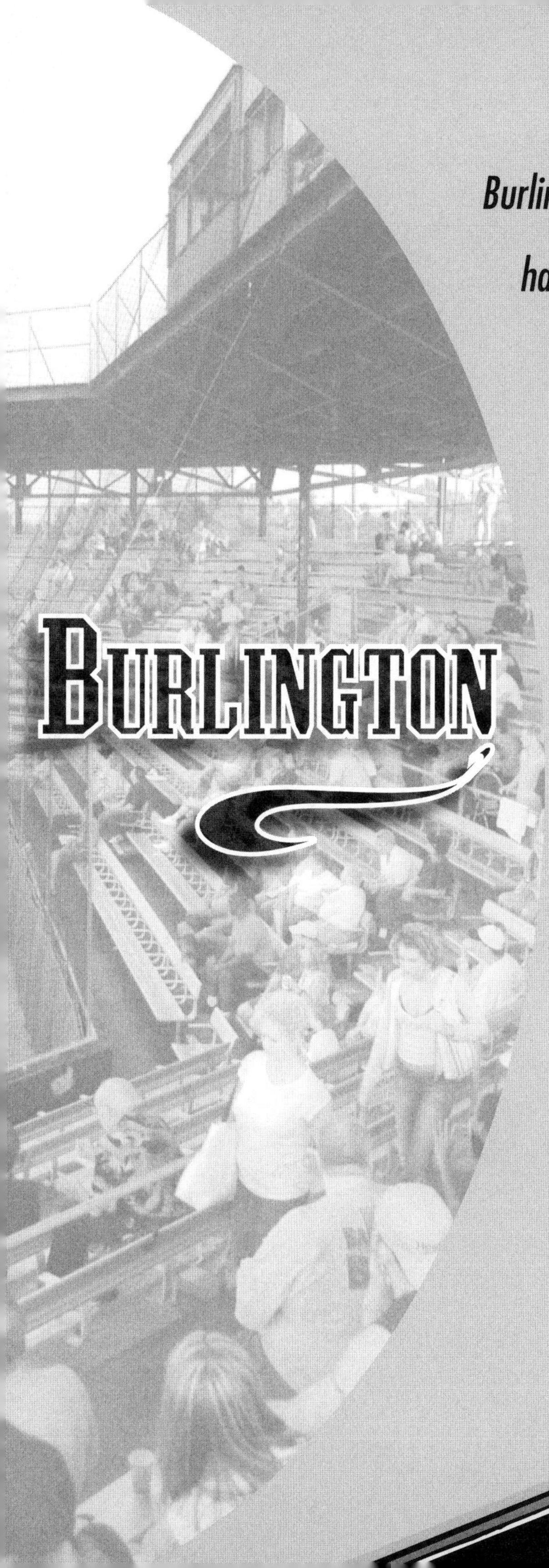

CHAPTER 10

BURLINGTON

Burlington Athletic Stadium has hosted minor-league baseball in two states — Virginia and North Carolina.

BURLINGTON ATHLETIC STADIUM

Opened: 1960 (in Burlington; opened 1950 in Danville, Va.)

Capacity: 3,500

Dimensions: 335L, 410C, 335R

Current Team: Burlington Royals, Rookie Appalachian League (2007-present)

Previous Minor-League Teams in Area: Burlington Indians, 1986-2006, Appalachian League; Alamance Rangers, 1972, Carolina League; Alamance Senators, 1965-71, Carolina League; Alamance Indians, 1960-1964, Carolina League

Website: burlingtonroyals.com
Phone Number: 336/222-0223
Ticket Prices: $3-6
Broadcasts: Online only, at team website
Online ticket sales: Yes
Parking: Free and abundant in adjoining parking lots

Have Ballpark, Will Travel: Danville's Loss was Burlington's Gain

Burlington Athletic Stadium, home to baseball in Alamance County for over 45 years, is a true classic with an authentic feel and a rich history. This is one of the last of the ballparks used in the movie *Bull Durham* still hosting minor-league baseball, and it has served as the home field to players ranging from Luis Tiant to Manny Ramirez. It also has a tie to one of minor-league baseball's most notable people, Miles Wolff, who has served as the club's president since the team's inception in 1986. Wolff, who previously owned Baseball America and serves as commissioner of the Can-Am League and American Association, revived the Durham Bulls in 1980 and is credited by many industry experts as having helped launch the minor-league baseball boom that continues today. (*For more on Wolff, see our chapters on Durham and The Movie.*)

While Wolff was enjoying great success with his Carolina League team in Durham during the early 1980s, he was hoping to add a South Atlantic League team in Burlington, just 35 minutes to the west. After Greensboro's ownership blocked Wolff's effort to purchase a team in the Sally League, Wolff nonetheless honored his commitment to the city of Burlington and commenced paying rent on an empty ballpark for several years. Finally, in 1986, he was awarded the management contract to operate the Indians' Appalachian League affiliate. After a 14-year absence, baseball was back at the old ballyard on Beaumont Avenue.

Formerly known as Fairchild Stadium, the park was renamed "Burlington Athletic Stadium," or "The BAS" in the style of the "Durham Athletic Park," a.k.a.

"The DAP." The facility required significant work to prepare for the return of professional baseball. When Wolff notified the city officials that he had finally secured a team, it was the middle of the offseason and there was only about five months until Opening Day.

Rotting wood planks were removed from the upper grandstand seating area and replaced with aluminum, while the old wood slat box seats were removed and also replaced with aluminum benches with seat backs and armrests. The concessions, offices, and locker rooms were also in disrepair, and the playing surface was a long way from professional standards. Despite all this, the park was ready and filled to capacity when the Burlington Indians took to the field for their first home game in June 1986.

From the outside, Burlington Athletic Stadium grandstand shows its age.

Burlington was ecstatic to have professional baseball again, and in those early years that initial excitement combined with some excellent teams to draw record crowds. Burlington's fans were rewarded with an Appalachian League championship in 1987, just the team's second year, with an eye-popping 51-19 record.

The B-Tribe also won their division in 1991, when they were led by a young outfielder named Manny Ramirez. The league MVP, Ramirez batted .326 with 19 home runs and 63 runs batted in, all in just a 68-game season.

Burlington won the Appalachian League championship again in 1993, but the next year began a decade-long string of losing teams. Despite the up-and-down nature of the team's on-field performance, an impressive stream of talent passed through Burlington during the Indians' 21 years as parent club, including Jaret Wright, Mark Lewis, Bartolo Colon, Richie Sexson, C.C. Sabathia, and Einar Diaz. In recent years pitchers Rafael Perez and Edward Mujica have advanced from Burlington to Cleveland in the space of just a few years, while Adam Miller projects as a front-line starter if he can stay healthy.

The facility was upgraded several times during the Indians' tenure, most notably when a new brick clubhouse building was constructed behind the third-base bleachers in 1995 in response to MLB's new facility standards. A new lighting system also was installed prior to the 2005 season.

The BAS has also seen some upgrades to the park's fan amenities, including a party deck down the first-base line, a new picnic building on the first-base side, and air-conditioned bathrooms added as part of the clubhouse construction. A recent addition to the restrooms is Chris Byerly's artwork. If you come by during the day, you may be able to see both the men's, featuring "lockers" of some of Burlington's famous alum, and the women's, which features paintings that are in a league of their own!

There's no doubt that it's no longer 1960, or even 1986 when you see a game in Burlington; there are Internet streaming of the games, online ticketing, souvenirs through the team's website, and even wireless Internet access in parts of the ballpark. You can even track the speed of every pitch thrown thanks to a digital radar board mounted on the third-base light tower.

Yet, despite these modern amenities, baseball in Burlington retains a charming, old-time feeling. The ballpark doesn't boast any single remarkable feature, but it is still truly notable as a quintessential old-style minor-league ballpark of the type rapidly disappearing from pro baseball.

Tidy and clean despite its advancing age, the BAS is tucked away in an older residential neighborhood. Across the street sits a massive, largely shuttered industrial complex that was the birthplace of Burlington Industries, the textile giant and the area's primary economic catalyst.

Known as Fairchild Stadium when it opened in Burlington in 1960, the ballpark is the only professional facility in the country to have been moved from another site where it housed a minor-league team. This grandstand was originally home to the Danville Leafs minor-league team,

Day game at the BAS.

as well as industrial-league teams operated by the Dan River Mill. Constructed in 1950 in the Schoolfields area of Danville, the park had become expendable by the late 1950s.

Burlington was also seeking a more suitable home for the area's Carolina League entry. The Indians' affiliate in the Single-A Carolina League, the Alamance Indians, were named for the county and played their home games at a high-school field on Pine Street in neighboring Graham. This park is still used by the local Legion team and is located just a few miles from Burlington Athletic Stadium.

Under the lights
at Burlington
Athletic Stadium.

(Directions from the BAS: take a left turn out of the parking lot onto Graham Street, follow round two snaking turns, turn right at the stop light onto Graham-Hopedale Road. Cross the train tracks, then turn left at the light and follow N. Main into downtown Graham, go halfway around the traffic circle around the courthouse, and at the next light, turn left onto Pine Street. The park is on the campus of Graham Middle School, which will be on your right.)

The City of Burlington purchased the Danville ballpark for $5,000 in 1959; the structure was disassembled and loaded on flat-bed trucks. The concrete foundations, locker rooms, and concessions underneath the seats were built from the scratch according to the Danville blueprints, while the steelwork, roof, and seats were the same ones used in Virginia.

The park was first occupied by the Carolina League's Indians, whose most notable player of that era was Cuban pitcher Luis Tiant, who would go on to an outstanding big-league career with Cleveland and Boston. While pitching for the Alamance Indians in 1963, Tiant set a Carolina League strikeout record later broken by Dwight Gooden.

Eventually, the Indians gave way to the Senators after four seasons. The Senators franchise spent eight years in Burlington, although during the final year (1972) the team became the Alamance Rangers, reflecting the parent team's move to Texas. The Senators/Rangers era produced a few notable players, including Toby Harrah, Dane Iorg, and Mike Cubbage. Attendance, though, was dismal, and the team moved to Wilson following the 1972 season.

Burlington and Alamance County's earlier baseball teams, the Pirates and Bees, lived a nomadic existence, playing at the high-school field in Graham and carrying the name "Bur-Gra," or Burlington-Graham. Some years the teams would play at Elon's old wooden ballpark next to the train tracks. The ballpark is long gone, but the site is easily identified; it's now an intramural field that sits directly across the street from the fire station at the corner of Williamson and Ballpark.

It was in the Graham ballpark in 1953 that a young catcher for the Bur-Gra Pirates named Jack McKeon became a local fan favorite. Despite his modest hitting abilities, he impressed a young lady named Carol Isley, who became his wife. Alamance County became his off-season home. McKeon would later assist in

BAS grandstand silhouette at sunset.

coaching the Elon College baseball teams in the fall while attending classes there and eventually earned his degree.

Burlington's first pro teams played in the 1940s at a park that is now the location of Blessed Sacrament Catholic School on Hillcrest Avenue, just west of downtown off Church Street. The Hillcrest Avenue field is also where a local nine took on a team of Navy pilots that was training in Chapel Hill. That Navy squad included an outfielder named Ted Williams. Already a big-league star, Williams was serving one of the two military stints that cost Teddy Ballgame five years of his Red Sox career.

After playing at parks from one end of the county to another, baseball had a permanent home when Fairchild Stadium was built. The ballpark was built within a larger complex known as Fairchild Park. A large community center and gym now sits beyond the right-field wall, and locals say that Manny Ramirez regularly parked home-run balls on its roof. There's also a BMX track and two softball fields beyond the outfield wall, with a walking track and youth baseball field next door.

As you can see when you visit, this is a classic regional ballpark. Typical of the era: the press box on the top of the roof. The PA man, scoreboard operator and official scorer have a real bird's eye view of the game, with the press box located on top of the front edge of the grandstand roof. Accessed by fire-escape-type stairs at the back of the grandstand, this is no place for anyone who's scared of heights.

Bingo the mascot remains, even though the team affiliation has switched from the Indians to the Royals.

The in-stadium atmosphere is festive and kid-friendly. There are some on-field promotions, but in keeping with the park and the fans' taste, they are not overdone. The focus here is on the baseball for a solid core of fans who turn out every night. Of course, there is a Speedpitch, a Sno-Kone stand, and lots of kids that give the concourse a lively carnival feeling. And the team's furry orange mascot, Bingo, keeps the younger fans entertained. Ultimately, though, this is an experience that a baseball purist can enjoy.

Concessions can be found throughout the ballpark. A large stand underneath the grandstand offers hot dogs, pizza, Chick-Fil-A chicken sandwiches, BBQ sandwiches, popcorn, funnel cakes, and more. Behind the grandstand is the aforementioned Sno-Kone booth, and there's another small concessions stand that just sells ice cream, candy, and Cheerwine slushies. You have to try one; they'll turn your teeth purple (temporarily) and give you a brain freeze, but they are delicious.

It sounds strange to single out such a standard food item, but the hot dogs are excellent. Beefmaster, a local company, provides the hot dogs. All-beef, these are the same hot dogs served at UNC football games, although Burlington has been serving them a lot longer. Add a little chili and some of the onions personally chopped by concessions stand manager Denise Matkins, and you've got a real treat.

You'll find cold beer at a bottled-beer stand on the third-base side. Draft beer, bottled beer, and wine are all served up by Dori the Beer Wench at the main beer counter behind the first-base dugout. The wine is provided by local vineyard Irongate Winery, one of five Alamance County wineries to offer tastings and tours (see **burlington-area-nc.org** for a list). You can also kick back on the deck, all the way down the right-field line (*see Insider's Tip*).

An era came to an end with the conclusion of the 2006 season as the Cleveland Indians decided to drop their Appalachian League affiliate. This ended a 21-year relationship that was one of the longest in baseball at the time. Fortunately for Burlington, Kansas City's new general manager, Dayton Moore, visited Burlington many times in his role within the Atlanta Braves organization, and he wanted to add an additional team to the Royals already fully stocked minor-league system.

For the foreseeable future, this means minor-league baseball will continue to be played in Burlington. For the serious baseball fan, the charming old park, a great history including the likes of Kevin Costner and Manny Ramirez, and Burlington's convenient, central location in the state, make it a must-see.

⌀ Insider's Tip

If you want to relax with a beer and a close-up view of the game, check out the deck down the first-base line. With a tiki bar that offers draft beer, bottle beer, wine, cable TV, chips, peanuts, and the company of Tom the Bartender, the deck is the ballpark's hot spot, especially from Thursday ($1 beer night) through Saturday. You can enjoy sitting under an umbrella at one of the tables, or you pull up a barstool facing the field. This is truly the best seat in the house; less than six feet from fair territory and close enough to carry on a conversation with the right fielder. And, you can get a fresh drink or a bag of peanuts and check out the big league scores on TV, all without getting up from your seat. No, it's not Iowa, it's Heaven! If I'm not in my seats in the front row of Section 6, come see me down on the deck.

Author's Note

During nearly 15 years in North Carolina I've been professionally tied to about a dozen of the ballparks described in this book and have visited nearly all of them numerous times. But after four years as general manager of the B-Tribe, the Burlington Athletic Stadium will always be my home field.

It was here that I finally had my own team to run. Throwing a party at the ballpark and having anywhere from 300 to 3,000 people show up gives a person a great feeling. But the games were just the most visible part, like the tip of the iceberg. Equally important was a community that embraced and valued their hometown team, and the chance to play post-game wiffle ball with my young sons on the same field where Manny Ramirez and Luis Tiant began their careers.

And last, but not least, when another 14-hour workday was done, there was the "post-game meeting" where the staff would enjoy the cool of the evening and break down the day's events, tell stories, and laugh over a couple cold beverages. The cast of characters was different every night with umpires, coaches, and assorted friends of the team dropping by, but it was always a great way to end the day. And to the front office staffers, dozens of interns, and too many other people to mention that made all that time at the ballpark something other than work, I'd like to simply say "thanks."

What to Do in Burlington

SHOP:

Burlington is known throughout North Carolina for its outlets, the first in the state. At exit 145, you'll find the "BMOC," Burlington Manufacturers Outlet Center. These are real outlets, not just dressed-down retail. There's a mall and a Wal-Mart at exit 143, as well as a wide variety of restaurants. You don't need to travel that far from the ballpark to find a Wal-Mart, as the retail giant opened a new store just a stone's throw beyond the center-field wall.

Burlington is in the midst of the BBQ Belt. The local favorite is Hursey's Bar-B-Q, located at 1834 S. Church St., at the corner of Alamance Road, two miles north of the freeway. North Carolina BBQ is pretty straightforward: trays and plates of chopped and sliced pork, pork and beef ribs, chicken, or flounder. Hursey's smokes its own barbecue onsite; check out the fire door in the brick wall facing the parking lot. If they're cooking barbecue, you'll be able to find the place by the fantastic smell.

EAT:

Burlington must have more restaurants per capita than any city in the state. Huffman Mill Road, between I-85/40 exit 143 and Church Street, is the hot spot, with a wide variety of chains alongside local favorites. Check out Longhorn Steakhouse for the best steaks in town.

GOLF:

Alamance County is home to five golf courses, and dozens can be found within a 30-mile radius. Locals are justifiably proud of their municipal course, Indian Valley, located a few miles north of downtown. It offers some beautiful scenic holes located along the Haw River, and it's reasonably priced. Call 336/584-7871 for tee times and directions.

VISIT DOWNTOWN BURLINGTON:

There's some history downtown, centered on the railroad tracks. Burlington was founded as "Company Shops, N.C.," when it was the primary maintenance and repair yard for the N.C. Railroad Company. Downtown features not one, but two train depots illustrating the area's railroad heritage. Visit the Historic Depot on the south side of the train tracks to see the original station that served the town up through the 1970s. Across the tracks on the north side, you'll see Company Shops Station, the current Amtrak stop. This station was created from an imposing turn-of-the-century-era engine-repair shop. The lobby area includes several historical displays, including a scale model of the town in the 1920s. There's also the Paramount, a restored 1920s movie house that hosts numerous live concerts and plays. There are several restaurants downtown, including lunch counters, sandwich shops, and an excellent Mexican restaurant named Mi Casa between the theater and depot that offers outdoor seating and a full bar.

VISIT CITY PARK:

Just west of downtown along Church Street is City Park, Burlington's answer to Central Park. The centerpiece of the park is a fully functioning antique Dentzel Carousel, complete with mechanical organ music. There's also a fantastic playground, a mini-train, and a handful of other amusements. If you're traveling with kids, it will be welcome chance for them to run and play and, if you're just a kid at heart, you'll want to plunk down your $1.50 and ride both the train and the carousel.

VISIT ELON UNIVERSITY:

Featuring one of the nation's prettiest campuses, Elon is now rated among *U.S. News and World Report*'s top five southeastern regional universities. There's a charming little downtown area adjacent to the campus centered on the intersection of Williamson and Lebanon. It's a perfect place to grab lunch (Sidetracks Grill) and take an afternoon stroll. Just head west on Church Street/U.S. 70 until you get to Williamson Avenue, take a right, and proceed about a mile. (*See our chapter on Elon on* *pahg 137*.)

Check out **burlington-area-nc.org** for more information on lodging, meals, golf and more.

N
W ✦ E **Directions**
S

From I-40/85:

Take exit 145. Head north on Maple Avenue and go approximately two miles. Take a right onto Mebane Street. Continue on Mebane Street for two miles. Take a right onto Beaumont Avenue. Follow Beaumont Avenue a half mile; the stadium is on the left.

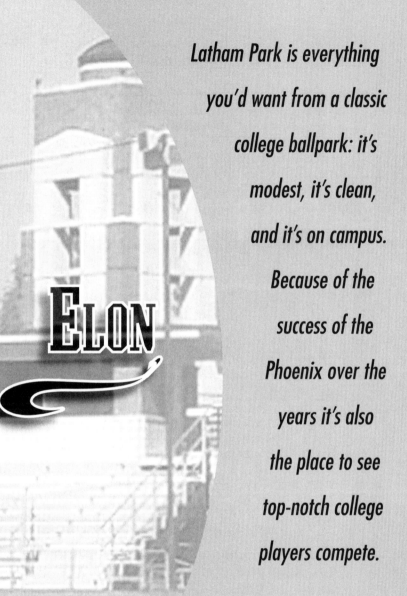

Latham Park is everything you'd want from a classic college ballpark: it's modest, it's clean, and it's on campus. Because of the success of the Phoenix over the years it's also the place to see top-notch college players compete.

CHAPTER 11

LATHAM PARK

Leading Off

Opened: 2001

Capacity: 2,000

Dimensions: 317L, 360LC, 385C, 380RC, 327R

Current Team: Elon University Phoenix (NCAA Division I; Southern Conference)

ESSENTIALS

Website: www.elon.edu/athletics
Phone Number: 336-278-6800
Ticket Prices: Free!

Where the Phoenix Keep Rising

The current home of the Elon University Phoenix, like the entire university campus, is pleasing to the eye and well manicured. The small, straight grandstand seats approximately 400 on aluminum benches, while small bleachers on either side can handle another 35 each. Concessions are run out of a trailer parked next to the third-base bleachers, with hot dogs, sodas, and candy on the menu. The press box is above the main grandstand in a two-story brick structure; it also houses bathrooms and serves as the main gate. This isn't a big, fancy ballpark, but Latham Park feels just right for Elon: newly built but with a classy, upscale look.

There's lots of brick and stone, and the area around the ballpark includes a bell tower marking the center of the athletics complex. The Phoenix's new 10,000-seat football facility, Rhodes Stadium, peeks over the first-base side. (That's quite the capacity considering the town's 2000 population was just 6,738.) A pond with a fountain and a huge bronze statue of a Phoenix are both set beyond the left-field corner. The best spot in the ballpark, though, lies outside the gates. While Elon does not charge to sit in the grandstand or bleachers, the bank beyond the third-base dugout is a prime spot for a lawn chair or blanket (*see Insider's Tip*).

Elon baseball traditionally has been the university's best athletic program, going back decades when the Elon College Fighting Christians competed in the NAIA. It's also been a launching pad for coaches, including Florida State's Mike Martin, although with Elon's climbing reputation it certainly has become less of a stepping-stone job than in the past.

Over the past decade Elon has moved from the NAIA to NCAA Division I as members of the Big South Conference. Most recently, the Phoenix stepped up again and became a member of the Southern Conference. The team's breakthrough year was 2006, when the Phoenix captured a Southern Conference championship and an NCAA berth. Regularly appearing on the schedule are national powers like UNC and South Carolina.

When the state-of-the-art lighting system was added to Latham Park prior to the 2005 season, it allowed the Phoenix the flexibility of scheduling nighttime baseball. Crowds have grown, too, as the evening start times proved more convenient for many fans. Prior to the new lighting, the Phoenix had played four or five games per season at the Burlington Athletic Stadium, the home of Burlington Royals of the Appalachian League.

As for the town, a picturesque one-block "downtown" features a few restaurants, a few coffee shops and, of course, a bar. As for the university, the Elon campus is a site to behold. Beautiful brick buildings ring impeccably manicured quads. Swans glide by the fountain in the middle of the lake. A stroll through the campus is well worth the time; Elon is routinely ranked as having one of the nation's most beautiful campuses. The school has also become much more highly regarded for its academics, now ranking among a top handful of Southeastern regional universities.

Coach Mike Kennedy, an Elon alum and former minor-league player, has been very successful with the Phoenix, and a number of his players from recent years have signed pro contracts. (They join the likes of Elon alumni Greg Harris and Greg Booker, who both reached the majors.) You'll find the baseball there to be excellent and the atmosphere pleasant. If your schedule allows, catch a game at Latham. You'll be glad you did.

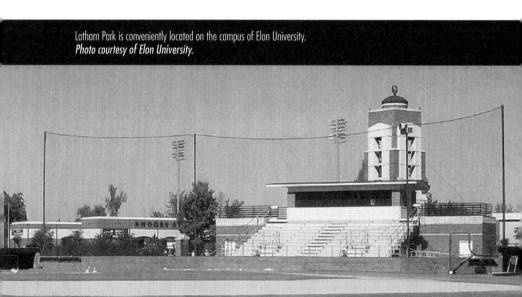

Latham Park is conveniently located on the campus of Elon University.
Photo courtesy of Elon University.

⬩ *Insider's Tip*

Bring your lawn chair and cooler when you come to Latham Park. Head for the bank beyond the third-base dugout and set up camp. Since this is outside the gates, you can bring your own food and even enjoy an adult libation if you're discreet. There's also a lively scene out on the bank; some of the students bring out couches and easy chairs, and there's an occasional grill. If you smell the smoke of an expensive cigar, look around for Elon's most famous resident, longtime big-league manager Jack McKeon. An Elon alum, Jack attends a handful of games each year, and he can usually be found talking baseball with the students while puffing away on one of his trademark stogies.

Sports Around Town

Elon is part of Alamance County and borders Burlington, home to the Appalachian League's Royals (*see Burlington chapter on page 125 for more information*). For scheduling convenience, Elon used to play a handful of games at the Burlington Athletic Stadium, but now play all their home games on campus since the installation of lights at Latham Park in 2005. Prior to the opening of Burlington Athletic Stadium in 1960, some of Alamance County's minor-league team played at Elon's old wooden ballpark, since demolished. The site is still visible, next to the train tracks and across Williamson Street from the post office and the fire station. This land is still used as an intramural practice field and as overflow parking for football and basketball games.

Dining

Need a caffeine pick-me-up? The Acorn serves Starbucks coffee, muffins, and sandwiches.

Acorn Coffee Shop
118 South Williamson Av.
336/278-5350

Grab a pasta dish, a bowl of soup, a sandwich, or a wrap, and wash it down with a soda or a beer alongside students, faculty, and visiting parents at Sidetracks Grill, an intimate eatery adjacent to campus. The prices are reasonable and the service (provided by Elon students) is always excellent.

Sidetracks Grill
110 West Lebanon Av.
336/584-1769

Notice a theme here? You may have figured out that both West End Station and Sidetracks are right next to the railroad tracks. This is your place in Elon for beer as a wide selection, from Bud to Blue Moon, is available on tap and in bottles. It's also the place to find pool and second-hand smoke. West End Station features good food, pizzas, wings, and such, but this is a student hangout first and foremost, and as such doesn't really get cranking until 11 p.m.

West End Station
138 West Lebanon Av.
336/585-1227

For additional area attractions, see our Burlington chapter on page 125.

Directions

From I-40, take University Drive (exit 140) and go north. Take an immediate right onto St. Mark's Church Road. St. Mark's Church will cross U.S. 70/Church Street and become Williamson Avenue. Continue straight on Williamson until you see the ballpark on your right; turn right into parking lot.

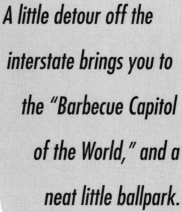

A little detour off the interstate brings you to the "Barbecue Capitol of the World," and a neat little ballpark.

HOLT-MOFFITT FIELD

Leading Off

Opened: 1938

Current Teams: High School and American Legion

Former Teams: Lexington Indians, 1937-1942, 1945, 1947-1949, 1951-1953, 1961-1962; Lexington A's, 1946, 1950; Lexington Giants, 1963-1966; Lexington Braves, 1967 (all Western Carolina League/Tar Heel State League/South Atlantic League)

Art, BBQ & Little Legion Ball in Lexington

Lexington may not come to mind when planning a baseball trip through North Carolina, but if you were mapping out a barbecue trip, this would probably be where you'd start. With the self-proclaimed title of "Barbecue Capital of the World," Lexington hosts the Barbecue Festival every October — the community's signature event. With over 20 barbecue restaurants in a town of around 20,000 people, there's no doubt they are serious about their barbecue. While Lexington no longer hosts minor-league baseball and the city's courtship with the Coastal Plain League was a near-miss, this charming small town with a ballpark just a few blocks from the main square is worth a visit.

Holt-Moffitt Field traces its history and name back to the Wennonah Cotton Mills, sponsor of textile-league teams in the '30s. When those industrial leagues gave way to minor-league baseball, the old Wennonah Park was replaced with Holt-Moffitt Field, named for the co-owners of the mill, who donated the land where the new WPA park was built.

Holt-Moffitt is still home to baseball in Lexington nearly 70 years later. The main seating area has been rebuilt, with a small, solid concrete grandstand in place of the larger original wooden structure. Minor-league baseball last called Lexington home in 1967, when the Lexington Braves, an Atlanta Braves affiliate in the Western Carolina League, limped home with a record of 55-63.

Of course, with Lexington's population of under 20,000 and its proximity to Winston-Salem and Kannapolis, it is a near certainty that this community will never again host minor-league baseball. But the ballpark came very close to fielding a team in the collegiate Coastal Plain League. In the late 1990s, when the CPL was in the midst of rapid expansion, Lexington was under consideration for a

franchise. Ultimately, while the city approved a lease, the potential local ownership group never came through. The league ultimately decided that an outside ownership group could not tackle the necessary political issues. Chief among these was the ballpark's location in close proximity to a church, which would have made obtaining a beer license potentially troublesome.

So, if you want to see baseball in Lexington, you'll need to check out a Legion or high school game. If you do, you'll be rewarded with a cozy little grandstand that looks over the same playing field that has been the home to baseball in this community since prior to

1965 Lexington Giants official program cover. *Image courtesy of the Notre Dame Rare Books collection.*

the outbreak of World War II. The outfield still has a unique old-school element; a steep bank rises from center field to left field and begins climbing well before you reach the outfield wall. Once common as a sort of early edition of the warning track, this bank is one of the last in the state. (You can see another in Thomasville's Finch Field.)

The original grandstand, built in 1938 with seating capacity of 3,000 and a roof over most of the grandstand, was made of wood and, sadly, is no longer with us. The current squatty, little concrete grandstand is functional and sturdy, but you'll want to bring your own stadium seat. The seating bowl here is NASCAR-style; just bare concrete with room for about 700 people. There's no roof, but the top row of the seating bowl is adorned with a little tiny wooden press box. Concessions are located right behind home plate, and a new freestanding concessions building is located just down the first-base line.

A small clubhouse sits a little further down toward right field, and pair of small bleachers (aluminum on the first-base side and wood on the third-base side) flank the field. Both are unusually far removed from the grandstand.

Some good players passed through Lexington; Ty Cobb once played at a mill ballpark in an exhibition game, and Bobby Bonds competed for the Lexington Giants. One of the most notable alumni of pro baseball in Lexington was not a player, but rather a Dartmouth student who arranged his schedule to graduate a semester early so he could seek a baseball broadcasting job. Bob Hager was the play-by-play voice of the Lexington Indians in 1960 and 1961. He switched to news reporting and is now better known as a correspondent for NBC News for 35 years before retiring in 2004. He later parlayed that two-year stint into a spot in the South Atlantic League Hall of Fame.

Even if you visit this park when there's no ballgame, go ahead and look anyway -- it's fairly open, with just chain link between you and the field most of the way around. Don't be afraid to take a little detour off the interstate, grab some barbecue and maybe a Bob Timberlake print or lamp, and check out a neat little ballpark. You'll be glad you did.

Sports Around Town

Lexington is best known for barbecue, but the town's other claim to fame is Bob Timberlake. The prolific painter who specializes in rural scenes has branched out into everything from decorative plates to a furniture line. His studios and gallery are located in Lexington, and you can visit his website at **bobtimberlake. com** or call 800/244-0095 (the ballpark directions will take you right by the gallery on Old 64/Raleigh Road.) In addition to being Lexington's most famous resident, Bob also has a connection to the town's baseball history.

Ty Cobb (pictured with a child on his knee) drew a good crowd when in Lexington to play an exhibition game at a cotton mill ballpark. *Photo courtesy of the Davidson County Historical Museum.*

Lexington's first pro team, a relocated franchise from

Forest City, N.C., was dissolved following the 1936 season, but when Lexington returned to pro ball with a new franchise the following year, the new owners were a pair of local businessmen, A.C. Fite and Edgar Timberlake, grandfather and namesake to Bob.

What to Eat

Barbecue, of course. And Lexington restaurants are best known for serving the definitive version of western North Carolina (tomato-based) style of barbecue, as opposed to the vinegar-based barbecue sauces used in the eastern part of the state.

And what makes Lexington barbecue so special? Just ask the folks from the Barbecue Festival: "The fare is pork, of course — and shoulder is the cut of choice in Lexington. The pork shoulders are cooked long and slow — about an hour a pound — over hickory wood until it is fall apart tender. The shoulders are basted with *dip*, a mixture of vinegar, ketchup, water, salt, and pepper. As the dip and fat drip onto the coals, smoke is created that rises up, surrounds and permeates the meat, and gives it a rich, smoky flavor. The meat is served chopped, although sliced can be requested with more of the basting sauce on the side." Hungry yet?

Barbecue Center
Sonny Conrad
900 N. Main St.
336/248-4633
barbecuecenter.com

John Wayne's Lexington BBQ
601 West Fifth Av.
336/249-1658
johnwaynesbbq.com

 **Directions**

From I-85:

Take exit 94 for Old U.S. 64/Raleigh Rd. West. Proceed to downtown Lexington, take a left on Main St. Turn right on 9th St., ballpark is on left. (The grandstand is located on the other side, near the intersection of S. State St. and S. Hargrave St.)

THOMASVILLE

Finch Field has been synonymous with minor-league baseball in Thomasville since the 1930s. But when the original ballpark burned down the locals came through with a replacement, and a complete renovation in 2006 turned the facility into a first-class summer-collegiate ballpark.

CHAPTER 13

HISTORIC FINCH FIELD

Leading Off

Opened: 1935, rebuilt in 2006 • **Capacity:** 2,200 • **Dimensions:** 325L, 350LC, 390C, 365LC, 330R • **Current Team:** Thomasville HiToms, Coastal Plain League (1999-present) • **Former Teams:** Thomasville Chairmakers, North Carolina State League (1937); Thomasville Orioles, North Carolina State League (1938); Thomasville Tommies, North Carolina State League (1939-42); Thomasville Dodgers, North Carolina State League (1945-47); High Point-Thomasville Hi-Toms, Carolina League (1948-1958); Thomasville Hi-Toms, Western Carolina League (1965-66); High Point Thomasville Hi-Toms, Western Carolina League (1968-1969)

Old is New Again in Thomasville's Finch Field

Thomasville's rich minor-league baseball history goes back to the 1920s and baseball notables like Curt Flood and Jack McKeon (*see interview, page 283*), but the city will almost certainly never see another affiliated team. Like many of North Carolina's smaller cities, Thomasville and the neighboring city of High Point are locked out of affiliated baseball, as they are too close to both Greensboro and Winston-Salem to be granted a franchise. The community has not been left without baseball, though.

In 1999, a Coastal Plain League franchise was placed at Finch Field, the former home of the High Point-Thomasville Hi-Toms. While visiting the ballparks of the CPL often means seeing great old historic stadiums, Thomasville unveiled a wonderful new grandstand in 2006. Don't despair: this cozy new park utilizes the same site, playing field, and scoreboard that have been a part of Finch Field since the facility's opening in 1935.

This team's unusual name can be traced back to Finch Field's former minor-league tenants. Originally known as the Thomasville Dodgers back when both High Point and Thomasville fielded teams, the club was renamed the Hi-Toms when the two cities decided to join forces in 1948. Finch Field is strategically located near the border between the two neighboring communities. While the CPL team originally carried the historical name "Hi-Toms" while under league ownership, the current group now uses the non-hyphenated variation "HiToms."

Finch Field — where High Point and Thomasville come together.

While the new park is a wonderful venue, baseball history buffs will be saddened to know that the original Finch Field, which featured a 3,000-seat roofed grandstand, burned down in a fire in the early 1980s. Local legend has it that the fire was started intentionally by a neighbor annoyed by the field lights and traffic, but no one was ever charged with a crime.

The city fathers rebuilt the ballpark, although in a very basic configuration. The outfield fence and manual scoreboard survived, and the same playing surface was used, but the new grandstand consisted of huge slabs of concrete. The overall impression has been described as "Stonehenge Ballpark."

A modest concessions stand underneath the home-plate section, a small press box, and ticket booth with one window were all deemed sufficient for a city that figured they were out of pro baseball for good. This simple, fireproof facility, seating about 750 people, served the city's high-school and American Legion teams well for many years, but when the Coastal Plain League HiToms began operation a number of modest improvements were undertaken. Box seats donated by the New Orleans Zephyrs were installed in the park's front row, and aluminum benches were bolted to some of the concrete seats above. Previously, fans had needed to bring their own cushions if they wanted to sit on anything other than a slab of concrete.

In recent years, a large neighboring building has been acquired with plans to convert it into an indoor batting facility, team offices and lockers, and a community center. Since the current ownership took charge of the team, a new main entrance with brick pillars and an arched wrought iron sign spelling out "FINCH FIELD" has been constructed. A modestly sized but modern concession stand with a patio seating area down the left-field line also has been added. All this, though, was just the warm-up act.

A majestic gate greets fans entering Finch Field.

Visitors to the "New Finch Field" will enjoy a comfortable, modern facility with about 1,500 seats — mostly in the grandstand. The new grandstand is roofed, featuring fold-down chair seats through the lower half of the seating bowl, and benches with seat backs above. While the ballpark is built of aluminum decking and not concrete or brick, the overall feel of the place is nearly perfect for a community of this size and for the scale of CPL baseball.

New concessions, souvenirs, bathrooms, and ticket offices are housed in a spiffy set of new brick and block buildings separated from the back of the grandstand by a small concrete concourse with inset brick detailing. In fact, the entire park is laced with newly poured concrete walkways, well-manicured grass, and crushed red brick. Follow one of these walkways down the first-base side of the ballpark and you'll find yourself on a

A fine view along the first-base line.

beautiful little berm providing the kids a place to roam and parents a place to park the lawn chair or blanket. HiToms owner and team president Greg Suire told us that the team hopes to expand the berm, as it's become so popular. Suire also let us in on the fact that the idea of the berm arose as a way to add seating space while conveniently disposing of the "clean fill" generated from the demolition of the old Stonehenge grandstand. A stroke of genius!

Suire's fingerprints are all over this operation. He took the lead on securing funding for this renovation from the city and the Finch Foundation, which was established by the ballpark's namesake family. These were the founders of Thomasville Furniture, the community's long-time major employer. While the local furniture business is no longer booming, the Foundation continues to fund community needs. The city government of Thomasville has also been a huge supporter of the CPL team, providing support in a variety of ways throughout the franchise's

Plenty of
grandstand
shade at
Thomasville.

existence, including office space in the municipal building during the team's first
off-season and regular airtime on the city's community access TV channel.

Notwithstanding all these changes, one of Finch Field's charms is that the playing
field is still the same one graced by 1978 Hall of Fame inductee Eddie Mathews,
free-agency pioneer Curt Flood, and Phillies pitcher and manager Dallas Green.

Former Royals, A's, Padres, Reds, and Marlins manager Jack McKeon managed a
team technically classed as a co-op team in 1968 but was actually a farm club for
the expansion Kansas City Royals, who officially took on the Hi-Toms affiliation in
1969. The '68 Hi-Toms, scouted and signed almost exclusively by McKeon, finished
two games under .500 but ripped through the playoffs, claiming the Carolina
League championship — an early demonstration of McKeon's winning touch both
in talent evaluation and field leadership.

Finch Field — upgraded for Coastal Plain League play.

⚾ Insider's Tip

Look out toward the home-run fence and you'll see something missing: a warning track. Instead, the ballpark has an embankment in front of the fence that warns outfielders they're close to a collision. The warning embankment — for lack of a better term — is also larger in right field than in left. Before the 2006 renovation the area in front of the warning embankment became a trough where rainwater would gather, making life interesting for outfielders after a good soaking rain.

Ballpark Sundries

Concessions offer the normal ballpark fare, including reasonably priced hot dogs, drinks, popcorn, and candy. The grill down the left-field line offers excellent hamburgers, and I highly recommend the cheese fries, a great buy at just $2.50.

Souvenirs are housed in a small walk-in shop that also includes the "Museum," featuring photos of recent and not so recent teams, and a small handful of other local baseball memorabilia. Souvenir offerings are somewhat limited: primarily reasonably priced t-shirts and caps and fairly expensive logo balls and mini-bats.

The new concessions and souvenir building features one truly modern touch: a pair of flat screen TVs running an endless loop of player interviews and sponsor ads, placed where fans can see them while standing in line for concessions or waiting for someone outside the bathrooms.

There is a small speed-pitch booth behind the first-base side of the grandstand where the kids can get a reading on the speed of their throw, as well as a nice picnic shelter down the third-base line.

While the history that was lost in that fire in the 1980s is impossible to replace, the current Finch Field retains some wonderful touches from the original park, including the old manual scoreboard. The new grandstand provides a much-needed step into the future for this

Finch Field — prior to the upgrade.
Photo courtesy of Dennis Bastien.

thriving summer-collegiate franchise, complementing the improvements already in place. For the visiting baseball fan, Finch Field will provide a great night of small-town baseball with some of the nation's best collegiate players. Its proximity to Greensboro, Winston-Salem, Burlington, and Asheboro also make a great stop on any Triad area baseball trip.

Author's Note

I'll never forget the day I drove into Thomasville to take a look at Finch Field. The park seemed like it could be at best a functional facility for the CPL with some improvements, and the town seemed to have a healthy business community, but the town is awfully small and awfully close to Greensboro and Winston-Salem. I went to visit the recreation director, Vaughn Black, who was a former minor-league baseball player himself. He had played briefly in the Appalachian League before military service ended his baseball career, but he had a passion for the game that was evident from the moment I sat down to talk with him. When informed that Thomasville might be able to have its own baseball team again, Vaughn had the look of a kid on Christmas morning.

Less than an hour later, we were sitting in front of the city manager, Sam Misenheimer, who was very nearly as enthusiastic as Black. They both instantly understood what a community asset Thomasville's own team could be and were on board from the first meeting. It's this type of enthusiasm that made it an easy

Smooth concrete was the seating arrangement previously at Finch Field.
Photo courtesy of Dennis Bastien.

decision for the league to put a team here despite it being a small town with a marginal ballpark, not to mention two established minor-league teams sitting less than 20 miles away in either direction.

Of course, that community support has manifested itself in solid crowds and a facility that is no longer marginal, but rather one of the CPL's better venues. With the planned improvements, it may soon be the league's best environment for player development, and offers fans one of the most pleasant game experiences in the league.

⟲ Insider's Tip

I recommend spending the extra money to buy box seats; the upper general admission portion of the grandstand has some obstructed views, and the patio and berm fill up fast. There's one small problem with this. The HiToms sell beer, but you are not supposed to carry it out of the grill and patio area down the third-base line. The beer is sold in cans, though, as are many of their soft drinks. Wrap your can in a napkin or, if you're really well prepared, a can koozy, and you'll be able to enjoy your adult beverage sitting comfortably in your box seats.

Sports Around Town

When the latest edition of the Hi-Toms were being established in 1999, many people doubted the community would support a baseball team. "This is a football town," many said. It's since been established that this a pretty solid baseball area, but it sure is a football town. And with good reason. The Thomasville High School Bulldogs have a tradition of success and won three straight state championships from 2004-2006, and it's the hometown of Carolina Panthers fan favorite Brad Hoover.

During the spring of 2007, Thomasville High School's Cushwa Stadium was also home to the Carolina Phoenix, a women's pro football team in the Independent Women's Football League. While Cushwa is an outstanding high-school facility, I think the jury is still out regarding whether Thomasville is *that* much of a football town!

What to Do in Thomasville

Any visit to Thomasville and High Point has to begin at "The Chair." The entrance to downtown Thomasville on Randolph Street is marked by an 168-foot-tall replica of a formal dining-room chair (a Duncan Phyfe armchair, to be specific). It's a tribute to Thomasville's history as a furniture manufacturing center. The longtime home of Thomasville Furniture Industries, this city's earliest minor-league team was named the Chairmakers.

Within site of the big chair you can enjoy free live music, if you time your visit correctly. On Thursday evenings in late June and July there are free concerts at the bandstand, right in the heart of downtown. Bring your chairs, picnics, and blankets. Coolers are allowed, as well.

Thomasville is also home to a very nice, affordable municipal golf course, Winding Creek. Call 336/475-5580 for updated greens fees and directions.

WHERE TO EAT
Don't miss Kathy's Restaurant, in the middle of downtown just a couple blocks north of the Big Chair. If it's Wednesday, you'll want to try their chicken pie. If not, don't worry about it — everything is good and cheap.

Kathy's Restaurant
14 West Guilford St.
336/475-0226

WHAT TO DO
High Point is Thomasville's neighbor to the north and former partner in baseball is called "The Furniture Capital of the World." Downtown High Point is a fascinating collection of ostentatious show rooms that sit empty most of the year, springing to life twice a year for the "Furniture Market," a massive gathering bringing retail buyers together with area manufacturers. You may notice a sprawling white building next door to Finch Field: that is an outlying furniture show room utilized during the Furniture Market.

Thomasville is also close to the Triad; see our Greensboro (*page 95*), Winston-Salem (*page 161*), Burlington (*page 125*), and Asheboro (*page 113*) chapters for additional attractions and amenities. Thomasville makes an excellent day of a Triad baseball trip. You can stay in the same hotel in Greensboro for several days and see games in Greensboro, Winston-Salem, Thomasville, Burlington, and Asheboro without ever driving more than an hour in one direction.

 **Directions**

From High Point/Greensboro via I-85 Business:

From I-85 Business, take the National Highway/Route 68 exit. At the bottom of the ramp, turn right onto National Highway (if coming from the south, turn left onto National Highway and pass back under I-85 Business). Proceed approximately 100 yards, then turn left into entrance marked with a hanging "Finch Field" sign. Despite its name, do not turn on Ball Park Road.

From Thomasville:

Take National Highway toward High Point. Pass under I-85 Business. Proceed approximately 100 yards, turn left into entrance marked with a hanging "Finch Field" sign. Despite its name, do not turn on Ball Park Road.

WINSTON-SALEM

Ernie Shore Field is a classic 1950s-era ballpark and home to the Winston-Salem Warthogs. The Warthogs will be moving from Ernie Shore to a new downtown ballpark, so you'd best take in a game there soon if you want to a real, old-fashioned Carolina League ballpark in action.

CHAPTER 14

ERNIE SHORE FIELD

Leading Off

Opened: 1956

Capacity: 6,000

Dimensions: 325L, 400C, 325R

Current Team: Winston-Salem Warthogs, Carolina League (1995-present)

Former Teams: Winston-Salem Twins, 1956 (Carolina League); Winston-Salem Red Birds, 1957-1960 (Carolina League); Winston-Salem Red Sox, 1961-1983 (Carolina League); Winston-Salem Spirits, 1984-1994 (Carolina League)

ESSENTIALS

Address: 401 Deacon Blvd., Winston-Salem
Website: warthogs.com
Phone: 336/759-2233
Ticket Prices: $7-$9

Check Out Ernie Shore Before the Sheriff Leaves Town

What can you say about Ernie Shore Field, home of the Winston-Salem Warthogs? Ernie Shore is a historic ballpark, one of the last real old-time Carolina League parks, but one with enough modern touches that it feels like it was built in the 1970s. Ironically, it's one of the only North Carolina ballparks still hosting Carolina League baseball, as that circuit has expanded far beyond the state. Over the last two years, the Warthogs management has come to define Ernie Shore Field more by what it's not than what it is. Namely, it's not NewBridge Bank Field, the stunning state-of-the-art ballpark in Greensboro. The two cities are less than 30 minutes apart, so there's a little regional competition involved as Winston-Salem sports fans observe the phenomenal success enjoyed by the Greensboro Grasshoppers.

In fairness, some of this talk had been started well before Greensboro's new park had even opened. Several years ago there had been an ambitious plan for downtown development put forward by Winston-Salem-based donut maker Krispy Kreme, but that project went stale when the company fell on hard financial times, and any hope for a new ballpark evaporated. In 2007 the Warthogs ownership and the city came to an agreement for a new ballpark project spearheaded by Hogs owner Billy Prim. The founder of the Blue Rhino propane cylinder company, Prim is putting up a significant chunk of his own money as part of this plan. As of this writing construction has started and current plans call for a 2009 opening.

The facility issue has been simmering in Winston-Salem for years, dating back to Don Beaver's ownership of the team. Beaver, who also owns the Hickory Crawdads and the Charlotte Knights, began to seriously consider selling the Warthogs in

2001. Fortunately for Winston-Salem, Prim and his partner and brother-in-law Andrew "Flip" Filipowski purchased the team in 2002 even though the team's prospects for a new facility weren't good and the team's financial situation in the current ballpark was lackluster. That all seems about to change, though, as the pair's commitment to their hometown will lead to a state-of-the-art downtown ballpark. Don't be too sad: the plan is for Ernie Shore Field to serve as the home of Wake Forest baseball, so there are no plans to tear down the place. Still, it's likely Wake Forest will scale back the ballpark (don't expect beer gardens and triple-level display advertising).

Insider's Tip

Newcomers to North Carolina may be confused when they see highway signs to Wake Forest in the Triangle; most know N.C. State, UNC, and Duke are there, but Wake Forest, too? The town of Wake Forest is just north of Raleigh, and that's where the university used to be located. The old Wake Forest campus is now home to a Baptist seminary. The original school relocated to Winston-Salem in 1956 — lured by an endowment and land provided by the Reynolds tobacco family — but retained the Wake Forest name.

For the time being, you can still enjoy the charms of Ernie Shore. A very nice arched brick façade houses the main entrance and the ticket offices (added as part of the 1993 renovation). Enter at the top of the seating bowl, and once you're inside you'll see an expansive concrete seating bowl spreading out below you. Box seats in red and blue are located in the center sections, flanked by long expanses of aluminum benches stretching well down each foul line. This park has enormous foul territory; "cozy" is not a word that comes to mind. There is a small covered concourse with concession windows and a small walk-in souvenir shop. The split press box, with an oddly modern-looking roof, sits in front of the covered concourse. A nice touch is a Hall of Fame area on the concourse, honoring Winston-Salem notables. The concourse continues beyond the roof on either side, and these open-air portions also boast a number of concessions windows with the usual standard fare, beer counters, restrooms, and vending locations.

Head all the way down the first-base side to check out the fishpond, a lovely little oasis sponsored by a landscaping company. You'll also see a nice little carousel at this end of the concourse. If it's not booked for a party, you'll also want to check out the two-level Blue Rhino Deck overhanging the bullpen and nearly reaching into fair territory in right field. Grab a spot on the front rail for a great, unique view of the game.

Down the left-field line you'll find a sort of food court with a number of concessions windows and a small plaza overlooking the field.

Parking at Ernie Shore will cost you a few dollars. The stadium sits in the same complex with Groves Stadium, the home of Wake Forest University football, and the Lawrence Joel Coliseum, home to Wake's basketball team. A tiny lot controlled by the team just outside the gates on the first-base side carries a parking fee, and you'll need to pay to park at the acres of surrounding parking. If you're frugal and don't mind a little walk, there are a couple of places to park across the street from the ballpark beyond the right-field wall. Be alert — there aren't any sidewalks.

The outfield wall at Ernie Shore is immense. A full three levels of signs, totaling over 24 feet in height, tower over the field. Unlike many parks where the first level of signs makes up the home-run fence, and second- and third-level signs are set back officially out of play, Warthog pitchers know over 75 of the team's advertisers are working with them to keep the ball in the park.

While Ernie Shore's towering wall is a relatively new phenomenon, the twin cities' baseball history goes back to 1905. The story of Winston-Salem baseball includes the colorful Wilmer "Vinegar Bend" Mizell, who pitched for the 1950 Winston-Salem Cardinals and went on to the big leagues. Later he was elected to represent North Carolina in Congress.

Other notable Winston-Salem players include Wilber Wood, Bill "Spaceman" Lee, Wade Boggs, Mike Greenwell, Sam Horn, and one legendary manager. You can't discuss the history of Ernie Shore Field and minor-league baseball in Winston-Salem without mentioning Bill Slack. He logged 13 seasons as manager with Winston-Salem during the Red Sox's 24-year run as the team's parent club from 1961 to 1984. A native of Canada, Slack played 11 years in the minors before he moved into the coaching ranks. He went on to manage for 17 seasons in the

A fine crowd takes in a Fourth of July game (2003) at Ernie Shore Field.

Wake Forest baseball team with young mascot from the early 1900s
Photo courtesy of the North Carolina State Archives.

Red Sox system, winning five championships, including four in Winston-Salem. Now retired, Slack lives nearby and often can be found at the ballpark, where he is enshrined in the team's Hall of Fame and has had his number 37 retired and mounted on the outfield wall. The Warthogs also present an annual award for community service named for Bill Slack.

Winston-Salem has also been a model of consistency with Ernie Shore hosting Carolina League baseball every single year since its opening in 1956. Even during the lean times of the Vietnam era when most other cities in the state couldn't support a team, Winston-Salem answered the bell.

And who's Ernie Shore, you say? Well, he's an area native and a former teammate of Babe Ruth's who came home to become Forsyth County sheriff. After the old Southside Park burned down, he led the fundraising campaign to build a new ballpark. In 1956, that new park opened and was named in his honor.

While Ernie Shore is not the most charming park in the state, it's comfortable, well run, and certainly worth a visit. With its proximity to Greensboro, Hickory, and Kannapolis, and its rich, uninterrupted Carolina League history, Ernie Shore Field provides a great chance to soak up some history and see multiple games without even checking out of your hotel room. And, with the new ballpark wave sweeping the game, you'll want to see this park while you still can.

Sports Around Town

When you're at the ballpark, you're really already there for most of the action. Practically all of Winston-Salem's sports venues are in the same complex, and if you come early you can check out Groves Stadium, home to the Wake Forest Demon Deacons football team. The football stadium is adjacent to Ernie Shore Field. Across the road from the baseball and football stadiums is the Lawrence V. Joel Memorial Coliseum, home to the Wake Forest basketball teams. A member of the ACC, Wake Forest's most notable basketball alum of recent years is Tim Duncan, who has followed up his stellar four-year career at Wake Forest with multiple NBA championships and an MVP season with the San Antonio Spurs. As with most sporting venues during their off-season, if you're discreet and friendly, you can likely get a look inside the arena, which features a parquet floor reminiscent of the one in Boston Garden.

The Wake Forest baseball team used to play baseball at Ernie Shore Field. The University now plays most of its home games at Gene Hooks Stadium (a bandbox located on the edge of campus), but the financing plan for the Warthogs' new ballparks include selling Ernie Shore to Wake Forest.

If you're a racing fan, or even just a stadium buff, Winston-Salem also includes one of the strangest combinations in all of sports. Located several miles south of the ballpark, Bowman-Gray Stadium is a horseshoe-shaped venue that was the home to Wake Forest University's football team until Groves Stadium was built, but now serves two very different tenants.

From spring through fall, Bowman-Gray continues operation as "NASCAR's Longest Running Weekly Race Track." It's an 18,000-seat minor-league NASCAR track. In the fall, Bowman-Gray serves as the home of the football team from nearby Winston-Salem State, a historically black university. Yes, black college football and stock-car racing. As odd as it seems, the partnership seems to work. The facility, while quite old, boasts some terrific modern touches like a state-of-the-art press box and hospitality space. And while some older college-football venues have a running track separating the spectators from the field, this stadium has an asphalt track and retaining walls. Strange, but it seems to work.

⏱ *Insider's Tip*

If you purchase your Warthogs tickets in advance, be aware the only covered seats are in the box seats immediately in front of the press box. This is Section F, and you'll want to be a few rows back from the field, particularly if you want to be safe from any liquid sunshine. This section has a unique configuration — two press boxes over the center section, one to the right and one to the left — and box seats and a walkway right down the middle. On a hot day, seats in the center of Section F and near the top will give you a little more air movement than in the rest of this sunken seating bowl.

Lodging

The Courtyard by Marriott is a nicely appointed property especially convenient to Ernie Shore Field and the Wake Forest University campus. This is the place to stay if you want an easy walk to the ballpark.

Courtyard by Marriott Winston-Salem University
3111 University Pkwy.
Winston-Salem, NC 27105
336/727-1277; 800/321-2211
marriott.com

The Quality Inn, located just off U.S. 52, is a short drive from the ballpark and many other area attractions. A well-kept older property, often this is one of the best values you'll find in the area.

Quality Inn – Coliseum
531 Akron Dr.
Winston-Salem, NC 27105
336/767-8240; 800/841-0121
qualityinnws.com

If you have a desire to stay at a full-service downtown hotel, two excellent choices are available along North Cherry Street — the newly renovated Embassy Suites and the Winston-Salem Marriott. Both are featured at **twincityquarter.com**.

 **Directions**

Take Business I-40 to the Cherry Street exit. Go north through downtown to Deacon Boulvard, then hang a right to the ballpark.

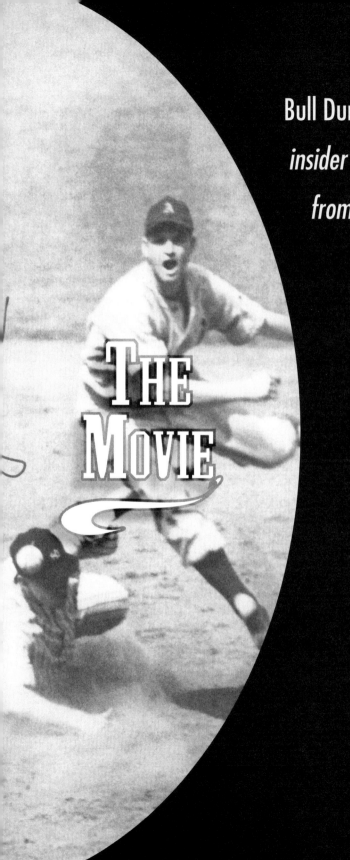

Bull Durham – *an insider's perspective from Miles Wolff.*

THE
MOVIE

Crash Davis at his home with a cutout of him from his college days.

For folks involved with baseball in North Carolina, you just have to say *the movie*. *Bull Durham* was filmed in Durham in 1986, with the Bulls' charming old ballpark serving as the primary filming location. Minor-league ballparks in Wilson, Asheville, Greensboro, and Burlington all made supporting appearances in the movie, which was filmed entirely in the Tar Heel state.

The film became a huge hit after its release the following year. It became such a monumental event for the Durham Bulls, their city, minor-league baseball, and stars Kevin Costner, Susan Sarandon, and Tim Robbins, that it's easy to forget that it was relatively small-budget movie with what were (at the time) minor stars. Written by Ron Shelton, a former minor-league ballplayer, and produced by Thom Mount, a Durham native who worked for Universal Pictures, this film is regarded by many as one of the greatest sports movies of all time. It also launched the superstar careers of Costner and Robbins and gave Sarandon her most notable role since *Rocky Horror Picture Show*.

What is now regarded as a major milepost in the sporting landscape began with a chance contact. It also changed the way we viewed minor-league baseball. Already in the early stages of a nationwide revival, the bush leagues became cool with poster-boy Kevin Costner. Fans wanted see if their local team had a real-life Nuke LaLoosh or Annie Savoy, and in the process rediscovered the simple pleasure of seeing a ballgame live and in person.

Miles Wolff was at the center of it all, just as he has been for nearly every major development in minor-league baseball over the past 30 years.

We spoke with Wolff about this cultural touchstone and his place in it.

MC: *Can you tell us how this all started?*

MW: When I was forming the Bulls, I didn't have any money. So, I started selling stock, and I called [fellow minor-league operator] Van Schley, who said he know someone from Durham who might be interested who worked for Universal Pictures. It was Thom Mount, a Hollywood producer. He had produced *Animal House* and was really a bright light in the movie business, and he put in $5,000.

That winter he came to the park with his wife, and, well, kind of played a bit of the Hollywood producer. He said, "We'll make a movie here some day." I said, fine, just so long as I have your money so maybe we can survive until opening day.

He was in fact a very active part-owner. He actually designed the logo the team is still using today, had it done by someone at one of the subsidiaries of Universal Pictures. He designed the uniforms, too. He'd come to games and really took a good interest in the team. I guess it was '86 and he called, and said, "I've got a writer doing a minor-league baseball screenplay, and I'd like him to come down and get some, you know, feel." Turned out it was Ron Shelton, who'd been a minor-league ballplayer and made it as far as Triple-A with the Orioles, had been a good minor-league player.

So, Ron came down for, I think, two weeks. Originally, the script didn't have it being the Bulls, and Thom told Ron, "You don't have to make it Durham, make it whatever team works best," but Ron came and fell in love with the old ballpark, and decided to make it the Bulls. It was Ron's first directing job.

MC: *This wasn't a big-budget thing, then, with a first-time director?*

MW: It wasn't a really high priority for the studio. The actors were not really big stars at the time. Costner had been cut out of his last movie, but you knew his name. Sarandon had done *The Rocky Horror Picture Show*, and Robbins was a complete unknown. This was a relatively small picture for Orion (a division of Universal), I think it was an $8-million budget, which even at the time was a relatively small film, and Ron said, "Let's do it in Durham."

But, they didn't have a title for it, so they said, let's put "Bull Durham" on it until we can come up with something better.

(The Bull Durham tobacco brand was strongly associated with Durham and baseball through their bull-shaped outfield billboards and other advertising in ballparks around the country. It was owned by the American Tobacco Company and controlled by the Duke family, for whom Duke University is named.)

So, I hired [former Bulls GM] Pete Bock to come back and help out. He had gotten "island fever" [after several years as the GM of the Hawaii Islanders] and needed to come back to the mainland. So he came back and was the baseball consultant on the movie. We called all the nearby minor-league clubs and asked if we could borrow their uniforms and use their parks.

MC: *What kind of deal did you have with them for use of the ballpark?*

MW: Thom paid us $10K to use the ballpark and all the uniforms, and we thought that was a pretty good deal for us at the time. They were running out of money at the end of the movie, though. They had painted the park from the blue to green, they wanted a more old-school look – that ballpark green. And then at the end, they didn't want to repaint it blue. They didn't have the money. We really had to push them to paint it back again after they were done.

We didn't think the movie was going to be much. And, by the end of the movie, I was pretty frustrated with it. There was one instance where they were going to film a big crowd scene and we ran some ads, sent letters to all our season-ticket holders, promised everybody free hot dogs. Well, we got a big crowd there, maybe two or three thousand people that afternoon, and then someone decides it needs to be a night shoot. They told us, "Just don't feed them, and they'll stay. We need to keep 'em here until eight o'clock." This was our fan base, our season-ticket holders, and they weren't happy about it, and neither were we.

MC: *So it was an education dealing with the movie people.*

MW: Yes, they made the decisions like that about that scene being a night shoot at the last minute. It's just like Pete [Bock] playing the role of the minister in the wedding scene. This was late in the movie, and they hadn't hired anyone to play the role, and Pete was the only one who fit the suit.

So, by the end, we didn't really know what to think of the whole thing. Then they had the premiere at the Carolina Theater, and we were all scared to death, you don't know if this is going to be something embarrassing. We all go dressed up, and we were watching. Everyone was nervous, we didn't really know if it was good, or what. It was a couple weeks later that my wife Michele and I went to see it in a regular theater, and we started laughing and enjoying it. We said, "Hey, this is really pretty good."

MC: *Were you involved in details like Max Patkin's appearance?*

MW: They had a character in there like Max Patkin, and they said, 'How are we going to find someone, a baseball clown, and I said, "Why don't we just get Max?" And Ron asked, "Is he still alive?" So I called Max, and we were able to get him, and that made his career for another 10 years. In fact, I've still got a copy of the original script, and the Max Patkin character died in a car wreck. He was supposed to be following the bus, but that changed. I guess him dancing with Susan Sarandon was enough.

MC: *What was the biggest challenge in the filming?*

MW: It was the coldest fall I had ever seen in North Carolina. Fall is usually gorgeous, but that year you could see people's breath, the leaves had already turned. It was the worst possible fall to do it, and poor Nuke almost froze to death out there in his jock strap. We also had to spray the grass green with food dye, since it had turned brown due to the cold weather.

We figured putting the team together was going to be a challenge. But, we got a lot of real ballplayers to serve as extras without too much trouble. There were players who had stayed in the area, and Pete coordinated it. And, the one thing I was really worried about was putting the players and the actors together. I thought there would be problems. I thought we'd have some macho ballplayer getting in a fight with an actor, but they got along great! In the end, I realized that they were very much alike, very much thinking short-term. They could be released tomorrow and not have another job, live for today, that kind of thing. And they got along great.

And, Costner was a real baseball player. He hit one out of the park in BP. Of course, Robbins was not. Scouts say he could never be a pitcher, that he had awful form.

In hindsight, it's funny to think that by the end, I didn't want anything to do with it. They really didn't understand baseball, and there were lots of unreasonable things they wanted to do like driving trucks on the infield, and things like that. I just wanted to get these people out of there.

MC: *Did you regret not having a percentage of the box office instead of a flat fee?*

MW: Actually, they were mad that they didn't have a piece of action on souvenirs. We went from $50,000 in souvenir sales to $500,000; we had an 800 number, had a store at the mall, we were doing huge business. This changed the way the licensing was done. All of a sudden, minor-league logos mattered. People started thinking about having their own name, instead of just carrying the parent team's name. Minor-league licensing was nonexistent to that point, and there were not really teams with well-known names except for maybe the Toledo Mud Hens with Jamie Farr and *M*A*S*H*. If there had been national licensing at that time, there's no telling what kind of sales we could have done.

MC: *Some of the scenes that people probably assume were done at the ballpark were actually filmed elsewhere in town, correct?*

MW: The interiors were done at an old tobacco warehouse next to the arts council, and they actually pulled a lot of stuff out of our clubhouse to make it look like a locker room. They looked at filming in the locker rooms at the park, but you just couldn't fit the cameras and crew in our locker rooms and have any room to move.

They shot all around town. They rented the house that was Annie Savoy's house in the movie and, of course, the exteriors like Crash walking the streets at night and shooting pool were all filmed in Durham.

MC: *How did the actors live while they were in town?*

MW: They rented houses, and I think Costner had his children here with them. There were locals who would go to the parties they would throw. It was a very natural thing; remember, these were still not big stars then. There wasn't any security keeping people out of the ballpark during filming. Remember, we were doing business, and people were coming and going, and they needed to have extras in the stands; the more the better.

MC: *How did the crew handle night filming?*

MW: I remember worrying about that, but they didn't bring anything extra in. In fact, I don't think our lights at the park were even up to Single-A standards at the time, but I guess it looked dark and minor league-ish. It certainly doesn't look like a major-league night scene, and I imagine that was what they wanted.

Crash Davis really did make it to the Major Leagues. At shortstop for Philadelphia (circa 1941), he forces out Yankee Buddy Rosar. This print, signed by Rosar and Davis, is on display at the North Carolina Baseball Museum in Wilson.

MC: *There was a lot of filming on the bus. Was that the team's actual bus with the tassels and the card table?*

MW: The bus in the movie is the one we owned. It was a 1966 GMC, and it had cost us $10,000. They got use of the bus as part of the deal.

MC: *What was the most tangible result of the movie for the team?*

MW: The best result for the ballpark was the snorting Bull. I think Shelton had read my other book, *Season of the Owl*, where they had an owl that came up over the wall with smoke coming out of it. That, and the image of the old

Bull Durham sign looming over the wall, combined to become the snorting Bull, and that became a great part of our park. It was recognizable from the movie and was something we hadn't had before. The film crew left it behind, and we continued to use it.

(The bull was pretty low tech. Built by local sign company Art Signs, it required a game-day worker to pull a rope to make the tail go up and down, flip a switch to make the eyes light up, and set off a fire extinguisher to make the smoke come out of his nose. The original bull was replaced with a much larger version when the team moved to the new park, but the original bull is wall-mounted along the first-base concourse of the new Durham Bulls Athletic Park.)

MC: *What was the more long-term impact on the Bulls?*

MW: We were drawing really well already, over 4,000 a night, but it pushed us over the top, to 6,000-plus, and really pushed us over the top in needing a new park. We'd been in business for seven years, and we had grown each year. We didn't have any capacity to grow in that facility. A lot of people wanted to say that movie "made" us, but we were already doing very well.

MC: *What was the long-term impact on the game?*

MW: It gave people a real look inside minor-league baseball. It was pretty accurate, and it gave people across the country a close-up look. So, then you have the guy from New York who says, "I think I'd like own a minor-league team. That looks like fun." This was already happening, but this really accelerated the increase in franchise values and the whole boom in the minors.

And, it was a pretty realistic, good look at minor-league baseball. Well, except maybe the part with Millie and Nuke in the locker room at the very start of the movie. I don't think that's ever happened, but otherwise, it was pretty authentic. Thom Mount said he was going to make a movie; he did, and it worked.

Miles Wolff: All Roads Lead to Durham

Miles Wolff

The resume is impressive: founder and owner of teams, commissioner of leagues, author, publisher, and more. He was named as both the 71st most important person in the history of baseball by Total Baseball and one of the 10 best sports owners of the last 25 years by ESPN, the only minor leaguer on that list.

But the bullet points don't tell the whole story. Since the late 1970s, Miles Wolff has been at the center of practically every significant change in the minor-league baseball industry. Call it coincidence if you want. There's no disputing the fact that he's been in the right place at the right time more than once. But there's something more at work here. Wolff's love for the game of baseball and business instincts have led him to jump in where others wouldn't go, and the business of baseball has been better for it in every instance.

Growing up in Greensboro, Wolff longed to play in the big leagues like every Little Leaguer, but he realized early that it wasn't in the cards. Instead, he began to notice the people who made a living running the business end of the game. As minor league baseball struggled through the sixties and seventies, Wolff regularly followed his hometown team, the Greensboro Patriots, and realized that this was terrific baseball. He also wondered why more people didn't turn out.

So after graduating with a bachelor's degree from Johns Hopkins and a master's from the University of Virginia, Wolff did a stint as a Navy supply officer, which he still credits with teaching him resourcefulness and creative problem solving. He then set out to see if he could do a better job at attracting a crowd. Wolff ran baseball teams in a number of cities around the south, including Jacksonville, Fla., and Savannah, Ga., and collected a Sporting News Executive of the Year award along the way. He also published two books, a baseball novel called *Season of the Owl* and a historical account of the Greensboro lunch-counter sit-ins, called *Lunch at the Five and Ten*.

Wolff ultimately set his sights on ownership, and founded the Durham Bulls, which was a tremendous success from their very first homestand. This was one of the beginnings of the minor-league baseball boom that continues to this day. The Bulls would also be front and center when the American movie-going public was reintroduced to minor-league baseball through the movie *Bull Durham*.

He would also own and operate Baseball America magazine, the groundbreaking industry publication, which sought to provide a level of coverage that minor-league baseball had not been getting anywhere else. He would also branch out into hockey, starting up a successful minor-league hockey team in Raleigh and getting out before that sport hit one of its periodic downturns. Wolff would also found the Northern League, the first of the modern independent leagues.

Once again, Wolff was at the forefront. A host of other independent leagues subsequently sought to imitate the success of the Northern League, and independent ball has become a vital and credible part of the baseball landscape. But once again, Wolff was the first to take the plunge.

In the course of his career, Wolff has also owned teams in Butte, Mont., Asheville, N.C., and Pulaski, Va. He sold the Bulls in 1990 and is no longer the owner of Baseball America. He currently serves as the commissioner of the Can-Am League and the American Association, and owns teams in Quebec City, Canada, and Burlington, N.C.

So, what's next for Wolff? That's hard to say, but it's almost certain to be something no one has done before.

RALEIGH–DURHAM

TRIANGLE

SECTION 3

DURHAM

Baseball fans swoon over Durham. Durham Bulls Athletic Park is a beautiful, modern facility with a healthy dose of old-time charm. Durham Athletic Park is best known to purists as the original home of the Bulls and to millions as the main stage for Bull Durham. For those who love college baseball, the admission price to a Duke game at Jack Coombs Field is right: free.

CHAPTER 15

DURHAM BULLS ATHLETIC PARK

Leading Off

Opened: 1994

Capacity: 10,000

Dimensions: 305L, 400C, 327R

Current Team: Durham Bulls, International League (1994-present)

ESSENTIALS

Website: durhambulls.com • **Address:** 409 Blackwell St., Durham
Phone: 919/956-BULL • **Ticket Prices:** $5-$8
Directions: From I-85 (U.S. 70): Exit downtown Durham (Mangum Street).
Continue on Mangum through downtown for two miles.
Follow the parking signs to ballpark.

Durham: One of the Best Game-Day Experiences Anywhere

Durham Bulls Athletic Park, or the "Dee-Bap," as it is sometimes called, is a beautiful, modern facility with a healthy dose of old-time charm. Built primarily of brick and steel, this stadium was originally the brainchild of Bulls founder Miles Wolff. As far back as the mid-1980s, Wolff saw Durham as a Triple-A market and had worked on a plan for a new ballpark to replace the charming but creaky DAP. Wolff's original plans called for a ballpark on the site that houses University Ford, less than 100 yards from the current park's location. The Durham City Council narrowly defeated the funding for that facility.

Ultimately, Wolff sold the team to local media mogul Jim Goodman, who owns the Raleigh-Durham CBS and FOX stations, as well as several radio stations. Despite the fact that the new park was delayed almost 10 years, Goodman's media empire gave him the resources to not only contribute toward the construction of the new park but also spearhead the development of the American Tobacco Complex across the street. Formerly a derelict cigarette plant, this complex is now the dazzling centerpiece of the ballpark district's revival. Complete with restaurants, shops, and office space, the complex even incorporates a stream that runs the length of the development's interior courtyard, adding a welcome cooling touch to steamy game days.

Prior to the development of the American Tobacco Complex, construction of the ballpark had already spurred some new investment. Goodman built an office building above right field housing his WRAZ TV station, and this addition also

Players watch the action from the dugout steps at Durham Bulls Athletic Park.

created a whole new outfield seating section — the Diamond View section. This construction offers an few added benefits for tenants: some of the offices look out directly over the field.

New in 2007 was a rebuilt "Blue Monster" leftfield wall featuring a massive new video board.

While the ballpark has excellent food and beverage choices, many fans bring a picnic basket and enjoy some of the public open green spaces within the Tobacco Complex before the game. The Bulls also play many of the their Sunday home games at 5 p.m., which leaves enough daylight for a post-game picnic or a round of catch.

Inside the park there are a very nice kids' playground and food choices ranging from standard ballpark fare to local signature items. Don't leave without trying a Flying Burrito, sold out of the concessions stand directly behind home plate.

You can try your golf skills by putting on the concourse overlooking the right-field corner, climb a rock wall, or send your kids down a huge inflatable slide. The slide is free, but the kids should be prepared to wait in a long line if there's a big crowd. And there's almost always a big crowd.

There's a nice walk-in souvenir stand on the lower concourse immediately past the park's main gates, featuring a dizzying array of souvenir items and a neat full-size replica of the Bulls mascot, Wool E. Bull. It's easier to get a picture of the kids with Woolly here than trying to capture the very active character "on-the-hoof" (though there's a designated area to meet the colorful mascot down the third-base line). The souvenir shop is also a nice place to cool down if you are attending a late-summer game when the heat can be quite severe.

With Wool E. Bull a featured attraction, the Bulls' in-game presentation is among the best in the game. The character is a big step up from the ragged Bull mascot plunked by Nuke LaLoosh in *Bull Durham*, and he's everywhere: driving around the warning track on a go-cart, shooting a T-shirt cannon and, of course, racing against a young fan rounding the bases. Woolly's efforts and the inventive on-field games are well choreographed, accompanied by appropriate sound effects and geared to creating family-friendly fun.

Until 2007, nearly every word heard by Bulls fans in the new ballpark had been uttered by the pleasantly reedy voice of Bill Law. Bill retired after the 2006 season and was replaced by his good friend and longtime local radio personality Tony Riggsbee, who has an equally outstanding set of vocal cords, and is a minor-league fan of some renown.

Parking used to be the one big hassle associated with attending a Bulls game, but the addition of sizable parking decks at the American Tobacco Complex solves that problem. Also, the decks have freed up lots of on-street parking for the thrifty and/or adventurous fan, although if you're on vacation, you'd be smart to just pay your money to park in the decks.

While many traditionalists were heartbroken to see the Bulls move out of the old DAP, it's clear now clear after a decade that Durham needed this facility. Although the Bulls were drawing great crowds at the DAP, there were real limits to the team's ability to serve the type of crowds they were drawing. The move up to Triple-A baseball has been a positive for the region as well, and a move that would not have been possible without the new facility. This is also a case where the subsequent development in the neighborhood took several years to get underway, but it has certainly exceeded expectations.

When you combine a fantastic in-park presentation and Triple-A baseball with the great new amenities in the neighboring American Tobacco Complex, you have one of the best overall game-day experiences you'll find anywhere.

Games at the Durham ballpark usually are well attended, especially on the weekends.

Durham Bulls
Athletic Park
was one of the
first ballparks
to feature patio-
style seating.

🎾 Insider's Tip

Fans traveling in for a game — particularly a weekend game — will want to order their tickets in advance: Friday and Saturday sellouts are quite common. If it's an early game or particularly hot, you'll want to avoid the Diamond View outfield seats. There's no shade in these seats, and the sun will be right in your eyes while it's setting over the grandstand roof. Most grandstand seats, except those far down the first-base side, will offer some shade or at least put the sun at your back.

Exploring Durham

The ballpark is located on the southern edge of downtown Durham, and the hardy
fan may want to make an afternoon of it. Walk two blocks north of the ballpark
on Blackwell Street and find the Self-Help Credit Union Building where you can
take the "Morgan Burkhart Tour" of Baseball America (**201 W. Main St., Suite 201;
baseballamerica.com**). Ask for Ronnie, and buy the latest Almanac or Super Register.
Choose from several sandwich shops or see what's playing at the Carolina Theatre
(**309 W. Morgan St.; carolinatheatre.org**) right in the middle of the downtown loop. It's not
far from the Durham Marriott (**201 Foster St.; marriott.com**), which often houses the

visiting teams. The Southern Book Exchange (**107 W. Chapel Hill**) may be the oldest independent bookstore in North Carolina, and it features a fantastic collection of used books.

Keep hoofing it (or driving — after all, you're on vacation!) north up Duke Street and you'll find your way to Parker & Otis (**112 S. Duke St.; parkerandotis.com**), which will forever be known as the place that used to be Fowler's. Fowler's was a Tobacco Road answer to Zabar's in New York City, and the new owners have kept the tradition of fine wine, cheeses, beers, and sandwiches. Next door is Brightleaf Square (**905 W. Main St.; historicbrightleaf.com**), Durham's pioneering downtown mall housed in a rehabbed tobacco warehouse, complete with rough brick walls and hardwood floors. A Brightleaf institution, Satisfaction's (located in the North Building) is a favorite of the Dukies for their delicious (and greasy) pizza, cheap pitchers of beer, and huge TVs.

If you have a little less time or energy, you can make an afternoon of it at the American Tobacco Complex, right next door to the ballpark. Grab a pizza at the Mellow Mushroom (**410 Blackwell St.; mellowmushroom.com**), which also features a huge

The downtown Durham skyline provides a backdrop for the larger, reconstituted in leftfield at Durham Bulls Athletic Park.

draft beer selection, or eat at Symposium Café (**318 Blackwell St.; symposiumcafenc.com**), where you can enjoy a game of catch on the lawn in the middle of the complex.

(Additional Durham restaurants are covered later in this chapter.)

Of course, you can always head to the ballpark early and soak up the history on the decorative banners throughout the concourse. Don't miss the original snorting Bull sign from *Bull Durham*, now mounted on the wall along the first-base side of the grandstand.

DURHAM ATHLETIC PARK

Leading Off

Opened: 1939

Capacity: 5,000

Dimensions: 330L, 365LC, 405C, 370RC, 305R

Current Team: None

Previous Teams: Durham Americans / Braves, CPL (1997-2002); Durham Bulls, Carolina League (1980-1994); Raleigh-Durham Triangles, Carolina League (1968-71); Durham Bulls, Carolina League (1945-67); Durham Bulls, Piedmont League (1920-1933, 1936-1943)

ESSENTIALS

Address: 400 Morris St., Durham

The Real Cradle of the Game

Durham Athletic Park, or "The DAP," as Bulls fans affectionately called it for decades, is a cultural touchstone. This park would be hugely significant just from its role as the primary filming location for the movie *Bull Durham*. That movie, after all, made the minors cool to a whole new generation of fans and made the Durham Bulls the nation's most famous minor-league franchise. This is the park most people think of first when you talk about minor-league baseball in North Carolina.

For people in the baseball business, the park is just as significant as the home of the Bulls' rebirth in 1980, one of the early harbingers of the current minor-league boom. When the Durham Bulls returned and drew large crowds — as well as generating some serious revenue — smart businesspeople figured out minor-league baseball could be a profitable investment if properly promoted and managed. This was a major reversal from the '70s-era thinking that people would rather enjoy televised big-league baseball in the air-conditioned comfort of their homes.

Despite this prominent place in baseball history, it had appeared in recent years that the DAP would quietly rot. The condition of the park, resulting from the City of Durham's complete neglect of this tremendously important historical site, is enough to bring tears to your eyes, especially if you remember it packed to the rafters when the Bulls last played there. The playing surface is worse than a cow pasture, the steelwork is rusting, and the wood home-run fence has been replaced with chain link, giving the place the look of an abandoned high-school field.

The old Durham Athletic Park turret housed team offices and the ballpark's box office.

The removal of the bleachers shortly after the Bulls moved to their new ballpark in 1994 had already given the park a diminished atmosphere. Further indignity was visited upon the place when the city tore the grass out of the infield in 1997 to accommodate the short-lived Women's Pro Fastpitch League. At that time, with a Coastal Plain League team and the WPF both using the park, there was at least some semblance of maintenance and upkeep, although the teams undertook much of that work. With the departure of the WPF after a lackluster two-year run, and the shutdown of the CPL franchise following the 2002 season, usage of the DAP was limited to a handful of high-school baseball contests, recreation-league softball games, and a pair of annual festivals.

It appears that a new dawn is on the horizon for the DAP, though. The funding for a package of renovations was approved in a recent bond referendum, with the goal of making the DAP the new home to the North Carolina Central University, which brought back baseball in the spring of 2007, playing at Durham Bulls Athletic Park. The ballpark is also envisioned as a museum dedicated to the history of minor-league baseball and a training school for umpires.

Land acquisition and fund raising are also under way for a center city park that would connect the DAP with the center of Durham's downtown business district, just four blocks to the south. The ballpark also borders a massive new development financed by former Duke basketball stars Christian Laettner and Brian Davis, which has created upscale condos in a number of former American Tobacco Company buildings.

The question now becomes whether the city can follow through on its plan and preserve this important cultural and historic site. Those familiar with the city's history have their doubts, but at least there is cause for hope. Current City Manager Patrick Baker is a sports fan and seems to understand the historic and cultural value of the park in a way his predecessors did not.

Rebirth of the Bulls

Of course, this park has risen from the ashes before, sometimes literally, sometimes figuratively. When the current Bulls franchise was born as an expansion franchise in the Carolina League in the fall of 1979, one prominent city official said the only renovations performed on the old park should involve dynamite. In the end, though, owner Miles Wolff convinced the city to invest $50,000 in the place, most of which went for new paint and a few other assorted repairs.

The condition of the park wasn't the only obstacle, though. People were reluctant to commit their sponsorship dollars, as minor-league baseball had failed the last time a team was placed in Durham. Despite this skepticism, Wolff and his young general manager, Pete Bock, a former minor-league umpire, struggled on. They managed to convince most of their suppliers to extend them credit and sold fence signs with no money due up front.

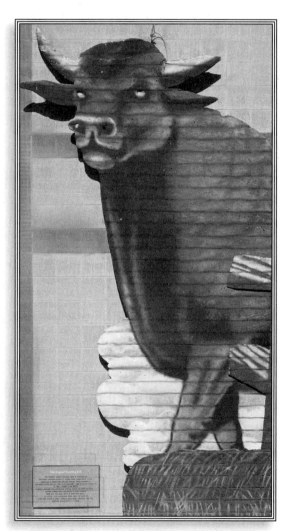

The original Durham Bull sign, created for the film, is mounted along the wall on the concourse of the new ballpark.

Then, just days before the opening of their first season in April of 1980, the team's uniforms were stolen. A replacement set of hand-me-down Braves jerseys and pants were rushed up from the "big club" in Atlanta, and the season was underway.

Team management learned about a number of the old park's quirks on Opening Night, but the most notable was in the middle of the game, when all the bathrooms in place backed up. It was a harbinger of things to come, as the place would show its age for the Bulls' entire 14-year run at the DAP. A bucket of ice with a fan kept the breaker panel for the field lights from overheating. There was a serious shortage of counter space: auxiliary concession stands, souvenir windows and beer taps were shochorned into every corner of the place. The playing surface had a persistent, recurring trough from the left-field corner to right-field bullpens.

Despite all these obstacles, the Bulls caught the front of a wave, providing a local rallying point for the residents of Durham. When Wolff and General Manager Pete Bock looked down the street on opening night and saw the line for tickets snaking around the block, they knew they had created something special.

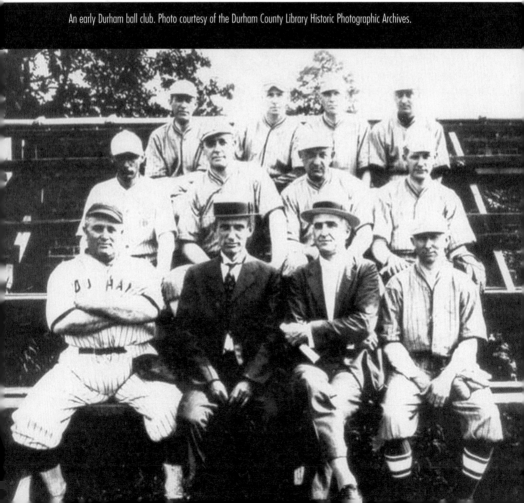

An early Durham ball club. Photo courtesy of the Durham County Library Historic Photographic Archives.

It's a good thing they drew a crowd, too. Both men had gone without a salary for several months prior to the season, as the club struggled to stay afloat financially until opening day. Bock, who had played college baseball at UNC prior to his minor-league umpiring career, was new to the business side of the game,

El Toro Park.
Photo courtesy of the North Carolina State Archives.

but he was a Durham native and gave the team some local credibility. Wolff, already a veteran minor-league operator from nearby Greensboro, originally had been the Southern League's Executive of the Year but longed to operate his own team.

Put together by league president Jim Mills, each had been led to believe that the other had some financial resources to bring to the table. Ultimately, Mills had to loan the pair half of the money to purchase the expansion franchise, which they acquired for about $5,000. For operating capital, they borrowed from friends, relatives, and virtually anyone who would put up some money.

In the end, it turned out to be a pretty good investment. When Wolff sold the Bulls to local TV magnate Jim Goodman in 1990, the sale price, while never made public, was rumored to be in the neighborhood of $4 million.

Rising from the Ashes

The beginnings of the modern Bulls franchise marked the second time the DAP had been reborn from the ashes. The first time, El Toro Park (as it was then known) was literally rebuilt from the ashes in the wake of a fire that destroyed the wooden grandstand in the middle of the 1939 season. The team went on the road for several weeks, and when they returned the grandstand that still stands today had been largely completed.

The most notable episode in Durham Athletic Park, allowing the sights and sounds of the DAP to reach more fans than any other minor-league park in history, was the filming of the movie *Bull Durham*, starring Kevin Costner as an aging catcher hanging on for one last shot, Tim Robbins as a clueless young fireballer, and Susan Sarandon in the role that made "Baseball Annie" a household term. The movie launched the Bulls brand into a whole new universe. Suddenly the Bulls, which had been largely a Durham phenomenon in their early years, were a nationally known team after the movie's release in 1988.

The movie was filmed the previous winter, and when the crew descended on the DAP they were greeted by brown grass, tiny locker rooms that didn't allow enough space to shoot, and weather so cold there is visible steam coming from the mouths

of the actors in several scenes. Vegetable dye was sprayed on the field, a "faux" locker room was constructed in one of the nearby warehouse buildings, and a wooden bull with glowing red eyes and smoke shooting from its nostrils was built above the right-field wall. (That bull is now located in the concourse of Durham Bulls Athletic Park.)

This iconic sign was a tribute to the advertising for Durham's signature product, Bull Durham tobacco. Known as the Bull City, Durham was home to American Tobacco, the company that made the Duke family rich enough to buy themselves a

The Sarandon suite, constructed for the film *Bull Durham*, still can be found directly behind the first base dugout at Durham Athletic Park.

university and a whole lot more. Bull Durham tobacco was advertised all over the minor leagues (take a look at scorecards from the 1940s and 1950s and you'll more often than not see an ad for Bull Durham chaw), and one of the theories on the origin of the term "bullpen" says the bull-shaped signs looming over outfield walls all over the minors provided some of the only shade in many of the parks. This supposedly created an inviting spot for the in which the relief pitchers could relax while awaiting the call to pitch.

If you get to visit the DAP, you'll see that this park has a couple of unusual elements still visible. The press box is located in a bunker sunken halfway below field grade, shielded with a plexiglass window. It's the closest view of a ballgame you'll ever see, although it's a strange angle; you lose the outfielders' legs up to the knee due to the crown of the field, and when a foul tip comes straight back, it's very difficult not to flinch.

Team offices were located where a press box would normally be, but there's also a small auxiliary press box above the offices. This cramped perch is where "The Voice of the Bulls, Teddy Garland" broadcast home games in the movie.

Also, the front-row box seats at the first-base end of the grandstand are mounted not on concrete, as the rest of the seats are, but rather on a wood platform extending beyond the concrete. Legend has it that the existing seats didn't

The trademark Bulls logo still watches over the DAP.

provide the right camera angles, and this small section was added specifically to accommodate seats for "Annie" and "Millie."

You'll also notice that the park seems much smaller than what's depicted in the movie; when the bleachers were removed shortly after the Bulls moved out the park's capacity was reduced from a total of about 6,000 seats to less than 2,000 seats, all of them located in the grandstand.

Although this park isn't what it once was, given its incredible history one can only hope that the City of Durham will step up to the plate and help this park rise from the ashes one more time.

⚾ Insider's Tip

When you watch *Bull Durham*, pay particular attention to the wedding scene. Shortly before the sequence was scheduled to be filmed, the casting director realized that they had neglected to hire anyone in the role of the minister. Former Bulls GM Pete Bock, who had left the team to run the Hawaii Islanders of the Pacific Coast League and subsequently returned to Durham, was serving as a baseball advisor to the production crew, and he was drafted for the job. Despite a suit that didn't really fit and a complete lack of any professional acting experience, Bock tackled the role. Note his bemused expression after he delivers his line, "You may kiss the bride." If the name sounds familiar, he's now the founder and president of the Coastal Plain League. For a day he was an actor, and he still receives royalty checks.

JACK COOMBS FIELD

Leading Off

Capacity: 2,000

Dimensions: 330L, 375LC, 400C, 375RC, 330R

Current Team: Duke University Blue Devils (NCAA Division I; Atlantic Coast Conference)

ESSENTIALS

Address: Whitfield Drive, east of Science Drive
Website: goduke.com
Phone: 919/684-2358
Ticket Prices: Free

The Other Blue Devils Roundball

There's a bonus to being in Durham in the early days of spring: Duke University Blue Devils baseball. Games at Jack Coombs Field are free, and even if the Blue Devils are struggling, the Atlantic Coast Conference usually features an array of good players, so you are bound to be entertained. While the Duke basketball team lives in the stratosphere of college basketball, the Devils baseball program has struggled along as one of the bottom feeders of the ACC for many years. While the school's rigorous academic standards pose a real challenge in recruiting, similar schools such as Vanderbilt and Rice have found baseball success in the last several years.

Despite these challenges, under new coach Sean McNally (a former Burlington Indians manager and owner of many of Duke's career hitting records) the Blue Devils have shown hustle and heart. And most importantly for the visiting fan the team faces fantastic opponents and the ballpark has a nice laid-back atmosphere. The grandstand has an odd wedge shape, much like the home-plate section of a larger grandstand that was never finished. This seating area is fully covered and has a capacity of about 1,200. The back of the grandstand features the same stonework appearance that is the signature of the entire Duke campus.

The biggest drawback to this park is the foul territory, which is enormous. This creates something of a disconnect from the action, and also probably helps explain why the press box is actually a counter built in front of the first row of seats; someone wisely decided that the official scorer didn't need to be put any farther from the field than necessary. The overall atmosphere, though, is very pleasant as some of the campus buildings peek over the right-field wall and a screen of pine trees provides the backdrop in left. The playing surface is lush and green.

The third-base side features a concrete plaza and entryway, as well as a new all-weather hitting facility. On the first-base side you'll find a big, grassy bank drawing a good portion of the crowd. Coombs Field added lights a few years back and night games are now a regular part of the schedule, but many of the early-season games are played in the afternoon to avoid the cooler temperatures at night. And, there's something particularly relaxing about seeing a game here in the afternoon. Much of the daytime crowd is made up of Duke students enjoying a nice spring afternoon with baseball as a definite afterthought. These are clearly not the Cameron Crazies!

Concessions are available from a trailer set up along the first-base plaza with standard items like hot dogs, sodas, and candy. That will get you through an attack of hunger pangs in the middle of a game, but if time permits, you'll want to try one of Durham's many and varied restaurants (*see below*). This ballpark, like all the college venues in North Carolina, does not serve beer, but one of the benefits of the laid-back atmosphere and open gates is that a discreet fan with a backpack can enjoy a beverage of his choice on the first-base berm. Bring an opaque cup or, better yet, support the home team by first enjoying a Coke in a Blue Devil souvenir cup.

The Duke campus itself is well worth a tour. The Sarah Duke Gardens are one of the Raleigh-Durham-Chapel Hill Triangle's most beautiful spots. Pack a picnic lunch, visit the Duke Chapel, and take a stroll of the main campus. Bring a blanket, stretch out, and watch some baseball too. You'll be glad you did.

Sports Around Town

Probably the best-known building in all of Durham is on the Duke campus, just a few yards from Jack Coombs Field. Cameron Indoor Stadium, the Blue Devils' basketball arena, sits right next door to both Coombs Field as well as Wallace Wade Stadium, the home of Duke football. When you leave Coombs Stadium, turn left and walk down the hill approximately 50 yards; Cameron will be directly to your left. Turn around, and you'll see Wallace Wade Stadium, which could be described as the Ohio State horseshoe's little brother: a vast, oval expanse of concrete steps and aluminum benches with one open end and the field encircled by a running track. Both venues are tucked away on the middle of campus, and looking from the exterior, Cameron is easy to miss. It looks like a big classroom building. The stonework look of the Duke campus is carried through to this arena, the former home court to such notables as Grant Hill, Bobby Hurley, Elton Brand, Mike Gminski, and many others too numerous to list. Housing a number of athletic-department offices, Cameron is generally unlocked during the day, and a lucky, discreet and polite fan might be able to get a glimpse of one of nation's best-known college sports venues.

Other Duke University Attractions

The Durham Life & Science Museum is a great outing for the kids. With hands-on science exhibits, a very popular butterfly exhibit, and a little train you and the kids can ride, it's a fun way to spend an afternoon.

Admission is between $7 and $10 and includes the Magic Wings Butterfly House and all indoor and outdoor activities except the train ($2 per ride).

Museum of Life and Sciences
433 W. Murray Av.
919/220-5429
ncmls.org

Hours: Monday-Saturday, 10 a.m.-5 p.m., and Sunday, Noon-5 p.m. Open 362 days, excluding Thanksgiving, Christmas and New Year's Day.

As mentioned earlier, the Duke University campus features beautiful stone buildings laid out in a series of quads. The main campus has such a classic look that it was used as a location in the college football movie *The Program* with James Caan, Halle Berry, and Omar Epps.

The Sarah Duke Gardens are a fantastic place for a picnic. A world-renowned garden, sometimes referred to as the "Crown Jewel of Duke University," occupies

1953 Duke University baseball team at the Raleigh-Durham Airport. *Raleigh News & Observer photo courtesy of the North Carolina State Archives.*

The sprawling American Tobacco Complex offering retail, restaurants, offices and a picnic area nicely complements the Durham Bulls Athletic Park across the street.

55 acres in the heart of the University's West Campus, adjacent to Duke University Medical Center. For more information, visit **www.hr.duke.edu/dukegardens**.

The Duke campus is also home to a center for the study of lemurs, the cute little tree-dwellers with the big eyes. The Lemur Center is open to the public by appointment only; call 919/489-3364, ext. 0, for more information. A gift shop is open to the public Monday through Friday, 8:30 a.m. to 4:30 p.m. Visit online at **lemur.duke.edu**.

The Duke Chapel is worth a visit. As with all the attractions on campus, the chapel can be easily reached on foot if you get around relatively well.

There is also a beautiful new museum on campus, the Nasher Museum of Art. With a varied collection of art that includes sculptures, visiting exhibits, and a nice gift shop and café, the Nasher is perfect stop for any art lover visiting the Duke campus (and it's air-conditioned). Visit online at **nasher.duke.edu** or call 919/684-5135.

Durham Restaurants

The Ninth Street area is adjacent to the Duke campus and a favorite of the student crowd. Two restaurants there are worth checking out: Parizade and George's Garage. With an upscale décor and terrific food, Parizade offers a varied Mediterranean menu and a great selection of wine and spirits.

Parizade
2200 W. Main St.
919/286-9712
ghgrestaurants.com

Owned by the same folks as Parizade, George's Garage is a casual alternative and offers a bakery, take-out buffet, sit-down restaurant, and nighttime dancing. Like at Parizade, the food is terrific, and the crowd ranges from professionals to college students.

George's Garage
737 9th St.
919-286-4131
ghgrestaurants.com

If you want to try some old-style barbeque in Durham, you'll want to find your way to Dillard's. This cafeteria-style restaurant has customers queuing outside the door before opening time. The décor is basic, but the food is outstanding, including a spicy, in-house sauce. Dillard's has also served as the official BBQ of the Durham Bulls.

Dillard's Bar-B-Que
3921 Fayetteville St.
919/544-1587

Durham Lodging

When selecting a place to stay in the Raleigh-Durham Triangle, keep in mind that the Triangle is fairly compact. Raleigh is only about 20 minutes away, depending on traffic, and Chapel Hill is less than 10 miles away. So, depending on how the schedule works out, you can pick what works best among the Raleigh-Durham-Chapel Hill area's cities and just stay put for several days. All other things being equal, though, I recommend staying in Chapel Hill to take advantage of the nice walkable downtown and lively nightlife.

The Radisson Hotel RTP may be the best bet if you want to be in the middle of it all — literally. Located just a few miles from RDU International Airport right on I-40, the hotel is between the two major cities, just a bit closer to Durham than Raleigh. A nice property with a unique octagonal shape, this Radisson also offers a free airport shuttle, tennis, fitness room, and an outdoor pool. If a Radisson isn't to your taste, there are several other airport hotels in the general area.

Radisson Hotel RTP
150 Park Dr.
I-40-@ Davis Drive, exit 280
Research Triangle Park, NC 27709
radisson.com

The Durham Marriott is downtown Durham's only full-service hotel. This is often where the visiting teams stay, so you may be able to pick up an autograph. This hotel is walking distance to the new ballpark and some of downtown's other attractions, like Brightleaf Square, but you'll want to be careful about walking around at night. You may want to get a cab after dark.

Durham Marriott at the Convention Center
201 Foster St.
Durham, NC 27701
919/786-6000
marriott.com

⊹ Directions

To Durham Bulls Athletic Park

From I-85 (U.S. 70):

Exit downtown Durham (Mangum Street). Continue on Mangum through downtown for two miles. Follow the parking signs to ballpark.

From I-40:

Take I-40 west to the Durham Freeway (Exit 279B), then to the Mangum/Roxboro Street Exit (Exit 12B). Keep straight up the hill for about 2 blocks (Willard Street). The ballpark is on the right.

From 15-501 North Bypass:

Exit Durham Freeway South. Exit Mangum/Roxboro Street (Exit 12). Cross Mangum Street. Go left on Roxboro. Follow signs for Durham Freeway North (stay to right). Cross Mangum Street again. The ballpark is on the right.

From I-540:

Take I-540 south to the I-40 exit. Take I-40 West until you reach the Durham Freeway (Exit 279B) to the Mangum/Roxboro Street Exit (Exit 12B). Keep straight up the hill for about 2 blocks (Willard Street). The ballpark is on the right.

⊕ Directions

To Durham Athletic Park

From Durham Bulls Athletic Park (the new ballpark):

Head up Blackwell Street (along the third-base line) away from the Durham Freeway. Continue on Blackwell Street through downtown Durham. The street name will eventually become Foster Street. Turn left on West Corporation Drive; the ballpark will be on your right.

To Jack Coombs Field

From RDU Airport and points east:

Exit the airport on westbound I-40. After 4 miles, merge onto NC-147N (Durham Freeway) toward Durham/Downtown, Exit 279B. After 8.5 miles, exit Chapel Hill Street, Exit 13. Chapel Hill Street becomes Duke University Road. Proceed to the dead end, and turn right on HW 751. At the next stoplight (Science Drive), turn right. Turn right on Whitford Drive; you'll see the ballpark.

From the north in I-85:

Exit 15-501 Bypass South. On 15-501, exit at HW 751, then turn left at the light. Proceed to the third light (Science Drive) and turn left. Turn right on Whitford Drive; you'll see the ballpark.

From the south on I-85:

Exit on HW 751, Exit 170. Turn right at the first light. Go three miles; at the fourth light, turn left on Science Drive. Turn right on Whitford Drive; you'll see the ballpark.

BUIES CREEK

Taylor Field may be small, but don't be fooled by the home of the Campbell University baseball team: it features a top-rate playing surface, and some very good players can usually be seen, either playing for the Camels or the visiting team.

TAYLOR FIELD

Leading Off

Opened: Late 1940s

Capacity: 1,000

Dimensions: 337L, 368LC, 395C, 375RC, 328R

Current Team: Campbell University Camels (Atlantic Sun Conference)

Website: gocamels.com/baseball/mbc_home.htm
Phone Number: 910/893-1354
Ticket Prices: $3-$5
Parking: free

Camels in Carolina? Only at Campbell

With the only team in any sport — collegiate or pro — nicknamed "Camels," Campbell University is worth a visit just to get a hat featuring a large "C" behind an image of a menacing camel in the school colors of orange and black. It's a great-looking hat, and you definitely will be the only one on your block to have one.

Campbell is a small Baptist college in the microscopic town of Buies Creek (2000 population: 2,215). Campbell University was a longtime member of the NAIA (National Association of Intercollegiate Athletics), but it transitioned to NCAA status in recent years, and Campbell is now a Division I program. The Camels' home field is a cozy little park with a truly outstanding playing surface and top-of-the-line field lights. In recent years, the two-story press box that could kindly be described as "rustic" was replaced with an attractive, modern building featuring air conditioning in the press space above and a small but modern concessions stand underneath. This renovation also included brick retaining walls from dugout to dugout, new bleachers, and new covered field-level dugouts.

The Camels' conference — the Atlantic Sun — is not as well-known or prestigious as those of the Camels' neighbors, the NC State Wolfpack of the ACC or East Carolina of C-USA. Nonetheless, Campbell has sent a number of players on to pro ball and has some big-league flavor in their history. Calvin Koonce, a member of the Mets' World Series team of 1973, once guided the Camels' program.
You can also walk across the road and visit the Camels' home gym, one of the smallest venues in Division I at 947 seats.

Campbell University Camels logo

You won't be likely to find yourself in Buies Creek by accident, but you may consider a visit if you're in Raleigh in the spring. (In fact, it's highly unlikely you'll be staying in Buies Creek; see our Raleigh chapter for information on lodgings and restaurants.) You'll find a real homespun college baseball experience. In past years, former Athletic Director Tom Collins (now a university vice president) was known to bring his pet camel to some of the team's home games. The Camels usually host some big-name foes, particularly when the northern schools are on their early season southern swing.

Parking is behind the post office and free, and all tickets are general admission. Concessions offerings are basic, but very affordable: hot dogs, soda, pizza, and some candy.

In the past Campbell hosted a summer-collegiate Coastal Plain League game. This has often been done in conjunction with one of the University's summer camps, complete with post-game fireworks. This has been a natural fit with Campbell typically placing many of their players in the CPL each year.

Directions

From Raleigh:

Take Route 401 south to Lillington, then take Route 421 east to Buies Creek. From I-95, take exit 79, then take Route 27 west through Dunn and on to Buies Creek.

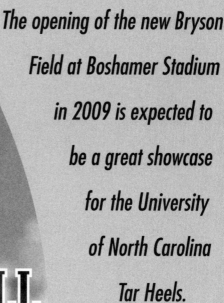

The opening of the new Bryson
Field at Boshamer Stadium
in 2009 is expected to
be a great showcase
for the University
of North Carolina
Tar Heels.

CHAPEL HILL

CHAPTER 17

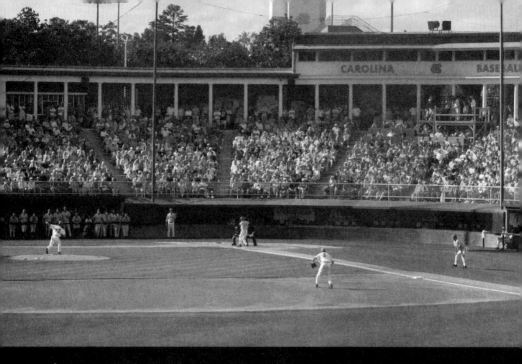

BRYSON FIELD AT BOSHAMER STADIUM

Leading Off

Opened: 1972

Capacity: 2,000, plus room for 1,000 on left-field berm

Dimensions: 335L, 370LC, 400C, 362RC, 335R

Current Team: University of North Carolina Tar Heels

(NCAA Division I; Atlantic Coast Conference)

ESSENTIALS

Address: Ridge Road, East of Stadium Drive
Website: tarheelblue.com
Phone: 919/962-2296
Ticket Prices: $5 for adults; $3 for students/seniors;
free for UNC students, faculty/staff, and children ages 6 and under.

My Blue Heaven

When a ballpark is part of a university campus, there is no finer compliment than to say it is in harmony with its surroundings. This is particularly true when the surroundings are as charming as Chapel Hill, known locally as the "Southern Part of Heaven." Boshamer Stadium, with its brick grandstand, sky-blue bench seats, and white columns supporting the concourse overhang, feels like it grew organically from the soil of the UNC campus.

That's a good thing in a green town like Chapel Hill, where organic foods are popular. Sports are a major preoccupation for the student body at UNC and the locals as well. While basketball most certainly is the highest-profile program on campus and the women's soccer team has built a dynasty, baseball is well supported. The baseball Heels have an illustrious history in their own right, including a College World Series team in the 1980s featuring B.J. Surhoff, Walt Weiss, and Scott Bankhead. Current Orioles star Brian Roberts grew up at Boshamer during his father's tenure as head coach at UNC and began his college career wearing the pale blue before transferring to South Carolina.

Current coach Mike Fox took the 2006 and 2007 teams to the College World Series championship round in Omaha, as well. Players like Andrew Miller (who rose quickly with the Detroit Tigers and then was traded to the Florida Marlins), Josh Bard, and Andrew Carignan led the way; Miller and Bard were both were selected in the first round of the June 2006 amateur draft.

The Atlantic Coast Conference is, of course, one of the nation's top college baseball conferences. The expansion of the league, begun in the 1990s after decades as an eight-team circuit, was based on strengthening its standing in football, but it brought in a powerhouse baseball program in Florida State and later added Miami to a group that has always been among the nation's best.

Tar Heel B.J. Surhoff shows the swing that resulted in a 19-season Major League career with the Brewers.
Photo courtesy of the University of North Carolina.

The focus at Boshamer is definitely on the baseball. When attending college baseball games, it's worth keeping in mind college programs are run by baseball coaches with the student-athlete as the first priority. For fans accustomed to dollar beer nights, playgrounds, burritos, and furry mascots of indeterminate species, this is a decidedly different experience.

You won't be able to see the Tar Heels at Boshamer in 2008, as the team will be playing at the new USA Baseball National Training Complex at Cary's Thomas Brooks Park while the ballpark is rebuilt. When Boshamer opened, it was considered among the best in the ACC and hosted five ACC tournaments between 1973 and 1983. Named for Cary C. Boshamer, who pledged the funding for the ballpark in 1970, the stadium hosted its first game in March 1972. (The photos in the chapter were of the original Boshamer Stadium.)

The new Bryson Field at Boshamer Stadium, which will be built in the same footprint as the existing field, will feature more than 4,000 chairback seats, premium seating, a wider concourse and new restrooms and concessions. Fans will also be able to enjoy a Hall of Honor celebrating the success of Carolina baseball through the years. New team facilities will include a 1,500-square foot clubhouse and a 2,600-square-foot weight room with adjoining training room. The facility will also feature a 4,500-square foot indoor/outdoor hitting and pitching practice facility. The upper deck will feature offices for the coaching staff, as well as a new press box with separate television and radio booths. Club-level suites will be available for lease.

Left-hander Andrew Miller finished his brilliant UNC career in 2006, was drafted in the first round in June, and debuted with the Detroit Tigers later that year. *Photo courtesy of the University of North Carolina.*

The courtyard at the new ballpark will be named the Steinbrenner Family Courtyard as a result of New York Yankees owner George Steinbrenner and his family donating $1 million to the project. There's a deep connection between the Steinbrenner family and UNC: Steinbrenner's daughter, Jenny, graduated from UNC, and Steinbrenner used to schedule exhibitions between the Yankees and the Tar Heels in the late 1970s and early 1980s. These contests drew overflow crowds; some area fans describe people hanging from trees to see the Major League superstars.

The park is shoe-horned into a small, uneven parcel of land, adding to its charm, but making it a tight squeeze on a busy night. A high-rise dorm looms over the left field wall, offering a "sky box" housing option for some lucky students.

Parking can be a challenge in Chapel Hill, as is the case on most college campuses, but normally enough spots are available at the lot down the hill from the right-field wall. This presents another obstacle for anyone of limited mobility, but numerous handicapped spaces are reserved right next to the main entrance.

Taken as a whole, seeing the Tar Heels play at Boshamer is a wonderful, relaxing outing, and we're sure the new ballpark will enhance the experience. Like Clint Eastwood says, "a man's got to know his limitations," and for the fan who is prepared for a purist's experience and some of the best college baseball you'll see anywhere in America's prettiest university town, Boshamer is a must.

Sports Around Town

While UNC produced the most famous basketball player of all time, Michael Jordan, many sports fans don't realize the Tar Heel football program also produced two of the all-time greats in that sport. Two very different players from two different eras — Pro Football Hall of Fame member Lawrence Taylor and two-time Heisman Trophy runner-up and College Football Hall of Famer Charlie "Choo Choo" Justice — both called UNC's Kenan Stadium their home field.

Taylor played defensive end and linebacker from 1977 to 1980. A consensus All-American his senior year, Taylor was known as a wild man on the field and off, making Franklin Street his personal playground during his years in Chapel Hill.

Justice was an elusive running back who played his college football in the late 1940s after two years of military service. Despite playing in a lightly regarded football conference, Justice was runner-up for the Heisman Trophy in both '48 and '49. From 1946-1949, the Heels went 32-9-1 and played in three major bowl games in what is still regarded as the "Golden Age" of Carolina football.

Justice is honored with a larger-than-life bronze statue at the west entrance to Kenan Stadium and was described by Athletic Director Dick Baddour as "one of the most beloved figures in the history of this great University." He died in 2003 at age 79 at his home in Cherryville, N.C.

Things to Do

VISIT THE DEAN DOME

The Dean E. Smith Center — home to the Tar Heels basketball program and known informally as the Dean Dome — is slated for a significant facelift over the next few years. Visitors who associate this program with championships and regular appearances on national TV may be surprised at the slightly rough-around-the-edges look of this arena's exterior and landscaping, but it's definitely worth a visit for the serious basketball fan. Visitors to the Memorabilia Room can view photos and at least one national championship trophy. Hours are Monday-Friday 9 a.m. – 5 p.m., subject to change for event preparation. The Memorabilia Room is located on the second floor of the Smith Center. The Concourse Level (third floor) is also open to visitors from 9-5 Monday-Friday, aside from events. For more information, visit goheels.com.

VISIT CARMICHAEL GYM

Many fans don't realize the Heels' most prominent alum, Michael Jordan, never played in the Dean Dome. During Jordan's time at Carolina, the men's team played at 8,000-seat Carmichael Gym, just a few hundred yards from Boshamer and adjacent to the soccer stadium. Now the home to the UNC women, this great old arena has seen some sellout crowds in recent years, particularly since the rivalry between the UNC and Duke women's programs has truly heated up.

GO TO FRANKLIN STREET

The town of Chapel Hill and the university are virtually synonymous, and the main student strip up and down Franklin Street offers a wide variety of inexpensive food and drink. It's also a great jumping-off point for a stroll around one of the nation's prettiest campuses.

There are several landmark establishments, including a great bar called He's Not Here. If you're lucky enough to visit Chapel Hill over a weekend when the weather's nice, He's Not Here often has live bands in the courtyard. Get a 32 oz. "Blue Cup" from the courtyard tiki bar, enjoy the often-dazzling scenery, and pretend you're back in college! Sometimes you'll pay a small cover charge if there's a band playing, but the music is usually pretty good. There's also an indoor bar at the top of the double stairs leading up from the courtyard. Check out the great vintage Budweiser light with marching Clydesdales hanging over the middle of the bar. You won't see any signs for this place: just look for the alleyway next to Caribou Coffee and Ben & Jerry's and enjoy.

He's Not Here
112 1/2 W. Franklin St.
919/942-7939

Franklin Street offers lots of fast food joints, pizza places, and Chinese restaurants, as you'd expect. But if you're looking for fast and cheap with some character, you'll want to eat at Time Out Chicken and Biscuits in the University Square shopping center, one of the only places in Chapel Hill with ample free parking for customers. It's right across the street from He's Not Here, and there's a fair amount of traffic back and forth, especially late at night. The chicken biscuit is out of sight, especially after a Blue Cup, and the "Bucket of Bones" is a favorite of the college crowd.

Time Out Chicken & Biscuits
133 W. Franklin St.
919/929-2425

If you want to go more upscale, head to the corner of Franklin and Columbia. Look at the tops of the buildings and head for the one with the gargoyles wearing basketball jerseys with the number 23 (an MJ reference, of course). That's Top of the Hill, as one recent UNC grad put it, "where all the rich alum go to eat before the basketball games." The menu has plenty of very affordable choices, including great personal pizzas, and their micro brews are excellent. Reservations aren't a bad idea on a weekend night.

Top of the Hill
100 E. Franklin St., third floor
919/929-8676
topofthehillrestaurant.com

The Carolina Brewery is another excellent brew pub and restaurant: Order the shrimp and grits.

Carolina Brewery
460 W. Franklin St.
919/942-1800
carolinabrewery.com

Spanky's is a great, centrally located option for a sandwich or a burger.

Spanky's
101 E. Franklin St.
919/967-2678
spankysrestaurant.com

Take a stroll around campus and visit the Old Well. This is UNC's iconic location, featured in university promotional materials and adapted for use by a variety of businesses courting UNC alum. It's also evoked at Boshamer by the columns supporting the concourse roof.

SEE ANOTHER BASEBALL GAME
Chapel Hill is less than 20 minutes from the home of the Durham Bulls (*see the Durham chapter on page 183*), about an hour from the home of the Carolina Mudcats (*see the Zebulon chapter on page 271*), and just 35-40 minutes in either direction from the home of the Burlington Royals (*see the Burlington chapter on page 125*) or the home of the N.C. State Wolfpack (*see the Raleigh chapter on page 239*). If the schedule works out right, you could potentially see two games in a day, or at least visit another ballpark.

Lodging
Although there many nice hotel properties in Chapel Hill, you want to stay at the Carolina Inn if you can get a room and it's in your budget. You are just a few blocks from everything that Chapel Hill has to offer, allowing you to enjoy the nightlife and walk home.

The Carolina Inn
211 Pittsboro St. (downtown)
Chapel Hill, NC 27516
800/962-8519; 919/933-2001
doubletree.com

Here are some other hotels worth checking out in the area.

Best Western University Inn
1310 Raleigh Rd. (NC Highway 54 East)
Chapel Hill, NC 27514
800/528-1234; 919/932-3000
bestwesternnorthcarolina.com

Courtyard by Marriott
100 Marriott Way (off NC Highway 54 East)
Chapel Hill, NC 27517
800/321-2211; 919/883-0700
marriott.com

Hampton Inn Chapel Hill
1740 N. Fordham Blvd. (US Highway 15-501)
Chapel Hill, NC 27514
800/426-7866; 919/968-3000
hilton.com

Holiday Inn Chapel Hill
1301 N. Fordham Blvd. (US Highway 15-501)
Chapel Hill, NC 27514
888/452-5765; 919/929-2171
holiday-inn.com

Sheraton Chapel Hill Hotel
One Europa Dr.
Chapel Hill, NC 27517
800/325-3535; 919/968-4900
sheraton.com

For detailed information on lodging choices, see the Chapel Hill/Orange County Convention and Visitors Bureau website at **chocvb.org**.

⊕ **Directions**

From Virginia and Points North:

Take I-85 South to Durham. Exit left at US-15/501 in Durham and follow 15/501 approximately 9 miles to Chapel Hill. Once in Chapel Hill, stay on 15/501 Bypass (Fordham Blvd.). At the 7th stoplight, turn right on Manning Drive. Continue on Manning until first stoplight. Turn right at light onto Ridge Road. Continue on Ridge Road approximately 1/2 mile to Boshamer Stadium on right.

From Points West:

Take I-85 North toward Durham. Exit just past Burlington onto NC-54 East (Exit 148, Chapel Hill). Follow NC-54 for approximately 20 miles to Carrboro. Go through two stoplights and stay on NC-54 until the next stoplight. Turn left at light onto Manning Drive. Continue on Manning until first stoplight. Turn right at light on to Ridge Road. Continue on Ridge Road approximately 1/2 mile to Boshamer Stadium on right.

From Points East:

Take I-40 West to Chapel Hill. Exit at NC-54 West (Exit #273A) and follow for approximately 4 miles. After the US-15/501 overpass, continue straight on NC-54 until the next stoplight. Turn left at stoplight onto Country Club Road. Make immediate right onto Ridge Road. Continue on Ridge Road approximately 1/2 mile to Boshamer Stadium on left.

From Points South:

Take US-15/50 North to Chapel Hill. Exit right onto 15/501 Bypass in Chapel Hill. Turn left at first stoplight onto Manning Drive. Continue on Manning until first stoplight. Turn right at light onto Ridge Road. Continue on Ridge Road approximately 1/2 mile to Boshamer Stadium on right.

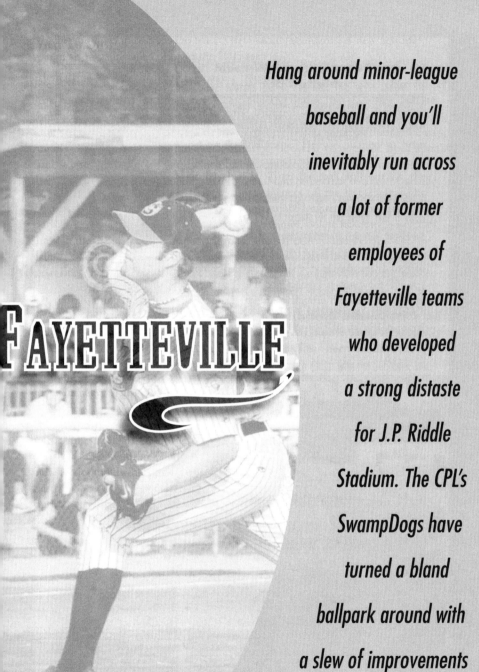

FAYETTEVILLE

Hang around minor-league baseball and you'll inevitably run across a lot of former employees of Fayetteville teams who developed a strong distaste for J.P. Riddle Stadium. The CPL's SwampDogs have turned a bland ballpark around with a slew of improvements and a raucous atmosphere.

CHAPTER 18

J.P. RIDDLE STADIUM

Leading Off

Opened: 1987

Capacity: 2,500

Dimensions: 330L, 375LC, 400C, 375RC, 330R

Current Team: Fayetteville SwampDogs (2001-present)

Former Teams: Fayetteville Generals, South Atlantic League (1987-1996); Cape Fear Crocs, South Atlantic League (1997-2000)

ESSENTIALS

Address: 2823 Legion Rd., Fayetteville
Website: fayettevilleswampdogs.com
Phone Number: 910/426-5900
Ticket Prices: $4-7

Riddle Me This: Baseball Success in Fayetteville

Fayetteville's J.P. Riddle Stadium is another of North Carolina's former minor-league ballparks where you can still get a cold beer and a hot dog and see some great baseball, thanks to the Coastal Plain League. While this is a pretty basic facility, it's a much better place to see a game than it ever was during the years it served as a minor-league ballpark. Fans who were upset at losing their professional team were pleasantly surprised to find the CPL provided great baseball and a much-improved facility.

The SwampDogs, like nearly every member of the CPL, will make it hard for you to remember you're not at a minor-league game. The game experience comes complete with a full slate of on-field games, lucky number giveaways and music. Add in what will inevitably be an entertaining game — SwampDogs co-owner Darrell Handelsman is one of the best summer-collegiate coaches of all time, with a signature aggressive style of play — and you've got a great experience.

The food at J.P. Riddle is varied and good. A full grill, two large concessions stands, and several beer counters make for short lines.

A steel girder and aluminum bowl ringed by concessions, souvenirs, and office outbuildings, this ballpark is reminiscent of Five County Stadium prior to construction of the new grandstand in Zebulon. A large asphalt concourse provides plenty of elbow room, even on the busiest nights. The largest of the buildings is a cinderblock structure on the first-base side housing the main concessions stand and rest rooms. These concessions windows offer the widest selection of foods. Since all the cooking is done in this building, your food will likely be fresher as well.

The ticket office is also housed in a permanent cinderblock building directly behind home plate. The clubhouse, also cinderblock, is located down the right-field line and is very comfortable by CPL standards. In fact, the clubhouse is another area where the facility is better now than it was as a minor-league park; the clubhouse is now air-conditioned, an upgrade since the professionals were in town.

J.P. Riddle grandstand
Photo courtesy of the SwampDogs

This ballpark was originally built as home to the Fayetteville Generals, the Detroit Tigers' affiliate in the Single-A South Atlantic League. Among the notable players passing through Fayetteville include Travis Fryman and Frank Catalanatto. The team was later affiliated with the Expos, and the name was changed to the Cape Fear Crocs during the franchise's tumultuous final four years in town.

The park has actually seen some significant improvements since the Sally League club bolted for Lakewood, N.J. after the 2000 season. The home-plate section was extended back by several rows and topped with a functional, modern press box replacing a two-story, wooden box that would have embarrassed most high schools. A roof was added over this center section a year later. This renovation provided the first park's first covered seating area, aside from the picnic areas on either side of the grandstand. You'll certainly appreciate the shade if you attend a game here. The sandy soil and the broiling heat can make it feel like this ballpark is located in a desert.

The landscaping was also significantly upgraded, and a new deck seating area dubbed the "Dog Pound" was added. This is another of the CPL's signature beer garden areas, with an old milk truck serving as a draft beer cooler, with a covered tiki bar and a nice, large wooden deck in front. While it's an outfield view, the deck is right on top of the field and provides a chance to heckle the other team's left fielder — which is not uncommon at SwampDogs games.

⚾ Insider's Tip

The Dog Pound beer garden area is a sun field. While it's a great place to watch the game, you'll be squinting right into the setting sun during the early part of the game. Enjoy the game from the first-base side of the grandstand with the sun at your back, or under the roof behind home plate. Wait until after the third or fourth inning to make your way down to the Dog Pound.

The elevated box seats are right on top of the action. The front row is about six feet above the ground and the foul territory is small. But if you like to roam, you'll eventually wind up in the Dog Pound. This is a lively place with a sports-bar atmosphere, and it's a favorite of the military crowd.

The former arcade building behind the third-base side of the grandstand was also renovated into permanent team offices in preparation for the SwampDogs' first season, making the 'Dogs the first team in the stadium's history to have administrative office space that didn't arrive on wheels.

Of course, upheaval and change was always the story of Fayetteville's Sally League franchise. When the South Atlantic League team arrived for the 1987 season, the ballpark wasn't ready. The team played its first handful of games at a county park as

A SwmapDogs pitcher delivers. A converted milk truck cooler in the background serves visitors to the Liberty Lounge party deck.

the original ownership group, including then-Major League scout Don Koonce and former department store executive Charles Padgett, struggled to get construction finished. Koonce and Padgett were so determined to place a franchise in Koonce's hometown of Fayetteville that they financed the construction of the ballpark privately. Local real estate tycoon Joseph Riddle donated the land in exchange for having the facility named in his honor. Ownership of the facility was later transferred over to Cumberland County, which was better equipped to handle the upkeep and maintenance.

When the ballpark was deemed fit for South Atlantic League play, it featured the aforementioned two-story wooden press box where the view of the game was cut in half by the back rail of the grandstand. Two large wooden bleacher sections with green seats and rusty metal supports were reportedly purchased from a circus and installed on either side of the grandstand. In the interest of fan safety, these bleachers have since been removed.

This was something of a family affair, with Don's brother Calvin serving as the general manager. Calvin Koonce had been a big league pitcher with the Mets, including the "Miracle Mets" team of 1969, and also coached at Campbell University in nearby Buies Creek. Cal has since passed away, but he remains the biggest baseball name in the history of Cumberland County.

Fayetteville is a military town, home to Fort Bragg and Pope Air Force Base. Together, these two bases make up the largest military installation in the world. Fort Bragg is proud home to the 82nd Airborne, a quick response unit that is often the first American "boots on the ground" in foreign conflicts. Approximately

Singing the National Anthem in front of a packed grandstand
Photo courtesy of the SwampDogs

50,000 service people and another 10,000 civilian employees work at Fort Bragg, and with the recent military reorganization, Fort Bragg is growing.

The military is the backbone of the town, and as you drive up Bragg Boulevard toward the base, you'll see endless rows of pawn shops, car accessory stores, and what we always liked to call "morally casual dance clubs." (Strip clubs, if you will.) The downtown area, though, has undergone some tremendous changes, and it is a far better place to visit than it was as recently as 10 years ago. A downtown clean-up and revitalization effort has yielded results (*see the Things To Do section for more information on downtown's attractions*).

Overhead view of J.P. Riddle Stadium *Photo courtesy of the SwampDogs*

The ballpark's neighborhood is nondescript with high-tension power lines and a modest housing development edging one side of the parking lot; and you may even think you've missed a turn by the time you see the signs. Yet, as a testament to the resiliency of baseball, this park is worth a visit, particularly in light of its proximity to Kinston and the Raleigh-Durham area.

Author's Note

In an aged Buick Skylark, with my mattress tied to the roof and all my worldly possessions crammed into the back seat, I pulled in to the EconoLodge at 3 a.m. one January day. That's how it all started for me in Fayetteville, where I worked my first baseball job over a decade ago. I was hired out of the job fair at the Baseball Winter Meetings in Louisville. After growing up in a tiny village in rural upstate New York, I had interned for both minor-league and major-league hockey teams and done a couple years of agency public relations work in New York City. Yet, nothing prepared me for Fayetteville.

Take note of the mobile home immediately to the left as you enter the ballpark parking lot. Most recently, it was a nail and hair salon. That was the team office for about 10 years, and it was where I reported for work the next day, in my best New York suit and polished wing tips. I trudged through the sand that passed for the office parking lot and walked up a couple unpainted wooden steps into what was once the trailer's living room. Matted carpet, two second-hand desks and cigarette smoke wafting down the hallway greeted me. I soon learned two important things: first, that one of those desks was going to be my work space, and second, that the office manager, the source of the smoke, carried a handgun in her purse, and could darn well do as she pleased.

I also learned that in Fayetteville you saved your best suit and tie for church, court, or a funeral. And, I found that people in the South wanted to take a little time to get to know you before they jumped into doing business. This definitely was not New York.

I was also startled to realize that this particular team wasn't the beloved local institution that I assumed all minor-league teams to be. This was a team that in its earlier years had stiffed vendors, angered sponsors, and created a general state of apathy in the community. It's a testament to the power of the great game of baseball that the team was still operating and retained any fans or sponsors at all.

In the end, the challenges of a subpar facility, a contentious relationship with the county, and a history of poor management cost Fayetteville its Single-A team. I was long gone by then, having headed to Raleigh to work for the minor-league hockey team that was, refreshingly, a beloved part of the community.

But my path would bring me back to Fayetteville. Seven years later, I was working at the CPL office when the Crocs made their much-anticipated announcement that they would move to Lakewood, N.J. We were dying to get into Fayetteville, and Cumberland County was dying to get rid of the Crocs. In the end, we had a lease in hand before the Crocs had even begun their final month of play.

One last note on that office/mobile home: It was just far enough from the ballpark that it made for an inconveniently long, hot walk, or a ridiculously short car ride. The team later moved their offices to a more modern modular unit just past the bathrooms on the first-base side within the ballpark area, but it was too late to save the starter on my old Buick or, for that matter, professional baseball in Fayetteville.

Sports Around Town

Baseball was once the only game in town, but since the Crown Coliseum opened in 1997 Fayetteville's fans have had a variety of sports teams to follow. This is a very modern and comfortable building, seating about 9,000 for hockey or indoor football. Built on the site of an existing civic-center complex, the name Crown Coliseum derives not only from the superstructure of the roof resembling a crown, but from the inability to find a buyer for the naming rights.

This arena hosted an NBA Developmental League team up through 2006, but, despite teams that included future NBA players Jason Collier and Devin Brown, the team was shut down for lack of interest.

The most successful of the arena sports has been hockey. The Fayetteville FireAntz play in the Southern Professional Hockey League, a circuit that has battled for stability, but the FireAntz have developed a solid following. Visit fireantzhockey.com for more information.

Things to Do

FOOD AND OTHER REFRESHMENTS

Screw the chains: the best places to eat the Fayetteville area are local establishments. Bruce & Mickey's is just a little way down Legion Road from the ballpark (technically in Hope Mills). It's a classic North Carolina barbecue restaurant with a very basic atmosphere, but great 'que. The pork is pulled and cooked in a vinegar sauce, and they offer a variety of sauces, including a sweet brown sauce that's almost Memphis-style. It's perfect for a pre-game meal.

Bruce & Mickey's
3154 Legion Rd.
910/424-3688

The Haymont Grill & Steakhouse has been a mainstay of the Haymont neighborhood for decades. The interior is like a time capsule, and the steaks are excellent. Just take Hay Street up the hill from downtown and you'll see it. Don't be confused by the big sign on the roof, which says "HAMONT."

Haymont Grill & Steakhouse
1304 Morganton Rd.
910/484-0261

The Mash House is Fayetteville's second brewpub, following in the footsteps of Huske Hardware House downtown. Located near the mall in a more modern setting, this will be a more convenient place for a post-game nightcap if you decide to stay at one of the hotels in the mall area.

The Mash House Restaurant & Brewery
4150 Sycamore Dairy Rd.
910/867-9223
themashhouse.com

This is a private club (see "Getting a Drink" in the Introduction) with lots of pool tables, a very long bar, sports on TV, video trivia, and some live music. This was a popular hangout for team staff in the past. It's convenient to the Holiday Inn Bordeaux, and also has fairly good pub grub.

Broadstreet Café & Billiards
Talleywood Shopping Center
Raeford Rd.
910/486-7832
broadstreetcafe.com

Louie's is a bar plain and simple, with no other aspirations. Volleyball courts out back, a dart board, one beat-up pool table inside, and lots of cheap beer.

Louie's Sports Pub
2417 Robeson St.
910/323-3373

VISIT DOWNTOWN FAYETTEVILLE

Once known as North Carolina's most notorious red light district, downtown Fayetteville has undergone an incredible transformation over the past 15 years. The strip bars and seedy nightclubs are gone, and in their place there's a brew pub, a museum, an art house movie theater, a coffee shop, and more. Ironically, but not coincidentally, the sprawling new police headquarters covers nearly an entire city block that once included Fayetteville's most notorious topless club, Rick's Lounge.

For people familiar with downtown Fayetteville's former reputation, the idea of "visiting" downtown would have been laughable. While there's still plenty to be done, constant renovations are underway to downtown's historic building stock. Today, it's a pleasant place to spend a few hours.

Have a meal and a beer at Huske Hardware House. In this renovated hardware store you will find Cumberland County's first and finest brew pub. The food is good and the beer is excellent.

Huske Hardware House
405 Hay St.
910/437-9905

The downtown centers on the old Market House, which sits in the center of a traffic circle. This building has been renovated and is considered by many to be a symbol of the city. Local government offices were housed in the upper floor, while the open air space on the first floor housed vendors of produce and goods. Others regard it as a stark reminder of a darker time when the open-air first floor is said to have been used as a slave market. Either way, its historical significance is undisputed; it was built in 1832 on the foundation of an earlier State House building. It's located at the intersection of Hay, Gillespie, Person, and Green streets; call 910/483-2073 for more information.

Downtown also features the Airborne and Special Operations Museum. This gleaming new facility is the centerpiece to the downtown's revitalization. Just across the tracks from the train station, the museum tells the story of America's Airborne and Special Operations forces. This is an official Army museum, and the highlight is a 24-seat simulator that lets visitors experience an extremely realistic re-creation of military operations, including jumping out of a plane with a parachute, a high-speed Jeep pursuit, and a helicopter attack.

Airborne and Special Operations Museum
100 Bragg Blvd.
910/483-3003
asomf.org

Built in 1911, the Atlantic Coast Line Railroad Station is a rare example of Dutch Colonial architecture. The outside passenger and freight platform and shelter date to World War I, and this train station may have sent more troops off to war than any other in the nation. The depot currently serves as an Amtrak passenger station and houses the Atlantic Coast Line Depot Railroad Historical Center.

Atlantic Coast Line Railroad Station
472 Hay St.
910/433-1612

OTHER ATTRACTIONS

When George Herman Ruth signed his first pro contract, it was with the minor-league Baltimore Orioles. The Orioles trained that year at the Fayetteville Fairgrounds. It's said that it was in Fayetteville he was nicknamed "Babe" by his teammates, reportedly due to his relative youth and baby face. Others say it was due to his fondness for the children who followed the ballplayers from their hotel to the field. It was at the Fairgrounds where Ruth hit his first professional home run. A historical marker shows the former location of the fairgrounds just east of downtown. While it's a nice historical tidbit, there is absolutely nothing to see there other than the marker.

Sadly, visiting Fort Bragg's 82nd Airborne Division War Memorial Museum is not as easily accomplished as it once was. Fort Bragg is impressive for its sheer size and once was an "open base" where civilian traffic passed without restriction through almost every part of the facility. In the wake of the Sept. 11 attacks on America, the base is largely closed to civilian traffic, but you can visit the 82nd Airborne Museum (not to be confused with the Airborne and Special Operations Museum downtown, mentioned earlier). The base museum houses more than 3,000 artifacts from World War I through Operation Desert Storm. Weapons, uniforms and aircraft are on display.

82nd Airborne Division War Memorial Museum
Ardennas & Gela streets
910/432-3443
bragg.army.mil/18abn/museums.htm

There's more golf in this part of the world than you can shake a stick at, including one course with the troubling name "Bayonet at Puppy Creek." The most convenient, though, is King's Grant Golf Club, located just a few miles north of downtown on Ramsey Street, near the Methodist University campus.

King's Grant Golf Club
347 Shawcroft Rd.
910/630-1114
kingsgrantgolf.com

Lodging

If you're interested in something out of the ordinary, check out the downtown Prince Charles. Built in 1924 and completely renovated in 1997, amenities include a fitness room, business center, free parking, room service, and free wireless and high-speed Internet. There's also a restaurant and bar called Charlie's. Just a few blocks from Huske Hardware House, this hotel also allows you to walk to all the downtown businesses, including a movie theater and a coffee shop, and visit the new Airborne Museum, all without getting in the car.

Clarion Hotel Prince Charles
450 Hay St.
Fayetteville, NC 28301
800/CLARION or 910/433-4444
choicehotels.com

The I-95 area is a very convenient area to find lodging, especially if you're coming in late. A few miles east of town, there are lots of hotels to choose from, and a good number of restaurants, too. Here are a couple of the hotel choices.

This one is a sentimental choice; it was the official team hotel when I worked for the Fayetteville Generals (see Author's Note). Well run, this is a nice, basic hotel room for what usually is a very basic price.

EconoLodge
1952 Cedar Creek Rd.
Fayetteville, NC 28312
800/446-0650 or 910/433-2100
choicehotels.com

Another of the many properties at Exit 49, this one offers the Hampton standards, free breakfast, a pool, and Internet access in all rooms.

Hampton Inn
1922 Cedar Creek Rd.
Fayetteville, NC 28312
910/485-1423
hilton.com

This Fairfield Inn was recently renovated and is definitely the place to stay if you're looking for the convenience of a major retail area. Located right in the parking lot of Fayetteville's largest indoor shopping center, the Cross Creek Mall, this may be a particularly good choice if the forecast is for stroke-inducing heat; you can walk around a little in air-conditioned comfort at the mall. The normal assortment of chain restaurants can be found in the mall and in the immediate area. The Fairfield has outdoor entrances on the first and second floor and interior hallways on the third floor.

Fairfield Inn
562 Cross Creek Mall
Fayetteville, NC 28303
910/487-1400
marriott.com

The Courtyard by Marriott is a nice, modern property near the mall, but not right in the parking lot.

Courtyard by Marriott
4192 Sycamore Dairy Rd.
Fayetteville, NC 28303
910/487-5557
marriott.com

If you're looking to stay close to the ballpark, the Holiday Inn Bordeaux will be your best bet. About two miles from the ballpark, it's definitely not walkable, but it's close by. Just turn right out of the parking lot on Legion Road, turn left when you get to Owen Drive, and the Holiday Inn will be on your right about a mile away. A Fayetteville institution, this property is full service with a restaurant and bar. You may be asking yourself, "Bordeaux?" Just across the street from the Holiday Inn you'll see a scaled-down replica of the Eiffel Tower in front of the "Bordeaux Shopping Center." The entire neighborhood is somewhat incongruously called "the Bordeaux" as a result.

Holiday Inn Bordeaux
1707 Owen Dr.
Fayetteville, NC 28304
800/325-0211; 910/323-0111
hibordeaux.com

For more information on lodging and attractions, go to **visitfayettevillenc.com.**

Directions

From I-95:

Take Business 95/Fayettevile exit. Stay on Business 95 until you see Crown Coliseum complex. Turn onto East Mountain Drive (away from the Coliseum) and then turn left onto Legion Road (also called Southern Avenue). The ballpark will be approximately one-half mile down on your left.

RALEIGH

Baseball in the state capital is limited to a nice little college ballpark: Doak Field at Dail Park, home of the N.C. State Wolfpack. Raleigh was also home to one of North Carolina's most fondly remembered (and colorfully named) ballparks, Devereaux Meadow.

CHAPTER 19

DOAK FIELD AT DAIL PARK

Leading Off

Opened: 1966; renovated in 2003-2004

Capacity: 2,500

Dimensions: 320L, 370LC, 400C, 375RC, 330R

Current Team: N.C. State University Wolfpack (NCAA Division I; Atlantic Coast Conference)

Former Team: Raleigh RedWolves, Coastal Plain League (1997)

ESSENTIALS

Address: 1081 Varsity Dr., Raleigh
Website: gopack.com
Phone: 919/865-1510
Ticket Prices: General Admission, $5;
Suites (seating up to 15), $240, plus $250-350 for catered concessions
Parking: Free if you park in the West Lot south of ballpark across Sullivan Drive

Doak Field: You'd Hardly Recognize the Place

Doak Field underwent a massive overhaul over the last several years. The result is a completely rebuilt grandstand on the same site as the prior version. The approximately 2,000 fold-down chair seats are surrounded by lots of brick and concrete. The new Doak takes its architectural cues from the surrounding campus, and the new grandstand blends well with the simple brick and concrete construction of much of the campus.

The old Doak was a pleasant place to watch a game but was, in reality, simply three large bleacher sections situated atop six-foot-high retaining walls ringing the infield. Bathrooms were almost nonexistent (before the renovation portable restrooms were employed in an effort to meet code). Concessions consisted of an 8-by-12 Coca Cola trailer with a hot plate, and the press box was located in a small stone and mortar building above first base. The playing surface was always excellent, though, and during the nine years of the Ray Tanner era the teams were normally excellent as well. The lack of any progress in upgrading the old Doak ultimately drove Tanner to accept the job at the University of South Carolina where he continues to field outstanding teams, including an appearance in the NCAA championship game.

Under current head coach Elliot Avent, the Pack have been successful in the always-tough ACC and have had notable postseason success. When he arrived from New Mexico State in 1996, Elliot said the old Doak was like a major-league stadium compared to his previous home field. Nonetheless, State desperately needed a major upgrade if they were going to keep up in the ACC baseball facility arms race. Avent's patience has been rewarded with the terrific renovation.

The old Doak Field also hosted a Coastal Plain League team in 1997, the CPL's inaugural season. Powered by four of Coach Tanner's finest, the Raleigh RedWolves went wire-to-wire to win the league championship under the guidance of Randy Hood, a former minor-league teammate of Michael Jordan's with the Birmingham Barons who made college coaching stops at Campbell and UNC Wilmington. Unfortunately, the crowds at many RedWolves games could be counted on your fingers and toes, and the team was relocated to Florence, S.C., where the RedWolves name is still in use.

The new Doak features modern, plentiful bathrooms, permanent concession stands, and a real press box located behind home plate. Athletes enjoy much-improved clubhouses, indoor and outdoor batting tunnels, and a player's lounge. As is the case at ECU's new facility, none of the seats are covered. In fairness, the weather is generally much more predictable during the colleges' spring season than it is during summer months when minor-league fans often have to seek shelter from sudden downpours or relief from the blistering heat of the sun.

Even on a cold, February day, vocal NCSU students make their presence known in the grassy area down the left-field line at Doak Field.

Overall, the new Doak Field is exactly what the N.C. State baseball program needed and deserved, and one that certainly puts them among the leaders in the ACC facilities race.

The new press box and suites are located behind home plate at Doil Park.

⚾ *Insider's Tip*

Definitely stop by Mitch's Tavern on Hillsborough Street, adjacent to the campus. For detailed information see our Carolina Mudcats chapter, but suffice it to say that Mitch's is where the bar scene in *Bull Durham* was filmed, and it's the only filming location from the movie that hasn't changed at all.

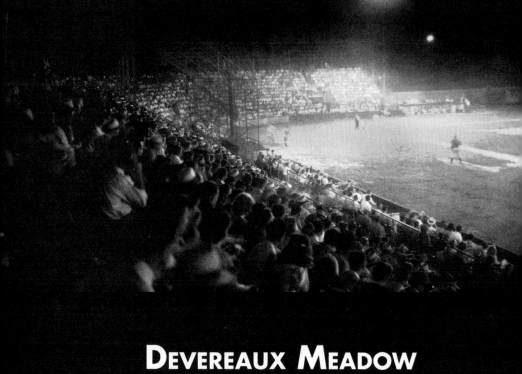

DEVEREAUX MEADOW

Leading Off

Opened: 1939(?)

Demolished: 1971

Former Teams: Raleigh Capitals, 1945-62; Raleigh Mets, 1964; Raleigh Cardinals, 1965; Raleigh Pirates, 1966-67; Raleigh-Durham Mets, 1968; Raleigh-Durham Phillies, 1969; Raleigh-Durham Triangles, 1970-71; all Carolina League

Raleigh's minor-league teams played at Devereaux Meadow from 1945 until 1971, the final season of the Raleigh-Durham Triangles. A struggling co-op team that split its home games between Raleigh and the Durham Athletic Park, the Triangles' withdrawal from the Carolina League signaled the end for this evocatively named ballpark. The park consisted of a large covered grandstand with a long run of bleachers down the third-base side, and doubled as a high-school football stadium.

The park reportedly opened in 1939, the same year that several other WPA ballparks were built around the state. Raleigh's new park, though, didn't attract a new minor-league team until 1945. The city's Piedmont League team had disbanded following the 1937 season. Locals remember Devereaux Meadow as charming but rickety in its final years, and city officials apparently wasted no time in demolishing this historic facility following the 1971 season. This must have been a sad day for minor-league baseball fans, but minor-league baseball was at such a low ebb that two sizable communities like Raleigh and Durham combined couldn't support even one Single-A team. The former site of the ballpark on Wade Avenue is now the site of the Jaycees Park and a maintenance garage where the city's trash trucks are parked.

Devereaux Meadow hosted some great teams and notable players over the years, including Carl Yastrzemski, Jim Bibby, Ken Singleton, Bob Boone, and Greg Luzinski, as well as a career minor-leaguer better known for playing with the Bulls, Crash Davis (yes, there was a real Crash Davis, *see chapter on The Movie*).

As explained in the Zebulon (Carolina Mudcats) chapter, the end of the Triangles and Devereaux Meadow likely signaled the end of affiliated pro baseball in North Carolina's capital. Both the Bulls and Mudcats are locked into relatively new facilities. Under current territorial rules, both the Bulls and

Red Sox great Carl Yastrzemski spent the 1959 season with the Raleigh Capitals.
Raleigh News & Observer photo courtesy of the North Carolina State Archives.

the Mudcats would need to agree to let a new team take up residence in Raleigh, and that is extremely unlikely.

For more information, see Raleigh information in the Zebulon chapter, page 271.

Sports Around Town

Sports history buffs will enjoy visiting Reynolds Coliseum. Once one of the major basketball arenas in the South, construction on Reynolds began in 1943 but stalled during World War II. When Everett Case took the reins of the N.C. State basketball program in 1946, he inherited a skeleton of an arena. He revised the blueprints, adding seating capacity to bring the arena capacity to 14,000. This revision gave Reynolds some odd sight lines as the increased seating was added to the both ends of the building, resulting in a long, narrow arena.

With the largest building in the region, N.C. State began hosting the Dixie Classic, where four of the nation's top teams would be invited to Raleigh to take on the "Big Four;" State, Carolina, Duke, and Wake Forest. At that time Wake Forest University was located in the village of Wake Forest, just a few miles north of Raleigh. (The same Reynolds tobacco family whose name is on Reynolds Coliseum later enticed the school to relocate to Winston-Salem in the 1950s.)

Reynolds predates the formation of the ACC, but it was also the long-time home of the ACC tournament and was the home court to N.C. State greats like Tommy Burleson and David Thompson, who led the 'Pack to the 1974 National Championship.

To get to Reynolds from Doak, walking will be your best bet. Parking is scarce on campus. Just keep the train tracks that run along the third-base side of Doak on your left, walk about 500 yards, and you'll see it.

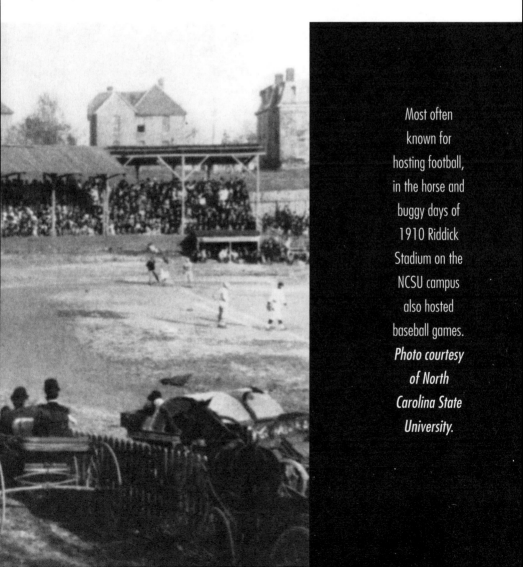

Most often known for hosting football, in the horse and buggy days of 1910 Riddick Stadium on the NCSU campus also hosted baseball games. *Photo courtesy of North Carolina State University.*

Author's Note

Some of State's notable players still make it to Raleigh regularly. When I was working for the Raleigh IceCaps minor league hockey team in the early 1990s, I went for lunch at the Arby's on Hillsborough Street near campus. Ahead of me in line was the tallest human being I had ever seen in my life. I cleared my throat (since I couldn't reach his shoulder to tap on it), and he turned

around. I knew this had to be one of two former N.C. State basketball players noted for their size: Tommy Burleson (7'4") or Chuck Nevitt (7'5"). Nevitt's name came to mind first, probably because he had played more recently. So, I looked up... and up... and up, and said, "I'm sorry to bother you, but are you Chuck Nevitt?"

The official 1899 team photo of the North Carolina College of Agriculture and Mechanic Arts (prior to its renaming as NCSU). **Photo courtesy of North Carolina State University.**

Well, this gigantic man looked down at me like I had slapped his grandmother,

and said, "Hell, no! I was way better than him!" Well, there was no arguing with him. This was Tommy Burleson, who helped N.C. State to a national championship, is regarded as one of the greatest players in ACC history, won an Olympic silver medal, and was named All-Rookie in his first pro season before his NBA career was derailed by a knee injury. Nevitt, on the other hand, was best known as a sort of human victory cigar whose entry into an NBA contest signified that his team had put the game out of reach.

I apologized for the mistake, and told him that I knew about the great State teams that he had played on. He proceeded to shake my hand and graciously add that it was nice to still be remembered 20 years after his college career ended. I did learn a lesson that day, though. If I'm ever in the same situation, I guarantee you that I'll guess Burleson first!

USA Baseball National Training Complex at Cary

If North Carolina is truly the cradle of the game, then the Town of Cary can now lay claim to its pulsating heartbeat. The city pulled out pretty much all the stops to attract USA Baseball to Cary, and the National Training Complex at Thomas Brooks Park is attracting top baseball talent at every stage.

The $11-million facility includes a stadium field and three training fields on 221 acres at Brooks Park. The stadium seats 1,754 and another 250 or so can be accommodated in the grassy area. All four baseball fields are maintained fully to Major League Baseball standards with dimensions of 330 feet down the line and 400 feet to center. All fields have easy access to the concessions building and restrooms. As a bonus, the facility will host UNC Tar Heel games while Boshamer Stadium undergoes major renovation in 2008.

Designed by architects Heery International, the stadium field has a press box that includes two suites, an official scorer's room, a sound room, and a press row. You can't help notice the pitcher-friendly spaciousness of foul territory, especially behind home plate where you can't miss the sprawling MLB logo.

USA Baseball came to North Carolina from Tucson in 2003, but the finishing touches on the project weren't complete until June 2007. Roughly 90 percent of the facilities cost was picked up the Town of Cary, along with $1 million in Wake County hospitality, prepared food, and beverage tax revenues.

USA Baseball is the national governing body of U.S. amateur baseball. The organization is affiliated all the way from Little League and American Legion ball through the ranks to the U.S. Olympic team and Major League Baseball in conjunction with the World Baseball Classic. USA Baseball selects and trains its collegiate-level National Team, Junior National Team (18-under), Youth National Team (16-under) and 14U National Team (14-under), as well as the USA Baseball

The National Training Complex at Thomas Brooks Park in Cary attracts top baseball talent at every stage of development. USA Baseball *photo by Brian Fleming.*

Women's National Team which participates at the international level. For more information on USA Baseball, visit **usabaseball.com**.

 **Directions**

To Doak Field in Raleigh

From I-40:

Take exit 295 (Gorman Street). Coming from the east, turn right at Gorman Street for several miles past Western Boulevard to Sullivan Drive at the following traffic light. Doak Field will be the second turn on the left (take a right turn to enter the West Lot).

To USA Baseball National Training Complex in Cary

From Interstate 40:

Take Exit 278 (Highway 55 exit). Travel toward Apex. Travel approximately 7.5 miles and make a right on Green Hope School Road at the stoplight. After approximately 1.5 miles make a left into USA Baseball National Training Complex.

From Highway 64 West out of Raleigh:

Take the Hwy. 55 exit. Make a right toward Durham. Travel approximately 3.7 miles and make a left on Green Hope School Road at the stoplight. After approximately 1.5 miles make a left into USA Baseball National Training Complex

From Highway 64 East towards Raleigh:

Take the Hwy. 55 exit. Make a left toward Durham. Travel approximately 3.7 miles and make a left on Green Hope School Road at the stoplight. After approximately 1.5 miles make a left into USA Baseball National Training Complex.

ROCKY MOUNT

Rocky Mount's Municipal Stadium was formerly the home field for Jim Thorpe, Buck Leonard, and Johnny Pesky, as well as 90 years of minor-league and summer-collegiate teams. But after a bad experience with the last Rocky Mount Carolina League team, city officials tore down the grandstand and downgraded the facility to a high-school field.

CHAPTER 20

GRYPHON FIELD
(FORMERLY MUNICIPAL STADIUM)

Leading Off

Opened: 1936 • **Current Team:** Rocky Mount High School Gryphons
Former Teams: Rocky Mount Railroaders, 1909-1910 (Eastern Carolina League); Rocky Mount Carolinians, 1915 (Virginia League); Rocky Mount Tar Heels, 1916-1917, 1920-25 (Virginia League); Rocky Mount Buccaneers, 1927 (Piedmont League); Rocky Mount Buccaneers, 1928-29 (Piedmont League); Rocky Mount Red Sox, 1936-40 (Piedmont League); Rocky Mount Leafs, 1941 (Coastal Plain League); Rocky Mount Rocks, 1942 (Bi-State League); Rocky Mount Rocks, 1946 (Coastal Plain League); Rocky Mount Leafs, 1947-52 (Coastal Plain League); Rocky Mount Leafs, 1962-72 (Carolina League); Rocky Mount Phillies, 1973-75 (Carolina League); Rocky Mount Pines, 1980 (Carolina League); Rocky Mount Rockfish, 1997-1998 (Coastal Plain League)

ESSENTIALS

Address: S. Howell St., at Oberry St., Rocky Mount

A Sad End to a Long Baseball History

The tale of Rocky Mount's ballpark and baseball history is a cautionary tale. With apologies to Charles Dickens, it's also a tale of two cities. Rocky Mount and Wilson (*see the Wilson chapter*), two towns of similar size, are located just 20 miles apart, both hubs of the eastern North Carolina tobacco trade. They were also linked for decades by minor-league baseball. The two communities boasted nearly identical ballparks, were usually in the same league and, most years, posted very similar attendance figures.

The Vietnam era is considered by most industry observers to have been the low point for minor-league baseball, and as the '70s ended Rocky Mount and Wilson were both without professional baseball. Wilson's last team had been an independent, nonaffiliated member of the Carolina League, the Wilson Pennants, which drew respectable crowds in 1973 despite their 52-88 record. Rocky Mount had struggled on as a member of the Carolina League until 1974 when their club folded.

Fleming Stadium sat largely empty, aside from a half-season played by the Carolina Mudcats in 1991 while construction of Five County Stadium was completed. The ballpark, which was in poor shape after years of disuse, was otherwise without a major tenant until the Coastal Plain League placed a franchise there in 1997. That team, the Wilson Tobs, quickly became a cornerstone of the league as a major renovation made Fleming literally better than new.

Postcard of Municipal Stadium, Rocky Mount

Rocky Mount, in the meantime, had one more go-round with the Carolina League, fielding an independent team named the Rocky Mount Pines in 1980. The Pines joined the Carolina League as an expansion team along with the Durham Bulls. Mal Fichman, who would go on to some renown during the independent-league boom of the '90s, managed them. His year in Rocky Mount, though, was an unmitigated disaster.

Mal's Rocky Mount club finished 24-114, one of the worst seasons in the history of minor-league baseball. Things were so bad in Rocky Mount that when the team finished its season neither Fichman nor any remaining funds were anywhere to be found. The team was scheduled to play its final series at Durham, where the Bulls were pulling in record crowds. The Bulls caught wind of the situation in Rocky Mount but were unwilling to give up on their last four home dates. They sent their team bus to pick up the Pines and paid their hotel bill and meal money through the end of the season.

With the bad taste of this experience still relatively fresh in their mouths, the city government of Rocky Mount managed to unload the old minor-league ballpark on the local school system several years later. With funds scarce for upkeep, the park deteriorated to the point that the school system became concerned for the safety of the public and their own liability, so the grandstand was torn down. Many residents of Rocky Mount feel that the ill will generated by the Pines' atrocious season, as well as their subpar business operation, created the climate for the eventual destruction of the old grandstand.

Rocky Mount had one more attempt at high-level baseball when the Coastal Plain League awarded the city one of the league's charter franchises. Municipal Stadium's playing surface was still being used, but in place of the grandstand were a large set of aluminum bleachers and a two-story concessions/press box building. The place also had been renamed Gryphon Field for the Rocky Mount High School's mascot, and few indications remained that this had ever been a minor-league ballpark. In the end, the lack of fan amenities and atmosphere combined with a skeptical business community, a marginal neighborhood, and bitter opposition from the local Legion boosters doomed this franchise to failure. After two unsuccessful seasons, the franchise was shut down.

Jim Thorpe's Fall and Buck Leonard's Rise

Rocky Mount's baseball history goes back to 1909 when the Railroaders were members of the Class D Eastern North Carolina League and has also included teams in the Carolina League, Piedmont League, and both professional and collegiate incarnations of the Coastal Plain League.

Perhaps Rocky Mount's most significant brush with baseball immortality has an ironic twist, as Jim Thorpe spent the 1909 and 1910 seasons playing for Rocky Mount. Thorpe went on to win the Olympic decathlon and pentathlon gold medals in 1912 and was hailed by King Gustav V of Sweden and many others as "The World's Greatest Athlete." He went on to play professional football and major-league baseball, but it was his two years of minor-league ball in Rocky Mount earlier in life that ultimately cost him his medals.

When Thorpe donned the uniform of the Rocky Mount Railroaders, he was certainly not the only "amateur" athlete who spent his summer playing minor-league baseball for pay. Most of these ballplayers took an assumed name for the summer, but Thorpe made the unfortunate decision to play ball under his real name. Sadly, Thorpe encountered real-life "railroaders," in the form of the International Olympic Committee, that stripped him of his medals in violation of its own set of rules.

By all reports, he was heartbroken over his removal from the Olympic record books, leading to deep despair later in life. His medals were restored and his records reinstated in 1982, but Thorpe wasn't around to feel any vindication: the moves came 29 years after his death.

Hall of Famer Buck Leonard's display at the North Carolina Baseball Hall of Fame in Wilson.

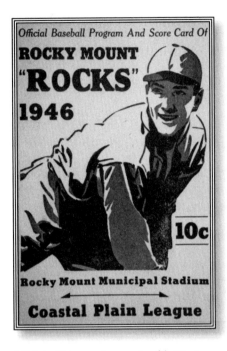

Official Baseball Program And Score Card Of

ROCKY MOUNT

"ROCKS"

1946

10c

Rocky Mount Municipal Stadium

Coastal Plain League

1946 Rocks official program. *Image courtesy of the Notre Dame Rare Books collection.*

Rocky Mount was also the hometown of legendary Negro League star Buck Leonard, who is generally regarded as the key player of the Homestead Grays dynasty that won nine Negro League championships from 1937-45. A Hall of Famer, "Buck" was born Walter Fenner Leonard in Rocky Mount on Sept. 8, 1907. Known for his loyalty, modesty, and good nature, Leonard retired to Rocky Mount, where died Nov. 27, 1997. A teammate of Josh Gibson, the pair was regarded as the toughest "one-two" combination in the history of the Negro Leagues. Leonard was recognized as a stellar fielder and, according to teammate Monte Irvin, trying to zip a fastball past him was like "trying to sneak a sunrise past a rooster." Displays honoring both Leonard and Thorpe can be seen at the North Carolina Baseball Museum in nearby Wilson.

Despite this rich history, it seems likely that Rocky Mount has seen the last of minor-league or summer-college baseball. One can only wonder what could have been if Municipal Stadium had survived long enough to be rehabilitated like Wilson's Fleming Stadium. Or, perhaps, what could be if the city ever saw fit to build a suitable baseball facility like the one in Thomasville.

⚾ Insider's Tip

You'll need to be a real hardcore history buff to visit this park. While it's the same field where Johnny Pesky played as a minor leaguer in 1940 and where Bill Kennedy notched an astounding 456 strikeouts in leading Rocky Mount to the Coastal Plain League pennant in 1946, there's just not much to see anymore. The old grandstand is gone; the outfield wall has been replaced by chain link; and, frankly, it's not located in the greatest neighborhood. Rocky Mount's baseball history is rich and features larger-than-life characters Jim Thorpe and Buck Leonard, but there's little of note in town recognizing that history except a park named for Leonard a few blocks from the baseball field and a historical marker recognizing Thorpe two blocks east of the ballpark.

Sports Around Town

The highest level of baseball being played in Rocky Mount these days is at Bauer Field on the campus of N.C. Wesleyan College. The Battling Bishops have a strong tradition of success in NCAA Division III, including 14 USA South Conference championships, 20 NCAA tournament bids, 12 regional titles, and two national championships (1989 and 1999) in the last 25 years. Wesleyan also boasts a notable alum in University of North Carolina coach Mike Fox, who directed the program for 15 years before taking over in Chapel Hill in 1999. The campus is north of town on Route 301. Visit the team's website at **annex.ncwc.edu/athletics/ baseball/index.htm** for schedule information.

Attractions and Lodging

See the Rocky Mount Travel & Tourism website at **rockymounttravel.com**.

W-◇-E **Directions**

From Raleigh:

Take U.S. 64 East. Take the Benvenue Road (N.C. 48) exit. Follow Benvenue approximately 1 mile, turn right onto U.S. 301. After about 1 mile, turn right onto Raleigh Road. Turn right onto Walnut Street, then right onto S. Howell Street. The ballpark is behind the Army National Guard Armory.

For a lesson on how to restore a ballpark, look no further than Wilson's historic Fleming Stadium. A WPA facility that's been updated in recent years, the ballpark is the recipient of lots of community love and affection. The best part: it's not retro — it's real.

WILSON

CHAPTER 21

FLEMING STADIUM

Leading Off

Opened: 1938, originally named Wilson Municipal Stadium

Capacity: 2,500

Dimensions: 332L, 405C, 332R

Current Team: Wilson Tobs, Coastal Plain League (1999-present)

Former Teams: Wilson Tobs, 1939-1941, 1946-1952 (Coastal Plain);

Wilson Tobs, 1956-1968 (Carolina League); Wilson Pennants, 1973

(Carolina League); Carolina Mudcats, 2001

(Southern League)

ESSENTIALS

Address: 300 Stadium St., Wilson
Website: wilsontobs.com
Phone: 252/291-8627
Ticket Prices: $3-$6

A Great Sense of History with an Inviting Touch of Newness

One of the shining jewels of North Carolina baseball, Fleming Stadium may be the most pleasant place to watch a baseball game that a fan can find. With a spacious covered grandstand of over 2,500 seats, a wide-open concourse, and lots of real estate down the lines, Fleming is comfortable and relaxing even on a busy night.

This park is so well maintained, so clean, and so bright with its gold-and-brown color scheme you could convince yourself that the place was just built. But it's not a "retro" park, it's the real deal. The team even wears throwback uniforms every night and, despite the national trend away from politically incorrect nicknames, Wilson embraces its heritage through the team's name and logo (the tail sweep under "Tobs" is a tobacco leaf), as well as their mascot — a tobacco worm named Slugger.

The main concession stand behind home plate offers a wide range of excellent food with a variety not typically seen at this level of baseball. Another smaller concessions stand and a café-style area with waitress service are located just past the grandstand down the first-base line.

A beer garden farther down the right-field line is built around one of the CPL's many milk-truck beer coolers. Yes, take a second look at the walk-in beer cooler: it's the back end of an old milk truck. Now, that's what you call authentic. You can also find these in Fayetteville, Gastonia, and Wilmington, while the original is in Burlington. One of the more unique features in this park is the bar the team built right up against the chain-link fence. Pull up a stool, sip your beer, and watch the action from the very edge of the field.

Easily accessible off I-95 and just a block away from the Wilson mall, this ballpark is also home to the North Carolina Baseball Museum. The museum's collection can be viewed at most home games, housed in a gleaming new building down the third-base line. You'll see baseball memorabilia from across North Carolina highlighting ballplayers such as Catfish Hunter, Hoyt Wilhelm, Gaylord Perry, Enos Slaughter, Rick Ferrell, and Buck Leonard, as well as a "Walk of Fame."

That Wilson's ballpark would be the site for a museum on the state's baseball history is very appropriate. Wilson's baseball history began in 1908 with a charter franchise in the Class D Eastern North Carolina League. Baseball has always been king in Eastern North Carolina, the largely rural part of the state stretching from I-

95 south and east to the coast. This was tobacco country, and while the central part of the state known as the Piedmont has always been a hot bed of college sports, particularly basketball, in towns like Wilson and Kinston, baseball was all they ever had.

Wilson's history is thoroughly intertwined with nearly every league that ever fielded a team in North Carolina and features some of the best-known characters to ever grace a baseball field. From the Eastern NC League in 1908 to the Carolina League, the Southern League to the Coastal Plain League: fans in Wilson have seen it all. Probable Hall of Famer Jack McKeon managed the Tobs in '60 and '61. And current Hall of Famer Rod Carew donned the Tobs jersey in 1966 — only one year prior to achieving American League Rookie of the Year honors with the Minnesota Twins. The pitcher said to have been the inspiration for Nuke LaLoosh (Tim Robbins) of *Bull Durham* was a 1958 Tobs flame thrower named Steve Dalkowski,

The field at Fleming Stadium in Wilson is already well-manicured several weeks prior to opening day.

who Ted Williams called the fastest pitcher he'd ever seen. His notorious wildness also led people in Wilson to tell the story about the night one of his throws tore a hole in the wire mesh backstop at Fleming.

Rod Carew played for the Tobs in 1966, and a bobblehead commemorating his year in Wilson is featured in the museum next to the field.

Back in the era when Major League teams barnstormed north after spring training, Fleming also hosted the Red Sox and Ted Williams versus the Philadelphia Phillies, although the largest reported crowd was 10,000 people at a game in 1940 where admission was free as part of a local festival, and New York Mayor Fiorella LaGuardia attended and addressed the crowd.

Another of the state's WPA-era ballparks, Fleming opened as a Coastal Plain League ballpark. Of course, that was the old Class D professional circuit, not the current summer-collegiate version, but the old CPL began life as a summer college loop, too. The current team name, Tobs, is short for "Tobacconists," the same name that most of Wilson's teams carried over the years in minor-league baseball. It's just one of the many things that create a palpable feeling of history repeating itself in this baseball-crazy community.

This is also another of the group of parks used during the filming of the movie *Bull Durham*, but by the late 1990s, when the current CPL was organizing, the stadium was in extremely poor condition. Broken glass, rusted steel girders, and a ramshackle perimeter fence greeted CPL founders on their first official visit. That is the same fence Crash Davis (Kevin Costner) smashed in with a baseball bat to create "a natural disaster" with the sprinklers at the park. The grandstand was also dotted with the remains of numerous small fires started by vagrants using the stadium's wooden seat slats. But the park was still in good structural condition, and the city was eager for a reason to renovate.

With the promise of a team in the yet-to-be-formed league, the City of Wilson went to work, undertaking a $300,000 renovation. The work was steered by a committee of locals, including restaurant owner Lee Gliarmis and Recreation Director Kent Montgomery, and the project was overseen by antique dealer Eddie Fulford, who significantly supplemented the budget by soliciting donations of supplies and labor. Envisioned by CPL founders as a cornerstone franchise, Wilson did not disappoint. More than 2,000 fans turned out for the first game, despite the stadium still being a construction site.

The city has undertaken regular upgrades since that first season in 1997 and has been rewarded with a very attractive and very busy facility. Prior to the 2005 opening of the Clark-LeClair Stadium at East Carolina University in Greenville, Fleming regularly hosted the Pirates' NCAA Regional brackets, drawing overflow crowds to the venerable venue. Wilson has also regularly hosted the Carolinas-Virginia Athletic Conference Tournament on behalf of their local school, Barton College.

With all this community support for baseball and the city's commitment to the facility, a person might ask, "How does a town like this lose its minor-league team in the first place? Why aren't they in the Carolina League with Kinston?" The answer parallels the rise and fall of minor-league baseball throughout the South and the nation. Many communities that hosted thriving teams during the Golden Era of

Fans in the grandstand at Fleming Field get plenty of weather protection from the large overhang.

North Carolina Baseball Museum

the '40s and '50s had great difficulty sustaining their teams during the Vietnam era. It was a time when many traditional things had fallen out of favor, and Wilson was no different, as dwindling attendance led to their Carolina League team relocating after the 1967 season. A Carolina League co-op effort called Wilson home for one season in 1973, but that was the end.

Wilson's last contact with professional baseball until the Southern League's Mudcats left Columbus, Ga. and made Fleming their temporary home while awaiting the completion of Five County Stadium in 1991. Single-A minor-league baseball, in the meantime, had begun a major shift from historic facilities in small towns like Wilson to newer, more elaborate ballparks in larger towns and suburbs. In this context, the chances a town of Wilson's size with an older ballpark lacking suites, club seating, and other modern revenue-generating amenities were very slim.

Fleming Stadium, home of the Wilson Tobs

Ironically, the Mudcats, who Wilson hosted in their hour of need, also present an insurmountable obstacle to Wilson's prospects of ever returning to pro baseball. Due to territorial rules, the Mudcats would have to approve any affiliated team that moved to Wilson, an unlikely proposition. For the fans in Wilson (and all across the state, for that matter), it seems that Coastal Plain League baseball fits the bill. The combination of a cold beer, a hot dog, and some of the best players from their favorite college programs — including ECU, NC State, UNC, and Barton, as well as some local kids most years — seems to be a recipe for success.

The Tobs are annually among the top draws in the Coastal Plain League, with crowds that would make some rookie-level pro teams jealous. In fact, many of the Tobs' more casual fans probably don't even realize they aren't watching minor-league baseball. After all, the

The upright display cases along the wall at the museum are devoted to the seven North Carolina natives inducted into the Hall of Fame in Cooperstown.

baseball is good, the beer is cold, and some of these guys will sign pro contracts. Most importantly, it's the hometown team. What more could any baseball fan want?

Sports Around Town

A visit to Wilson isn't complete without a meal at Dick's Hot Dogs on Nash Street, near downtown. Run by superfan Lee Gliarmis, Dick's has been serving fast, cheap meals to the people of Wilson for over 80 years. During that time, Lee and his family have also acquired a collection of team photos and autographed memorabilia from local and national sports figures that makes Dick's Hot Dogs the unofficial Wilson Sports Hall of Fame. Check out the picture of Bob Uecker and Lee Gliarmis taken in front of Dick's. Lee's son was a placekicker at Carolina, so he's happy to talk football, or you can find out anything you ever wanted to know about baseball history in Wilson. Their hot dogs and chili are both local products: you'll love 'em as much as you'll love the atmosphere!

Dick's Hot Dog Stand
1500 Nash St. N.
252/243-6313

What to Do While Waiting for the Game

Bill Ellis' pork is raised locally at his hog farm.

Wilson is also well known for its barbecue. Your best bet is Bill's Barbecue, on Route 301. This is the Eastern North Carolina version, pulled pork in a vinegar-based sauce that's just delicious. If you prefer the Kansas City style or the Western North Carolina tomato-based sauce, Bill's has a sweet brown sauce on the side that'll make your mouth water, too. The hush puppies are also renowned and, like any good NC BBQ joint, they've got sweet tea with enough sugar in it to make your teeth hurt.

Bill Ellis' Barbecue
3007 Downing St.
252/239-4372
bills-bbq.com

If you're traveling with the kids, Toisnot Park (Corbett Avenue and Lawndale Drive) has a neat little train ride and, of course, the standard swings and playground equipment that help tire out the little rascals.

Wilson is well-known for the quality of its antique shopping. More than 30 dealers provide a wide range of items and prices. There's a complete listing of the area's antique shops at wilson-nc.com/antiques.cfm, but we'll recommend one. Fulford's Antiques is owned and operated by a Wilson native, Eddie Fulford, who can offer you recollections of selling Sno-Kones at Fleming Stadium as a kid, playing baseball there as a teenager, and playing a major role in pulling together the renovations that made the Tobs' return possible in 1997.

Fulford's Antiques, Inc.
2001 Highway 301 S.
252/243-5581
Hours: M-Sat. 9 a.m. - 5 p.m.

The North Carolina Baseball Museum is a testament to the dedication of a group of baseball supporters, most notably former Tobs owner Leonard Turnage (who has since passed on), as well as several of the people who were instrumental in bringing the Tobs to town, including Parks Director Kent Montgomery, Lee Gliarmis of Dick's Hot Dog (see listing above), and local businessman Eddie Fulford.

Showcasing baseball memorabilia from across North Carolina, the museum spreads over 3,328 square feet. Memorabilia comes from ballplayers that played in the state, including Catfish Hunter, Hoyt Wilhelm, Gaylord Perry, Enos Slaughter, Rick

Ferrell, and Buck Leonard. Players that have played at Fleming Stadium include Ted Williams, Richie Ashburn, and Robin Roberts. A "Walk of Fame" area has brick pavers featuring player memories, honors, and recognition. The museum is open year-round and is run by volunteers.

North Carolina Baseball Museum
Fleming Stadium
300 Stadium St.
252/296-3048

Imagination Station is a science and technology center located in the Historic Wilson Federal Courthouse. Built in 1928, the building has been transformed into a science center for the new century. Renovations and improvements completed after a fire in 2000 have significantly updated the building, making Imagination Station a better experience for visitors. You can learn why and how things work with more than 200 hands-on exhibits related to space, health, and the environment; see live animals up close, take a spin as a human gyro, walk inside a giant mouth, or watch your hair stand on end from 10,000 volts of static electricity.

Imagination Station
224 E. Nash St.
252/291-5113
imaginescience.org

For a change of pace, check out the Southern National Speedway. The track features 70' high-banked curves, 16 speedway club skyboxes, trackside tailgate spaces, and full concessions. An average of 4,000 fans attend each race.

Southern National Speedway
8071 Newsome Mill Rd.
Lucama, NC
252/284-1114

Lodging

The hotel closest to the ballpark is the Best Western. It's not a new property, but you could walk to Fleming Stadium if you wanted.

Best Western
817A Ward Blvd. SW.
Wilson, NC 27893
800/528-1234, 252/237-8700
bestwestern.com

 **Directions**

From North and South:

Take Route 301 to Wilson. Turn onto Ward Boulevard (also Route 264 Bypass); turn left if coming from the south, right if coming from the north. Go through several lights. As Parkwood Mall approaches on the left, turn right onto Tarboro Street. The third right is Stadium Drive: turn right on Stadium and Fleming is on the left.

From West:

Take Route 264 to Wilson, turn right onto Ward Boulevard (also Route 264 Bypass). Parkwood Mall will be on the right: turn left onto Tarboro Street and follow as above.

From East:

Take Route 264 to Wilson, turn left onto Ward Boulevard (also Route 264 Bypass).

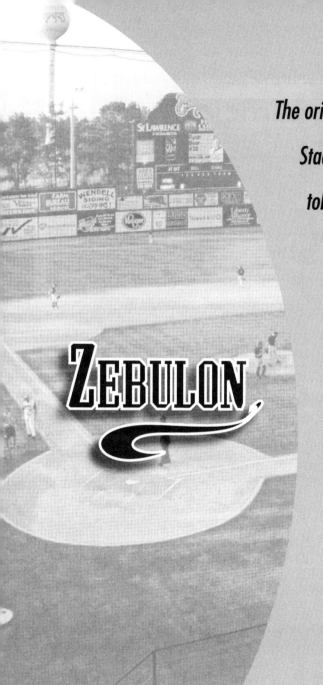

ZEBULON

The original Five County
Stadium rose from a
tobacco field...just as
Kevin Costner's
"Field of Dreams"
was carved from
an Iowa cornfield.

CHAPTER 22

FIVE COUNTY STADIUM

Leading Off

Opened: July 1991

Capacity: 6,500

Dimensions: 330L, 365LC, 400C, 369RC, 330R

Current Team: Carolina Mudcats, Southern League (July 1991-present)

Five County Stadium: Build it and They Will Come

Of all the places for Double-A baseball in the state of North Carolina, Zebulon may be the most unlikely. Zebulon was a town of less than 10,000 people when the Mudcats moved from Columbus, Ga., amid a wave of "Build It and They Will Come" press coverage in 1991. While Zebulon and the surrounding area have grown tremendously over the last decade, it's still a relatively remote location for a team that most strongly identifies itself with Raleigh, the state capital and home to North Carolina State University, about 20 miles away.

The original Five County Stadium rose from a tobacco field in a matter of months, just as Kevin Costner's "Field of Dreams" was carved from an Iowa cornfield. And they came in droves. Despite its remote location, the people of Zebulon and the surrounding towns embraced the team, having never had such big-time entertainment in their backyards.

The original Five County Stadium was built quickly, but not quickly enough, as the Mudcats began their first season in North Carolina playing in nearby Wilson, breathing temporary new life into a vacant and decrepit Fleming Stadium (*see our Wilson chapter on page 259 for more on that historic facility*). About halfway through the season, the Mudcats finally moved into Five County, which was dubbed an "interim stadium." It was basic: no roof, just steel girders on concrete pilings holding up rows of aluminum decking and red chairs. It was, in fact, a bit of a stretch to call it a ballpark, as the "grandstand" was actually three separate sections: one behind home plate, with sections flanking either side hugging the baselines. There were bleachers beyond each end of the main grandstand, and the press box was a trailer-like box on stilts behind the home-plate seats.

Concessions, souvenirs, restrooms, team offices, and locker rooms were all located in a variety of modular outbuildings ringing an asphalt concourse. Fans paid a couple dollars to park in a pair of huge gravel lots on either side of the grandstand.

Other than the field, the one permanent item was the scoreboard, which at the time the park opened was one of the largest in all the minor leagues. With an impeccable playing surface and the image of Muddy the Mudcat peering out from the brightly lit scoreboard, the view from the seats was first-class minor-league baseball. The view from the concourse, though, was more county fair, with a small-town feel and an intimacy that gave the park an atmosphere unlike anything else in the state.

Five County Stadium, named for the surrounding counties — Wake, Johnston, Franklin, Nash, and Wilson — was finally made permanent 10 years later. The "New Five County Stadium" opened in 2002 with the construction of a 5,000-seat concrete and steel grandstand at a cost of approximately $12 million. The influence of owner Steve Bryant, a North Carolina State University alum, is clearly evident in this facility: it's as if Carter-Finley Stadium, NCSU's massive concrete football facility, had been remolded to fit around a baseball field.

You'll want to sit in the lower box section: four rows of seats at field level are covered from rain and sun by the overhanging upper deck. If you can't get lower-level seats you may want to buy bleacher seats, especially if you like to roam the ballpark or if you have any problems getting around. The bulk of the seating in the main grandstand is a sort of upper deck that overhangs the field-level box seats. This main seating area is fairly steep and can only be reached by climbing a short flight of stairs. On the plus side, the angle of incline in this upper grandstand does give you the feeling of being right on top of the action.

The food at Five County is fantastic and unique. A catfish sandwich is the "must have" item on the menu, but a wide, well-prepared selection is available, as well as an ample choice of beers, including some local brews. The Mudcats food has always been excellent, but it has only gotten better since they moved into the modern concessions facilities in the new grandstand.

Five County also boasts the only fine-dining restaurant housed in a ballpark in the state of North Carolina, named Cattails. If you want a culinary experience that is far from the ordinary ballpark meal, come out early and dig into a five-course feast served on fine china and spotless white linens. But bring your wallet: while it's fairly reasonable for the fine-dining category, dinner at Cattails definitely is in a different price range than chili dogs and draft beer.

The Mudcats have always prided themselves on their souvenirs, and the Mudcat logo continues to rank among the top sellers in all of minor-league baseball despite the proliferation of creative, merchandise-friendly team nicknames. Choose from a huge selection of merchandise in the new, walk-in Bait Shop souvenir store.

While the game experience at Five County is a social scene with old friends reconnecting and regulars enjoying the camaraderie of the ballpark, the star of the show is definitely Muddy the Mudcat. What's a Mudcat, you say? Well, in this case, the long answer is that it's a six-foot tall figure, dressed in a baseball jersey with a big fish tail emerging from the back of his specially tailored baseball pants, and a huge, whiskered catfish head

Down the line at Five County Stadium.

sporting a huge baseball cap. The short answer is that it's a catfish. Muddy is an active, enthusiastic mascot always in evidence, from the artwork on the scoreboard to his frequent on-field appearances each game. Muddy was among the first mascots in minor-league baseball to include gimmicks like riding a four-wheeler around the warning track, and he's always got a fresh costume, prop, or skit.

Another key element to the fan experience has been PA man Duke Sanders, who has been announcing the batters for the Mudcats since their arrival in Zebulon. Duke brings a friendly, down-home sound to the microphone with a folksy delivery on announcements ranging from commercials to fans' birthdays, and individualized theme music for each player. His signature bit, though, is a chant of "Mud!" and then "Cat!" that pits the two sides of the stadium against one another like a "Tastes Great"/"Less Filling" beer commercial.

You'll pay to park at Five County; despite the new ballpark, the lots are still gravel. But there's no other place else to park, since the ballpark is out in the country, just off Route 264 east of Raleigh. Just watch for the lights and the huge water tower painted like a baseball, and you'll know you're there.

You're probably still asking yourself, "Why Zebulon?" To get to the bottom of that, we'll have to take you back to 1990 when Steve Bryant, owner of a successful Raleigh-based billboard advertising company, decided that Raleigh and Wake

Only a handful of grandstand seats benefit from overhang shading at Five County Stadium.

County needed their own minor-league baseball team. He was not satisfied to follow the Durham Bulls (*see our Durham chapter on page 183*), who were drawing tremendous crowds and marketing themselves as the Raleigh-Durham-Chapel Hill "Triangle's Team." Bryant also remembered the time of his youth when both Raleigh and Durham had fielded teams in the Carolina League. In fact, Raleigh's last minor-league baseball team had been the 1971 Raleigh-Durham Triangles, a shared team that split their home games between since-demolished Devereaux Meadow (*see our Raleigh chapter on page 239*) and Durham Athletic Park.

Seeking to trump the Bulls' Single-A Carolina League status, Bryant purchased the Double-A Columbus (Ga) Astros of the Southern League and renamed them the Columbus Mudcats prior to the 1989 season. The name and logo were a sensation, and Bryant had hit the merchandising jackpot before even moving his team to its eventual home.

Bryant began discussions with his alma mater, NCSU, about a shared facility to replace the Wolfpack's home field, a then-substandard Doak Field. A site was selected next to NCSU's Carter-Finley Stadium in west Raleigh, less than 20 miles from Durham Athletic Park. (The site that Bryant and NCSU agreed upon did eventually serve as the location for a joint-use facility housing a university team and a professional sports franchise, but it's not baseball. That piece of land became the location of the RBC Center, the arena housing both the Wolfpack basketball team and the 2006 NHL Stanley Cup champion Carolina Hurricanes.)

The plans failed when Bulls owner Miles Wolff and the National Association of Professional Baseball both reminded Bryant of the Bulls' protected territory, then defined as a circular area radiating out 35 miles from home plate. That territorial protection has since been expanded to include such a large area that almost every team in North Carolina is within another team's protected territory, including both the Mudcats and Bulls. Yet, even at that time with the smaller territories, Bryant's proposed facility was squarely in the Bulls' protected home turf.

Bryant's challenges to the Bulls' territorial rights eventually failed, and the search was on for a location that would allow Bryant to fulfill his dream of bringing Double-A baseball to Wake County and remain as close as possible to Raleigh, while staying outside the 35-mile radius from Durham. Seeking easy highway access and available land, the Zebulon site was chosen.

Five County is one of the newest minor-league facilities in the state, and it is an unusual example of ballpark architecture. The lack of retro details like brick and wrought iron, and the unique layout of the main grandstand make Five County a must-visit for the true ballpark aficionado. Make sure to walk around the back of the grandstand before entering; the rear façade is impressive. Muddy the mascot and the catfish sandwich make the trip worthwhile, but you'll likely want to stay in Raleigh, where an abundance of hotel choices and entertainment options await you before and after the game.

⚾ Insider's Tip

Be sure to account for rush-hour traffic when planning your trip from Raleigh to Zebulon. The new 264 Bypass has made getting to Zebulon a lot easier, but you'll still want to time your trip to avoid the 5 p.m. peak rush hour on a weekday. If you leave early, hang a right on down past Lizard Lick and make your way to downtown Wendell. In the midst of this sleepy row of storefronts, you'll find the Mortex Factory Outlet, a sportswear retailer. This is a real outlet, selling leftovers and seconds from the company's nearby manufacturing plant. You'll find gym shorts for 50 cents, high-quality sweatshirts (including those featuring Duke, ECU, and NC State) for $5-10, and T-shirts for schools from anywhere in the country for a dollar or two. You can cover all your souvenirs for the folks back home, and you'll spend a quarter of what they thought you spent.

Mortex Factory Outlet
42 N Main St., Wendell
919/365-3946

Sports Around Town

Other than high-school football, there aren't any other sports to speak of in Zebulon. On the other hand, nearby Raleigh is rich with sports entertainment. The North Carolina State University Wolfpack, a member of the Atlantic Coast Conference, plays football at the newly upgraded Carter-Finley Stadium. An impressive new football building looks out on the Trinity Road side of the stadium, and a massive new video board looms over the opposite end zone, visible from the road.

Behind the football stadium, and visible from the Wade Avenue split off of I-40, is the RBC Center, the arena that houses both the NCSU Wolfpack basketball team and the 2006 Stanley Cup Champion Carolina Hurricanes. While the 'Canes had been a definite second fiddle to the Wolfpack since this building opened in 1999, the NHL team runs the building. After some struggles during their early years in North Carolina, the Hurricanes appear to building a solid fan base on the strength of two appearances in the Stanley Cup Finals since opening the RBC Center and, of course, their championship season in 2005-2006.

It's a little-known fact that Hurricanes owner Peter Karmanos visited Raleigh to see a hockey game played long before he packed the moving vans and brought his Hartford Whalers to North Carolina. His son played for the Raleigh IceCaps of the East Coast Hockey League, considered at the time to be roughly Double-A-level minor-league hockey. He sustained an eye injury while playing for the IceCaps that ended his career, but it certainly couldn't have hurt Raleigh's chances to land the Hurricanes that Karmanos had seen sellout crowds cheering for pro hockey. The IceCaps played at grungy old Dorton Arena, a 5,700-seat cattle exhibition hall on the NC State Fairgrounds that was a nearly perfect minor-league-hockey venue. With its elliptical cable suspension roof this glass-walled arena was dubbed the "Big White Potato Chip" by hockey fans. It's located on the Hillsborough Street side of the Fairgrounds complex, just west of downtown and adjacent to the Carter-Finley Stadium and the RBC Center.

The Wolfpack basketball team draws consistent sellouts for their conference games. Nonetheless, a restless alumni base drove former coach Herb Sendek to leave for Arizona State after a string of five straight NCAA tournament bids. Sendek's teams had not been able to meet the expectations created by the team's success during the Jim Valvano era.

What to Do in Raleigh

We are assuming you'll want to stay in Raleigh rather than out by the ballpark. Raleigh has evolved from a sleepy state capital to a thriving city; add in a major university and you have a city worth making your home base.

Raleigh's downtown is bustling with nightlife, including the pioneering downtown entertainment district, City Market and Moore Square. A neighborhood of historic buildings was redeveloped in the late 1980s and early 1990s to house a collection of bars, restaurants, live entertainment venues, shops and galleries. The restaurant lineup includes Big Ed's, the place in Raleigh, for a hearty country breakfast or lunch, as well as Woody's Sports Bar, Vic's, and Rum Runners. Moore Square is also home to an excellent Irish bar and restaurant named Tir Na Nog, which comes complete with Guinness, Murphy's, and its own decorative stone wall and thatched roof inside. There's a free concert series on the first Friday night of each month with local bands playing in front of Big Ed's City Market Restaurant. For more information and up-to-date info on events, visit **citymarketraleigh.com.**

A few blocks north of City Market a portion of Glenwood Avenue has developed into an upscale nightlife district known as "Glenwood South." Named as one of the nation's top 40 nightlife spots by *The New York Times,* this area is bristling with clubs, boutiques, restaurants, live music and, increasingly, condos and luxury apartments. One of the best spots for a sports fan is Hi-5. They've got tons of TVs and a selection of over 200 beers. Stool Pigeons is another affordable, fan-friendly option, popular with both college students and young professionals.

Hi-5
510 Glenwood Av.
919/834-4335
hi5raleigh.com

Stool Pigeons
410 Glenwood Av.
919/831-0400
stoolpigeons.biz

CAMPUS AREA EATS AND NIGHTLIFE
The neighborhood around the N.C. State campus, most notably the Hillsborough Street area, offers a friendly, walkable cluster of inexpensive eateries and bars. This is a particularly convenient place to wrap up your evening if you stay at one of the two Hillsborough Street hotels listed below.

Mitch's Tavern is a must. Located in the second floor of a funky stone building in the middle of the Hillsborough Street student strip, this eatery and bar is marked by just a small sign hanging over the door. Climb the stairs, and you'll recognize the setting from the bar scene in Bull Durham. Grab the booth against the wall to your left as you reach the top of the stairs, and you'll be sitting where Kevin Costner sent the round of drinks to baseball's clown prince, Max Patkin, and Susan Sarandon. The menu, available at the tavern's website, features good sandwiches and unique chili, but the atmosphere is the reason to visit. The ceiling and walls are hung with everything from a surf board to one of the famed stenciled glass windows reading "Mitch's" that Nuke broke with a baseball before his fistfight with Crash. In addition to the classic booths, the tables and chairs are a mismatched collection that includes two church pews. But it's the dark, aged wood in the beams, floors, tables, and wall paneling that really gives the place its character. It's as comfortable as your favorite old pair of jeans.

Mitch's Tavern
2426 Hillsborough St.
919/821-7771
mitchs.com

East Village Grill has a menu that includes burgers, sandwiches, wraps, and heavy appetizers. The beer selection ranges from Pabst on tap to Killian's and Blue Moon. The atmosphere here is definitely laid back. There's a main bar room inside, and an enclosed patio area with a bank of TVs to catch the big game. But people know East Village for its deck. Built around a mature shade tree, this deck offers some of Hillsborough Street's only outdoor dining. While it's not a terribly scenic location, it's still a great spot for people-watching and relaxing.

East Village Grill
1 Dixie Trail (at 3000 Hillsborough St.)
919/821-9985
eastvillagegrill.com

FAMILY ENTERTAINMENT
Downtown Raleigh has an IMAX Theater and a big selection of museums, including Marbles, a children's museum right across Moore Square from Greenshield's, and a great Museum of Natural Sciences with exhibits that really engage even small children. Sports fans will enjoy the NC Sports Hall of Fame, housed in the North Carolina Museum of History. The NC Sports Hall honors a number of baseball figures, including legendary Negro Leaguer Buck Leonard and iconic North Carolina basketball coach Dean Smith.

Marbles Kids Museum
201 E. Hargett St.
919/834-4040
marbleskidsmuseum.org

North Carolina Museum of Natural Sciences
11 W. Jones St.
919/733-7450
naturalsciences.org

North Carolina Museum of History
5 E. Edenton St.
919/807-7900
ncmuseumofhistory.com

See Another Game

While staying in Raleigh, it's easy an hour-long drive to see the Wilson Tobs (*see our Wilson chapter on page 259*), while the home of the Durham Bulls (*see our Durham chapter on page 183*) is about 30 minutes away. If you're in town between late February and May, you could also explore some of the area's college-baseball venues. Campbell University (*see our Buies Creek chapter on page 211*) is about an hour away by country roads, and N.C. State's newly renovated Doak Field is well worth a visit (*see our Raleigh chapter on page 239*). The homes of the UNC Tar Heels (*see our Chapel Hill chapter on page 215*) or Duke Blue Devils (*see our Durham chapter on page 183*) are also just a 30- to 45-minute drive away, depending on traffic.

Lodging

While you certainly can find cheaper places to stay in Raleigh, there aren't many like the Velvet Cloak Inn, where you also can park the car and walk to nearby restaurants and bars. With wrought-iron railings that will make you think of New Orleans, this is a distinctive property and a popular choice for state legislators and other governmental and academic travelers, including some who make it their home for extended stays.

Velvet Cloak Inn
1505 Hillsborough St.
Raleigh, NC 27605
919/828-0333
velvetcloakinn.com

The other convenient campus-area hotel is the Holiday Inn Brownstone. Just a few blocks from the Velvet Cloak, the Brownstone is another local institution, and it also puts you in walking distance to a variety of restaurants, nightlife, the NCSU campus, and Cameron Village. This is a nice option for both dining and shopping if you're looking for something less student-oriented that's still within walking distance.

The Brownstone also has free wireless Internet and a full service restaurant in the hotel. The hotel is also adjacent to the Raleigh YMCA, and use of their facilities is included with the room. Like the Velvet Cloak, the Brownstone will set you back a bit, but hey, it's not much more than you'd pay at any of the chain hotels on the interstate, and you're on vacation, right?

Holiday Inn Brownstone
1707 Hillsborough St.
Raleigh, NC 27605
919/828-0811
brownstonehotel.com

If you are looking for convenience, free parking, and an overall good location straddling downtown not too far the NCSU campus, the Clarion Hotel State Capital fits the bill. While this aging property has seen better days, the front-desk service is helpful and the room rates are reasonable, especially when you consider the prime location.

Clarion Hotel State Capital
320 Hillsborough St.
Raleigh, NC 27603
919/832-0501
choicehotels.com

 **Directions**

From Raleigh:

Take the I-440 Beltline to Exit 14 for the new US 64 East/US 264 East Bypass (Mudcats Expressway). Exit onto U.S. 264 East. Take second exit (Hwy. 39) and turn right: the ballpark is on the right.

From Rocky Mount/Emporia, Va. and points north:

Take I-95 to U.S. 64 West to Stadium Exit at Hwy. 39. Turn left and follow Hwy. 39: the ballpark is 3 1/2 miles ahead on the right.

From Smithfield and points south:

Take U.S. 301 to Hwy. 39 (just north of Selma). Turn left and follow Hwy. 39: the ballpark is on the left.

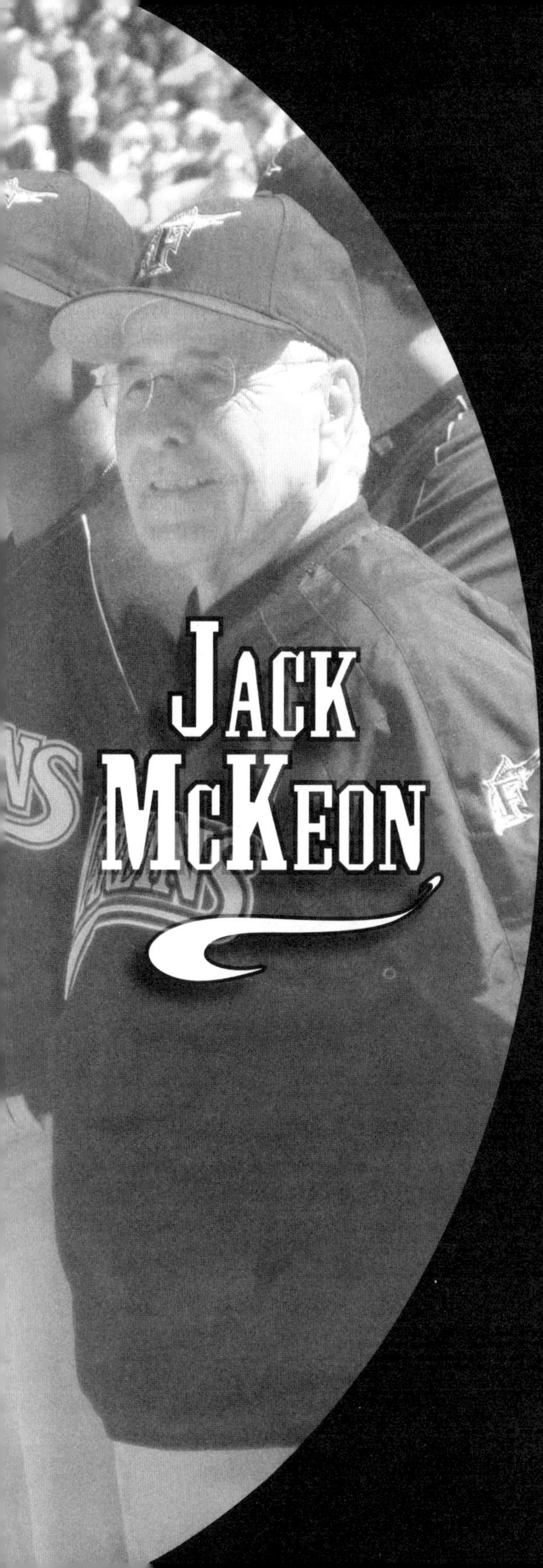

JACK McKEON

An interview

with one of

North Carolina's

biggest lights

in the

baseball world.

Jack McKeon accompanied the Florida Marlins in Greensboro for a 2005 exhibition game.
Photo courtesy of Elon University.

John Aloysius McKeon was born Nov. 23, 1930, in South Amboy, N.J. Known as Jack, he picked up the nickname "Trader Jack" while wheeling and dealing the Padres from the cellar to the World Series in just four years.

While McKeon is best known today as the manager of the miraculous 2003 Florida Marlins, his overall managerial career in baseball spans goes back more than a half century, as he worked his way up the baseball ladder. Early in the 2003 season, McKeon took over a losing team. When the season ended, they were World Series champions, having defeated the mighty New York Yankees. McKeon was named National League Manager of the Year for his efforts.

When he retired as manager of the Marlins following the 2005 season, he was 74 years old, the third-oldest manager in major-league history. McKeon's first major-league managing job was with the Kansas City Royals from 1973-75. He went on to manage the Oakland A's for the legendary Charlie O. Finley in 1977-78.

In 1981, he took over as general manager of the San Diego Padres, who had finished 19½ games back the previous year. The Padres won the National League pennant in 1984. McKeon guided the Padres as GM until 1990 and also served as manager from 1988 to 1990.

The Cincinnati Reds hired McKeon to serve as their manager in 1997, and he won his second NL Manager of the Year in 1999 before being fired in 2000. In his 15 years as a big-league manager, McKeon won 1,011 games and lost 940, for a winning percentage of .518.

Like so many field generals, McKeon was a catcher during his playing days. He spent his entire minor-league career in the minors, primarily in the Pirates organization headed by the legendary Branch Rickey. He played minor-league baseball in the Burlington area, and his first managing job was with a non-affiliated team in Fayetteville. He would also manage in Wilson and Thomasville.

As a minor-league skipper, McKeon managed teams for the Washington Senators/Minnesota Twins franchise and later for the Kansas City Royals. He managed Kansas City's "unofficial" affiliate in the Carolina League in 1968. McKeon broke into the big leagues as the Royals' manager in 1973 after winning two league championships while managing their Triple-A team in Omaha in 1969-72.

But it's his North Carolina history we're most interested in here. Jack McKeon has been an off-season and between-jobs resident of Alamance County for over 50 years, interrupted only by a stint when his entire family lived in San Diego while he was serving as the Padres' general manager.

During that time, McKeon has become well known in the area and certainly does not hide behind the walls of a gated community. He can be found at the local YMCA most days, and he is generous with his time where local causes are concerned. He is particularly generous with the local Catholic church, Blessed Sacrament, to whom he recently donated a rental home he had owned for many years.

I first met Jack McKeon shortly after I started work as the general manager of the Burlington Indians. I knew that Jack was Alamance County's most notable baseball figure, and I thought he was someone I should know. I called Jack and asked him to meet me for lunch. When we got together, I began getting to know the hometown Jack McKeon. He offered to help in any way he could and proceeded to suggest potential sponsors, fill me in on the local "who's who," and tell great baseball stories.

At that time he had no designs on managing again, telling me, "No, they think I'm too damn old." I was looking forward to seeing him at the Burlington Indians games, smoking cigars and sitting at the end of bleachers, but it wasn't mean to be. A few months later, the struggling Florida Marlins called, and Jack was back in business. The story is well known. He guided the Marlins to the best winning percentage in baseball after he took over, qualified for the playoffs, and won the World Series against the Yankees, going against the "book" by pitching Josh Beckett on short rest in the decisive Game Six in Yankee Stadium.

I didn't get to see Jack as much as I had hoped I would, but it was sure exciting to see one of Alamance County's own hoisting the World Series trophy on television. It was a rare treat to speak with him in the off-season and hear about his motivation strategies, the personalities, and how appreciative and humble he was about his accomplishment. I heard him on several occasions that you have to be both good and a little lucky to win a World Series.

Jack also gave a speech at an area appearance following his World Series win where he told the primarily local audience that he was their neighbor and their friend, just like he had been for 50 years. It was an impressive and humble statement from a man who has won more than he's lost in a game that can breed outsized egos.

I got together again with Jack for lunch, this time to talk about his years in North Carolina as a minor-league player and manager. Just four years removed from his World Series triumph, Jack is still happy to help a friend. He is still a robust figure and exhibits incredible recall and clarity regarding events from last year or 50 years ago. One can only hope someone will have the guts to give him one more chance. After all, he was already too old in 2003, but even today, at 76, he is simply a winner.

MC: *How did you wind up in North Carolina the first time?*

JM: I was with the Pittsburgh Pirates and had started out in '49 in Greenville, Alabama, then I was in York, Pennsylvania, in '50 in the Tri-State League. That was when Willie Mays was breaking in with Trenton. I got to a point where I wasn't playing regularly, so I said send me somewhere I can play. They sent me down to Gloversville (N.Y.) in the Can-Am League, Class C.

Then I was in the military service for a year and half, and when I came out, I went to Hutchinson, Kansas, in '52. Came to Burlington in '53, and I did most of the catching.

In '54, I was gonna be in Burlington, but I didn't go to spring training; I was gonna join 'em here. They had this big catcher coming in, so I was gonna be a player-coach.

MC: *So, you already had your mind set toward coaching?*

JM: Yeah, and things were going fine in Burlington, but then [Pirates General Manager Branch] Rickey calls me to manage in Hutchinson. Well, it turns out when I get there, you wouldn't believe it, there are three managers, including the original manager, George Genovese.

It all started one day when I'm at the [Bur-Gra Pirates] ballpark in Graham working out on my own, and the team owner Red Fowler calls me in his office and says, "Mr. Rickey called — he wants a favor." Well, we're in first place; we've got Stan Wentzel as the manager; I'm coaching third, playing a little, had my eyes on being a manager.

Fowler says, "Mr. Rickey wants you to go to Hutchinson. They're trying to make the playoffs. He's going to call back in an hour for your answer." So, I wanted to manage, and I figured it couldn't hurt to do Rickey a favor. So I tell him, "OK, I'll go." Ricky then tells me that he wants me to manage in Hutchinson, he just wanted to see if I would agree to go first.

I knew I wanted to manage, and now I thought I had my chance. Rickey says, "You'll take over when the team comes in off the road, meet them in Ponca [City], Oklahoma." I jumped in my '49 Plymouth and drove like hell. So, I get there, play a few games, and I go out to lunch, and see in the paper, "Larry Dorton named manager of the Hutchinson Elks!"

I was fit to be tied. Well, I was mad as hell. Dick Wagner was general manager; he comes by and says that Mr. Rickey forgot to tell the farm director that he had offered me the job. Well, I'm stuck. I'm pissed. Mr. Rickey flies in and he gets me up in the hotel room; says, "It's my mistake, nothing we can do now. I'll give you a choice, you can go back to Bur or stay here or go to Williamsport." But, he promises me that I'd be the manager there next year. He'd like me to stay there, so I'll stay. Well, the league folded before the next season. Some managing job!

MC: *So, that didn't quite pan out as you first managing job.*

JM: No. That's how I wound up in Fayetteville. They were called the Highlanders and an independent team. I got my release from the Pirates after the '54 season. Aaron Robinson is the player/manager in Fayetteville, and I go in, I'm playing great, batting like .285, best I've ever hit. Well, cut-down day comes, May 15, and the GM comes and says, we've got to cut down, and I've got to cut you, but I want you to stay around for the next two weeks. If Aaron Robinson doesn't play, you're back in.

Well, I get a call from Johnny Murphy with the Red Sox. "Our big catcher Jerry Zimmerman in Greensboro is hurt. We need you there." OK, but I tell him that I got a chance to manage, so I'll catch for him in Greensboro, but if the managing thing comes along, I'm gonna go. He says that's OK.

So, I'm catching every day, three weeks pass, and Fayetteville calls. "We need you come down, we're gonna fire this guy," they tell me. Well, I can't come tomorrow, I've got to tell the Greensboro people what I'm gonna do, and let them get somebody in here. So, I catch that night and tell them, and they say, we'll give you manager's salary to stay. Well, I've made a commitment, a bird in hand, you know. They promised me I'd manage the next year, but bird in hand....

I go to Fayetteville, and they're in last place, and I take over. We've got a makeshift team. I'm playing every day; we take a big jump. We're in first place by the All-Star game. I had Bobby Lyons, the leading hitter in the league, get hit in the head — up in Danville, he's done for the year. I had my big first baseman get hurt.

Well, I had a makeshift team. My big first baseman, he runs the YMCA in Greensboro; Ken Deal works at Western Electric. Another guy, he's got a construction company in the eastern part of the state, he only shows up when he's gonna pitch. Hal Woods from Asheboro, he's the football coach.

We went to the ballpark with 12 guys sometimes; whoever the hell shows up!

Then I get a bad bone bruise in my hand. It's swollen out to here. The doctor tells me that I need to take a week off or I could lose the hand. Well, I keep playing, but I'm only catching when Ken Deal, our knuckleballer, pitches. So, we just sweep Burlington in a doubleheader, but the owner tells me, you can't play, we don't pay (McKeon laughs)....So, I'm out, and Jack Sanford is in. Sanford is one of my players; he's the Elon coach. So, now I'm out of a job.

MC: *That was it for you that year?*

JM: Oh, yeah, that was it. There were only three weeks left in the season by then. So, the next winter, I went to the winter meetings in Louisville with Bill Jessup (then Carolina League president). Dick

Wagner's there, and he knows I got screwed in Hutchinson. So he's trying to help me. He's recommending me to Hank Peters, different people. I talk with a lot of people but nothing comes through right then.

I go back to Elon, and I'll never forget it, I'm taking a final exam in health from Mrs. Griffin. (McKeon began taking college classes in the off-season at Elon College in exchange for helping coach the baseball team in the fall. He eventually completed his bachelor's degree at Elon.) I get a phone message: please call your wife right away. I called her at work, and she said, "You got a wire — Nick Mariana, Missoula Montana; Need a hustling young player-manager." So, I walked right out of that exam.

I get on the phone with Nick. He says, "I just bought the Ogden franchise. I've got three players, no place to train. Can you get me players?" "Yeah, I know some people." "Can you get a place to train?" "Yeah, yeah," I tell him. "Well, I'll pay you $3,600." "OK." So I took the job.

MC: *So you were in charge of securing the players?*

JM: Yeah. I go to spring training, start rounding up some players. I got us a place to train in Newton [North Carolina]. This guy had a baseball school and he lets me have the facilities, he's got a boarding house, fed the players, and we used it as our training site. It was a tryout, too. We signed some of those players. Hey, I was scouting director, farm director, arranged transportation. We all drove out there.

I knew Phil Howser from Charlotte. Through him I was able to get a bunch of Cuban players from the Senators. I guess I did a good job with 'em, because the next year, we had a working agreement with Washington, which then became Minnesota. I stayed in Missoula three years. I was making my own trades. I was doing it all: personnel director, scouting, everything. There was no one there to be GM. That was my start at Missoula.

MC: *After Fayetteville, the next time you had a job that brought you back to North Carolina wasn't until High Point-Thomasville, right?*

JM: That's right. I had been working for the Twins as a scout. Lou Gorman with the Royals calls me. They're an expansion team at the time. I take a job with them. I agree I'll be a scout for a year, and then I was going to go to Omaha to manage the Triple-A team there.

In the meantime, High Point can't get a manager, and [Carolina League president] Bill Jessup called me.

He says, "You've got experience as a general manager. How about managing the Hi-Toms?" I told him I got a scouting job with the Royals. I say, let me think about it. So I call Gorman. I say, hey, we can't have any teams, but if I take this job, I can sign guys to the High Point club, you pay the salaries, and we give High Point a working agreement the next year. So that's what I did, I kept signing these guys. And that's how we did it.

I had all these retreads. I got Tony Solaita from the Yankees, 'cause they had Ron Blomberg, who was a number-one pick. We won the pennant. We had no pitching, but we had some hitters. We had five guys off the team make the big leagues: four players, one umpire. Solaita [11 years in the majors], Tommy Ragland [who played parts of six seasons in the big leagues], Jim Clark [parts of two big-league seasons], Monty Montgomery [parts of two seasons], and Daryl Cousins [who went on to umpire in the major leagues]. All these guys who everyone said couldn't play.

MC: *What was life like for a player in the Carolina League at that time?*

JM: When I was playing, there were families who'd rent a room. There were rooming houses, a new guy comes in, hey, we've got a room over here. When I broke in, nobody had cars. If you had 18 guys on a team, maybe two or three had a car. By the time I'm managing in the Carolina League, maybe half the guys had cars.

MC: *What was the Thomasville ballpark like?*

JM: It was about the same size as the park today, but all wood. There was a trailer park behind there. One night, I'm missing one of my players. It's game time, and turns out he's over in the trailer park, "visiting" with some girl....

That's also the ballpark where Daryl Cousins got locked in the clubhouse one night. We were on the bus, and one of the guys had to go back in to get something he forgot, and Cousins went in, too. I didn't know it, so I lock the dugout door. We headed to Raleigh, and halfway there someone says, "Hey skip, Cousins is still in the clubhouse." Well, tough [luck].

Lucky thing, there was an American Legion game that night, and the owner of the team was a big Legion booster. So, he's walking down the walkway and hears all this banging. He had a key so he let him out.

MC: *What were the best and worst places to play in the Carolina League?*

JM: Wilson was good, Durham, Winston-Salem. I played at old Southside Park in Winston that was nothing, like a semi-pro field, one of the worst. High Point wasn't bad, but that burned down. When I came back in '68 they had a grandstand that ran all the way around. They were like bleachers. It was open underneath, and you could go back there, and guys would sometimes take a leak back there, or something, and every once in a while, a guy would come back, and say hey, that one doesn't have any drawers on!

MC: *Travel was a challenge in that era. What was the most unusual experience you had on the way to a game?*

JM: One time, on the way from High Point to Wilson, I know where the ballpark is, and [our driver] is going the wrong way, almost hitting cars. Well, we check, and he's so drunk he can barely stand. So we put him out of the driver's seat, and one of the players took the bus.

There was another time when I was managing Wilson and we were on the way to Greensboro. The driver was Bob Bates, he had a wooden leg, we called him Peg Leg Bates. We get as far as Hillsborough, and the players are agitating the bus driver, and he's getting really ticked. He starts giving it back to 'em, and I said, hey, just drive the bus. He says, "I'll pull this bus over and get out." I said, fine. He pulls over, he gets out, and I say, who the hell can drive this bus? Chuck Weatherspoon, Spoonie, he was my favorite. Spoonie, I carried him with me nine or 10 years, used to come visit me in Houston all the time. Well, he jumps into the driver's seat and drives us away. We leave the guy by the side of the road. The guy shows up at the ballpark later that night, and apologizes....We didn't have any more problems with him the rest of the year.

MC: *What were the ballparks like in North Carolina when you were starting out?*

JM: Some of them were just terrible. I was managing the Hi-Toms, and [newspaper reporter] Moses Crutchfield in Greensboro wanted to do a story. Well, I was hot. Sitting on the bleachers at the Greensboro War Memorial, it was terrible, I was getting splinters in my ass. I told him, All-America City, my ass! Well, I ripped 'em, and it was a big deal. So, next thing you know, they started renovating....

I got some big renovations when I was in Omaha. I was speaking at a Lions Club, and I didn't know the mayor and some other people were there. Well, Omaha only worried about the College World Series. I tell 'em, you finally get back into baseball, and you're gonna lose it. And I tell them, hey, you guys were out of baseball for seven years, and things deteriorated. Lots of things hadn't been painted in seven years. I said, you finally got baseball, and now you're gonna lose baseball. Look at Albuquerque, they built a new ballpark, they're ready to lease it to a ballclub for $1 a year. So, the next day, the papers say, "Team's Goin' To Albuquerque!" So, they started fixing it up, we got new seats...and the team's still there today.

MC: *Was it any different dealing with those types of ballpark issues in the big leagues?*

JM: Hell no. In San Diego, I had a running battle with the city manager on the front page of the paper the year we went to the World Series. The field [currently Qualcomm Stadium] was so bad they had to dye it with vegetable dye. [Outfielder Kevin] McReynolds slides to catch a ball, and he comes up with his pants all green.

Well, we won the pennant, and we're supposed to be playing the World Series and they're getting ready for a football game on Sunday. We're getting ready to get out of town, and I go out there, and they're digging these holes in the outfield for where they roll the stands out. Well, when they set back up for baseball, balls are going this way and that. I go nuts. We wind up in front of the stadium commission. Finally, we got rid of that groundskeeper and brought in Bill Wilson. Smooth sailing then.

After we were in the Series, Ballard Smith, the president of the club, was negotiating a new lease, and he's gonna bring in this gal from the PR firm. Well, he and Dick Freeman are working on this thing, and Freeman doesn't want to make anyone mad, he likes being invited to the Poinsettia Bowl and all the black-tie cocktail parties. I said, let me negotiate it. I'll just tell them we're going to Denver. Freeman says, "No, you can't do that…." I tell him, I won't tell them, I'll just, you know, insinuate…

Let me give you an example of how bad our situation was there. They had all these extra rooms in the stadium and the Chargers had everything, but we didn't even have a batting cage under the stands. These guys finally got a room we could use, but the team winds up spending $325,000 converting it into a batting cage!

In the end, he and the PR firm did the lease, and I said, you'll wish you had let me negotiate it. So, 10 years later, they sold the club, and Larry Lucchino comes in and says the team has the worst lease in baseball!

MC: *Other than your time in San Diego, you've always lived in Alamance County during the off-season. Marrying Carol was the main reason you settled in the Burlington area, right?*

JM: Yeah, I played in Burlington in '53 and '54, and Carol and I were married in '54. I tell, you, though, I could've been happy in Missoula, Hutchinson, any of the places I played. Well, anywhere but Greenville, Alabama. The ballpark was a dump, and there were snakes coming out of the ceiling in the clubhouse. And hot. Anywhere you went, no air conditioning. So you open the window, in comes the bugs and the heat. Keep 'em closed, it's hot….it was terrible.

MC: *How did you and Carol meet?*

JM: I met her at the drugstore downtown. We'd go hang around there, try to meet the girls. One of my teammates was dating her sister, and I met her. She was nice.

Then, one night, the other team's catcher kept interfering with my bat. I was trying a new stance [McKeon holds his hands up, demonstrating a batting stance that held the bat flat, pointing straight back]. Well, he clips my bat with his mitt, and it's strike one. I told him if he did it again, he was gonna be sorry. Well, he did it again, and I take another strike. This time, I tell him he's gonna be sorry and make sure it's loud enough that the umpire can hear. Well, the next pitch is on the way, and I reach back, and instead taking a cut at the ball, I bop him in the head with the bat. He goes down, the ball hits the ump, it's strike three, but the ball gets away after it hits the ump, and the run scores from third. The catcher gets up and comes after me, and we fight. The umpire tossed me out of the game. I go get showered and went and watched the rest of the game in the stands with Carol.

MC: *So, on one play, you got an RBI, an ejection, a fight, and a wife?*

JM: Yeah, I guess you could say that.

MC: *You were regarded as a pretty hard-nosed player?*

JM: I was hard-nosed. I knew how to play. I was good at blocking the plate, but I paid the price. I've still got bad ligaments in the ankles. I didn't back down from anybody. And I could catch. Today, I could've hung around the big leagues 10 years on my glove. I just had the instinct. I knew the game.

MC: *Other than ballparks, what are the other major differences you've seen in life in the minors?*

JM: Medical care was really different. You got a raspberry, you went to the drugstore on your own, bought some zinc oxide, that was that. Now, they see real doctors, you got training staff, and all that.

MC: *So, did a manager or coach tape guys, that kind of stuff?*

JM: [McKeon laughs] We didn't know nothing about taping anything. Only thing we used the tape for was keeping up our socks. Yeah, we even had to buy our own sanis [socks]. Someone would go over to Conover and buy a gross. You want three pairs of sanis? OK, here's a buck….

We bought most of our equipment, too, when I started. Team might give you six bats; you could break those in a day. So you'd go down to the store and buy your own.

MC: What's changed regarding player development?

JM: These days, player-development people are afraid to make a mistake and afraid to release guys. That's why you've got these big rosters in the low minors and all these guys hanging around.

In the minors, my goal was to develop players. I wanted to develop players, and I thought if I make this guy 10 percent better, and this guy 10 percent better, well, the winning will come. I also wasn't afraid to let a guy work out of a jam. A guy gets into the sixth and has a couple guys on base, and now they take him out. I'd let a guy work out of the jam. Maybe he loses today's game for you, but he'll win one down the road. Keep in mind, we only had 17, 18 players, too. There weren't 10 guys in the bullpen waiting to pitch.

I had a 17-year-old Jim Kaat in Missoula, pitching 250 innings in his first pro season. I'd have lost my job for that today, but he went on to pitch 25 years in the big leagues. The big-league brass comes to see him and they say, he doesn't have the stuff to pitch in the big leagues. I said, I'll bet you he's in the bigs in two years. Well, six months later, there he is.

MC: I bet motivating players is a little different today. You told a story on Letterman after the Marlins won the World Series about a player in Wilson who kept running through the stop sign at third base.

JM: Yeah, I had this Cuban ballplayer, every night he comes tearing around third base, and I give him the stop sign. Well, he keeps running through the sign, paying no attention. So, I'm walking around downtown one day and I see this starter's pistol in the window of this pawn shop, and I get an idea. I buy the pistol and load it with some caps. I put the gun in my pocket. Sure enough, that night, here comes this guy running toward third base, showing no signs of stopping, even though I'm giving him the stop sign. So I pull out the gun! He sees it just as he's rounding third, and I aim the thing at him, and he's still running. I fire off four or five shots, scared the living hell out of him. He never ran through the stop sign again!

MC: So, other than the fact that you can't shoot at the players anymore, are the ballparks the biggest change in the game?

JM: Absolutely. You go to the new ballparks like Greensboro, and it's a joy. Wide aisles, good food, everything's clean, you can mingle. You're seeing cities really catch on to the value of professional baseball. It's a great promotional vehicle for the cities, it's recreation for the people, and it gives the kids something to do. You can't beat it.

MC: *Thanks, Jack. I couldn't have said it better myself.*

Jack McKeon's Complete Managerial Record

Year	Team	Classification & League (Major League Affiliate)
1955	Fayetteville Highlanders	Class B Carolina League (independent)
1956	Missoula Timberjacks	Class C Pioneer League (independent)
1957	Missoula Timberjacks	Class C Pioneer League (Washington Senators)
1958	Missoula Timberjacks	Class C Pioneer League (Washington Senators)
1959	Fox Cities Foxes (Appleton, Wis)	Class B Three-I League (Washington Senators)
1960	Wilson Tobs	Class B Carolina League (Washington Senators)
1961	Wilson Tobs	Class B Carolina League (Minnesota Twins) League Champions
1962	Vancouver Mounties	Class AAA Pacific Coast League (Minnesota Twins)
1963	Dallas-Ft. Worth Rangers	Class AAA Pacific Coast League (Minnesota Twins)
1964	Atlanta Crackers	Class AAA International League (Minnesota Twins)
1968	High Point-Thomasville Hi-Toms	Class A Carolina League (independent)
1969	Omaha Royals	Class AAA American Association (Kansas City Royals)
1970	Omaha Royals	Class AAA American Association (KC Royals)
1971	Omaha Royals	Class AAA American Association (KC Royals)
1972	Omaha Royals	Class AAA American Association (KC Royals)
1973	Kansas City Royals	American League
1974	Kansas City Royals	American League
1975	Kansas City Royals	American League (succeeded by Whitey Herzog during the season)
1976	Richmond Braves	Class AAA International League (Atlanta Braves)

Year	Team	Classification & League (Major League Affiliate)
1979	Denver Bears	Class AAA Pacific Coast League (Montreal Expos)
1980-1990	San Diego Padres	National League, General Manager, National League Champions, 1984
1988	San Diego Padres	National League (took over for Larry Bowa during the season)
1989	San Diego Padres	National League
1990	San Diego Padres	National League (succeeded by Greg Riddoch during the season)
1997	Cincinnati Reds	National League (succeeded Ray Knight during the season)
1998	Cincinnati Reds	National League
1999	Cincinnati Reds	National League National League Manager of the Year
2000	Cincinnati Reds	National League
2003	Florida Marlins	National League (succeeded Jeff Torborg during the season) World Series Champions, National League Manager of the Year
2004	Florida Marlins	National League
2005	Florida Marlins	National League

DOWN EAST &

THE COAST

SECTION 4

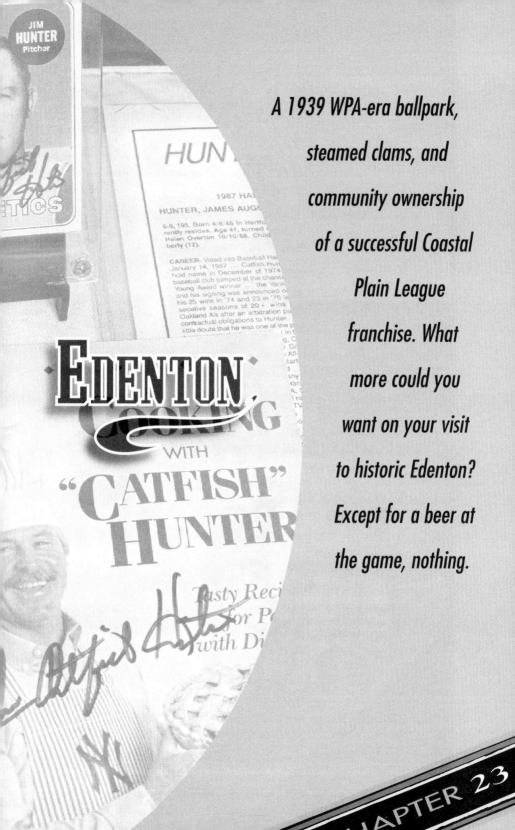

A 1939 WPA-era ballpark, steamed clams, and community ownership of a successful Coastal Plain League franchise. What more could you want on your visit to historic Edenton? Except for a beer at the game, nothing.

CHAPTER 23

HICKS FIELD

Leading Off

Opened: 1939

Capacity: 1,200

Dimensions: 300L, 336LC, 350C, 330RC, 198R

Current Team: Edenton Steamers, Coastal Plain League (1998-present)

Former Teams: Edenton Colonials, Virginia State League (1951), Edenton Colonials, Coastal Plain League (1952)

ESSENTIALS

Address: 111 E. Freemason St., Edenton
Website: edentonsteamers.com
Phone: 252/482-4080
Ticket Prices: $4-$5

Tender Loving Care Brought Back a Great Ballpark — And You Win

If ever there was a ballpark guaranteed to take you back in time, it's Hicks Field in Edenton. Built in 1939 as a Depression-era Works Project Administration project, Hicks Field is one of the last of the wood ballparks still standing in North Carolina (*see our Salisbury chapter on page 77*), and no wooden grandstand in the state is older. Located on the banks of the Albemarle Sound, Edenton was North Carolina's first permanent settlement and served as the colonial capital. Known as "The South's Prettiest Town," Edenton boasts a history that runs through nearly every building in the town's historic district. From the Chowan County Courthouse, built in 1767 overlooking Edenton Bay, to the lovingly restored Edenton Cotton Mill, to the beautiful old churches and homes that line Edenton's main thoroughfare, there is a charm and gentility to the place that lies somewhere between Mayberry and Tara.

Drive into downtown on Highway 17 and you'll want to take a right as soon as you hit Broad Street. Park in front of one of the shops there and take a stroll through Edenton's picturesque downtown. You'll almost certainly find yourself drawn to the water, where you'll see the Barker House, which dates to the town's earliest days and once served as the customs house for goods coming in from England and other European countries. Head to the end of the landing, and if you're lucky you'll see a blue heron, but in any case you'll see the beauty of the Albemarle Sound. Turn around and head away from the water, and you'll have your choice of several distinctly different restaurants. For a nice, upscale lunch at a reasonable price, stop at Waterman's Grill. Head upstairs for a cozy feel that will make you think you're eating in the captain's quarters. For a burger and fries, Snooker's will

Panoramic view of Coastal Plain League action at Hicks Field. Photo courtesy of Edenton Steamers Baseball.

be just the ticket. Or, you can hit the lunch counter at Mitchener's Drug Store for a grilled-cheese sandwich.

If you can handle a half-mile's walk, leave your car downtown and continue up Broad Street. You'll pass by a church that is one of the oldest structures in Chowan County (and the state). If you ask politely at the municipal building, they might show you the old jail out back, where heavy iron bars and primitive stonework bring to mind visions of Oliver Twist slurping his gruel.

Shortly, you'll be closing in on the ballpark, although not before walking past one of Edenton's truly excellent B&Bs, the Governor Eden Inn. If you are staying overnight to see a ballgame, the Governor's Inn offers a short walk home after the ballgame and a wonderful little second-floor balcony where you can watch Edenton's nightlife unfold. This balcony is also the best place in town for a quiet post-game beer (since you won't find one at the ballpark), and you'd be hard pressed to find anyplace open in downtown by the time the game ends, other than the Short Stop convenience store or maybe Waterman's.

The ballpark is a block over from the main road. If you see John A. Holmes High School, you're about to miss it. Like many of North Carolina's small-town ballyards, Hicks Field also serves as the high school's home field. Unlike many of these parks, this one was in place long before the high school was ever built. There can be no doubt, though, that it was the high school's proximity and their use of the playing surface that kept Hicks Field alive.

Originally, Hicks Field served as the home to a successful semi-pro team in the Albemarle League, known as the Colonials and led by the hard-drinking "Gashouse" Parker. Their success in the semi-pro ranks led Edenton to step up into minor-league baseball, first as a member of the Virginia League in 1951 and then as a member of the original Coastal Plain League in 1952. The Edenton Colonials had the good fortune to win the CPL championship in 1952, but had the bad luck of joining the league for what would be its final season.

These two seasons in affiliated ball weren't Edenton's only brush with organized pro ball, though. During the 1940s and 1950s Hicks Field also served as the

spring-training home for Double-A and Triple-A teams and hosted a number of exhibition games, including one during World War II featuring Hall of Famer Bob Feller, who was playing for the Norfolk Naval Yard team while serving in the military.

In addition, a black team, known as the Quick Steps, called Edenton home and barnstormed from South Carolina to New York, complete with its own musical band.

After the departure of the Coastal Plain League team the park continued to host baseball, including a short-lived re-creation of the Albemarle League, as well as American Legion and high school ball. Unfortunately, the simple little wood grandstand proved difficult to maintain, and by 1997, only the lower four rows of seating were safe for spectators. The remainder of the grandstand had been fenced

Dusk at Hicks Field.
Photo by Bill Miller.

Youngsters accompany Steamers players for the game introduction.
Photo courtesy of Edenton Steamers Baseball.

off with chain link, and the place was literally falling to pieces. County Manager
Cliff Copeland maintains that the only reason the park is still standing is that "we
didn't have the money to tear it down."

It was that fall, with the first season of the new Coastal Plain League in the books,
that league president Pete Bock and Outer Banks Dare Devils owner Blake Cullen
decided to meet somewhere between Norfolk and Raleigh to discuss some financial
matters. They hit on the idea of Edenton as a good meeting point, with Bock
holding a vague notion of seeing what he was told was an old ballpark in town.

During their meeting at a downtown restaurant, someone overhead the baseball
talk and told Bock and Cullen that Edenton was a great baseball town. Before long,
someone from the restaurant had fetched Copeland, the county manager, who had
been searching for added activities for the community, both for tourism and as a
quality-of-life enhancement.

After several subsequent meetings, the Coastal Plain League announced that it was
placing an expansion franchise in Edenton for the 1998 season. Chowan County,
the City of Edenton, and the local school system teamed to share the cost of a
$300,000 historically accurate renovation of Hicks Field. The Steamers were born
and, from the start, it was a community enterprise. As with most college summer
teams, local families hosted the players for the summer. The teams dressed and
showered in the high-school locker rooms next door. Much of the concessions
cooking is still done in the cafeteria kitchen, but don't worry, this isn't cafeteria fare
– don't miss the Steamer Plate, featuring (what else?) steamed clams.

Alcohol is not served, initially due to legal hurdles involving the proximity to the school and later by choice. After two very successful years as a league-owned team, the Steamers were purchased by the Edenton-Chowan Community Foundation and became the Green Bay Packers of the CPL. As a community-owned club, all proceeds from the team's operations go into youth sports in the area. This has no doubt helped maintain the community's enthusiasm for the team and is reflected by the number of game workers who are volunteers.

The ballpark itself is squeezed into a snug footprint, land donated in 1723 by one Robert Hicks for a public common. The main grandstand behind home plate is roofed and faces straight out to centerfield, holding about 400 fans. A small press box at the top of the grandstand was added during the most recent renovation, but it blends right into the original park, as does the office added behind the grandstand. The renovation also included the addition of a pair of open-air bleachers built to match the style of the main grandstand and a small concessions stand down the first base line.

This marvelous throw-back atmosphere is capped off by a wooden plank perimeter fence rebuilt using the same concrete posts outlining the park since 1939, with a huge manual scoreboard looming over the right-field wall, like an inverted image of Fenway's Green Monster. Some young fans chase home-run balls on the access road behind the short left-field fence, and it's one of the few parks where you will in fact see "knothole kids" peering through the outfield wall for a peek at the game.

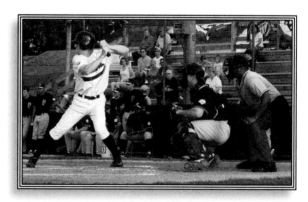

Alex Pascual bats lead-off in a June 2006 game against Peninsula Pilots for the then two-time defending CPL champion Steamers.
Photo courtesy of Edenton Steamers Baseball.

Although the remote location may lead you to consider skipping Edenton, you won't regret making this trip. The community spirit, the historic beauty of the town, and the friendly confines of Hicks Field make this one a must-see.

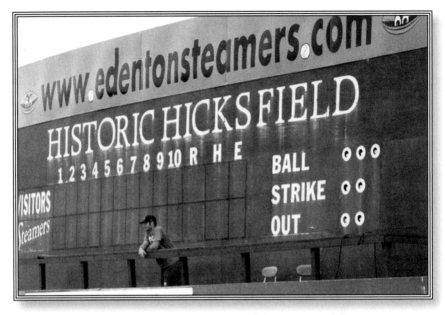

Historic Hicks Field features a manual scoreboard in right field. *Photo courtesy of Edenton Steamers Baseball.*

⚾ Insider's Tip

Hicks Field has a small grandstand and backstop — and there's not much to stop a foul ball, particularly if you're sitting in the bleachers. If you plan on soaking up the atmosphere and doing some people-watching, I'd recommend sitting behind the backstop netting. By the same token, you'll be well advised to park your car a few blocks away from the ballpark or, better yet, walk.

Sports Around Town

While "Gashouse" Parker is remembered as the leading figure in Edenton's minor-league and semi-pro baseball history, nearby Hertford was home to Hall of Famer Jim "Catfish" Hunter. Known locally as Jimmy, Hunter played youth and high school baseball at Hicks Field before becoming a Major League star with Charlie Finley's A's. (The nickname "Catfish" was actually one of Finley's fabrications, designed to make the unassuming Hunter seem more colorful to the baseball media and fans.) In a career that included time with the Kansas City A's, Oakland A's, and the New York Yankees between 1965 and 1979, Hunter won 224 games and five World Series rings while being named to eight All-Star teams and winning the 1974 AL Cy Young Award.

Hunter is also regarded as the first of the big-money free agents in baseball. He accepted a multiyear deal from the Yankees that totaled over $1 million, a paltry sum by today's standards.

Hunter is remembered fondly in northeastern North Carolina, and while he died of Lou Gehrig's disease in 1999 when the Steamers were barely two years old, the Hunter family is nonetheless connected to current CPL team. Jim's son Todd served several years as the Steamers GM and only fulltime employee, and he helped establish the team's strong connection to the community.

Where to Eat

For anything from a quick lunch to a nice dinner with a bottle of wine, you can't go wrong at Waterman's Grill. Owned by Steamers President Katy Ebersole, Waterman's is one of the only places in town that serves beer and wine. The atmosphere is absolutely Edenton; exposed brick and hardwood floors, seafaring knick-knacks, and friendly service make this my favorite place in town.

As a youth, Jimmy Hunter often played at Hicks Field long before he entered the Hall of Fame. This Catfish Hunter display can be found at the North Carolina Baseball Museum in Wilson.

Waterman's Grill
427 S. Broad St.
252/482-7733

Just a few doors down from the movie theater, the hardware store, and the barber, Snooker's is another little piece of a vibrant downtown. Edenton fought off Wal-Mart's efforts to build a superstore in the area a few years back, and their downtown is a testament to the thriving local economy. Snooker's is your place for a burger or a sandwich.

Snooker's
204 S. Broad St.
252/482-7517

Forget your toothbrush? Stop by Mitchener's and grab a sandwich, too. The simple menu includes grilled cheese, ham sandwiches, sodas, and chips. It's not gourmet, but if you want a quick snack and a taste of a bygone era, a meal at this old-time lunch counter will take you back.

Mitchener's Drug Store
301 S. Broad Street
252/482-3711

Where to Stay

If you go to Edenton and don't stay in one of the town's many cozy historic
inns, you are missing a wonderful opportunity to enjoy the unique charms of this
community. There are more lodging choices on **visitedenton.com**, but these are my
favorites.

Just a short walk from both downtown and the ballpark, the charming Governor
Eden Inn bed & breakfast features an imposing entry framed by pillars that bring
to mind Tara. The second-floor balcony looks out over Broad Street and offers the
perfect place to finish off a day of sightseeing and baseball. With private rooms
and baths, a delicious breakfast, and a friendly atmosphere, this inn is also located
just two blocks from the Historic Edenton Visitor Center.

Governor Eden Inn
304 N. Broad St.
Edenton, NC 27932
800/348-8933, 252/482-2072

If you long to be near the waterfront, this is your place. Just three blocks from
the sound, this is another beautifully renovated historic home. As with most bed
& breakfasts, the personal touch of the owner/managers will provide you with a
memorable stay.

Captain's Quarters Inn
202 W. Queen St.
Edenton, NC 27932
800/482-8945, 252/482-8945

If the inns are all full, or if you just have to have the amenities of a chain
hotel, you'll like the Hampton Inn. This is the area's newest property and offers
predictable quality.

Hampton Inn Edenton
115 Hampton Dr.
Edenton, NC 27932
252/482-3500
hilton.com

What to Do

You can spend all day enjoying Edenton's restored historic 18th- and 19th-century
homes and buildings. Edenton's boosters say that their historic district surpasses
Williamsburg, Virginia because the homes and buildings of Edenton are original,
not reconstructed. Nearly thirty different homes and public buildings comprise the

North Carolina State Historic Site, and the waterfront is also a favorite spot for walking tours.

Guided walking and trolley tours available. Visitor Center features exhibits, gift shop, maps, and a short presentation on the history of Edenton.

The Visitor Center is open year round. Call for up-to-date operating hours and tour prices.

Historic Edenton State Historic Site
108 N. Broad St.
252-482-2637

For more information on lodging, dining, and attractions in Edenton, visit visitedenton.com.

Directions

From East and West:

Take Route 64 East to Williamston. Follow signs for Routes 13 and 17 North. In Windsor, Routes 13 and 17 will split. Stay on Route 17 North. After crossing the bridge over the Chowan River, follow signs for Route 17 Business and take Route 17 Business into Edenton. Turn left onto Broad Street and go five blocks and turn right onto Freemason Street (there will be a barbershop on the corner). Hicks Field is one block ahead on your left.

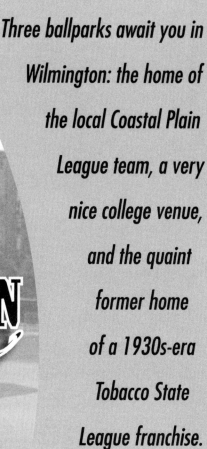

WILMINGTON

Three ballparks await you in Wilmington: the home of the local Coastal Plain League team, a very nice college venue, and the quaint former home of a 1930s-era Tobacco State League franchise.

CHAPTER 24

BUCK HARDEE FIELD AT LEGION STADIUM

Leading Off

Capacity: Approximately 6,000, including 3,500 in the grandstand

Dimensions: 336L, 366C, 339R

Current Team: Wilmington Sharks, Coastal Plain League (1997-present)

ESSENTIALS

Address: 2149 Carolina Beach Rd., Wilmington
Website: wilmingtonsharks.com
Phone Number: 910/343-5621
Ticket Prices: $4-$8

Cozy Up with the Sharks

Let's party! That's the mood at Buck Hardee Field, a tiny American Legion ballpark converted into a tiki-bar kind of ballpark. There's certainly no shortage of kids running around and the atmosphere is very family-friendly, but head down to the beer garden past the first-base bleachers and it's time to kick back.

Recent renovations have made a world of difference in Wilmington, where the team's first year saw the front-office staff working out of a 350-square-foot construction trailer and a stadium concourse that was more sand than concrete. Parking was an adventure, as the potholes threatened to swallow anything smaller than a midsize sedan.

Now there's a sea of level parking with islands and curbs. Large, modern restrooms and a new concession stand offer amenities that Sharks fans could only dream of during the team's first few seasons.

Wilmington's recent history with professional baseball can best be described as star-crossed, but the city's first team dates back to 1901, the first year modern professional baseball was played in the state. With franchises off and on over the intervening decades, Wilmington was without pro baseball from 1950 until the mid-1990s.

The Southern League was hunting for a home field for a franchise displaced by expansion, and a planned move to Puerto Rico was voted down. Wilmington seemed like a promising alternative, as Mudcats owner Steve Bryant agreed to run the Southern League's "orphaned" franchise, christened the Port City Roosters, for the '95 and '96 seasons. If the Roosters were successful, Bryant had plans to acquire a Sally League team for Wilmington.

The Roosters played their home games at Brooks Field on the campus of UNC Wilmington with no beer sales, inconvenient parking, and a location hidden away in the midst of campus. A few notable players took the field for the Roosters, though. Future Red Sox World Series heroes Jason Varitek and Derek Lowe both played for what was then a Seattle Mariners' Double-A team during the 1996 season.

Roosters 1995 inaugural season program

The Roosters eventually found a permanent perch in Mobile, Ala., and a new name, the BayBears, beginning in 1997, when a new ballpark was opened. It seemed unlikely that Wilmington would see any type of high-level baseball outside of the UNCW Seahawks, the university's Division I team. Wilmington was being courted again, though, as the Coastal Plain League began moving from the drawing board to reality.

Although frustrated by their unsuccessful efforts to secure a lease for Brooks Field, league officials were directed to Buck Hardee Field by a former Roosters staffer. Despite a minimal grandstand, tiny bathrooms and concessions, and the city's initial reluctance to allow the CPL to sell beer, a lease was quickly secured, and the Sharks were born.

Improvements were made year by year, and the team became one of the CPL's cornerstone franchises. A large set of bleachers that had stood near the battleship USS Wilmington (see "Attractions") was moved to Buck Hardee, adding over 1,000 seats. Beer sales were allowed after that first year, and the beer-garden area beyond the first-base dugout became the park's hot spot. The crowds grew each season.

Eventually, though, that success attracted the attention of the South Atlantic League when one of their planned expansion cities fell through at the 11th hour. In what could have been dubbed "Port City Roosters II, the Sequel," a Dodgers' Single-A affiliate – the Wilmington Waves – was dropped into Brooks Field for a disastrous one-year run in 2001. Disastrous not just because of the team's dismal attendance, but because of the suffering inflicted on the Sharks. While the Roosters had been a failure, they at least had the market to themselves. When the Sharks refused to be pushed aside, Wilmington area fans enjoyed an abundance of baseball, but both teams suffered as advertising and fan dollars were split.

In time, the Waves packed up and bolted for Albany, Ga. just weeks before the beginning of the 2002 season. They pulled the same stunt in Albany, departing for Columbus, Ga. in spring 2003, where they are now known as the Columbus Catfish. Despite the difficulties that these minor-league teams have had in Wilmington, UNCW has been the real winner, as they've left behind hundreds of thousands of dollars in improvements, including new box seats, expanded bleacher seating, improved lighting, and upgraded clubhouses.

The Sharks, in the meantime, hung tough and emerged in 2003 as the only game in town once again. It was also around this same time that the major renovations to Buck Hardee were completed, providing Port City fans a much-enhanced fan experience.

Wilmington Sharks logo

When locating Buck Hardee Field, you need to know that it is part of a complex most commonly referred to by locals as Legion Stadium, although that is actually the name of the city football stadium that stands between the main road and the baseball field. There's also a municipal pool, but the football stadium stands out. It's a big concrete grandstand that underwent a dazzling overhaul just prior to the improvements at Buck Hardee Field. Legion Stadium used to host most of the city's high-school football games, but as the schools began to construct their own on-campus facilities it has become home to a variety of other events, including the Wilmington Hammerheads semi-pro soccer team. The baseball field is also the home of New Hanover High School and has housed the city's American Legion baseball team for many years. The baseball field is named after Buck Hardee, a legendary New Hanover High School coach who led the Wildcats to 13 conference championships.

The football and baseball fields share parking, as well as some locker space located behind the outfield wall between the two fields. Behind the home-run fence is also another of Buck Hardee's landmarks: team offices located in the second story of a former concessions and storage building.

Today, the Sharks continue to offer Wilmington area sports fans their only chance to see baseball with a cold beer and the full complement of minor-league fun and games. The park is cozy and lively, and with just a little imagination you can likely visualize it like it was when there was just a playing surface, lights, and the tiny grandstand. For the ballpark buff, the combination of this park, Brooks Field (see below), and another former minor-league park (see Godwin Field, further below), wrapped up with some of the finest beaches along the East Coast, make this a mandatory stop for any baseball trip through eastern North Carolina.

ⓘ Insider's Trivia

In the 1999 CPL All-Star Game, a light-hitting and unheralded catcher named Kevin Youkilis was added to the East Division's roster only after another catcher was injured. He proceeded to hit the game's decisive home run, which bounced off the roof of the team's little office building behind the centerfield wall. The game was broadcast on HTS (the Orioles' cable flagship and the predecessor to Comcast) and the announcers for the game famously (in CPL circles, at least) repeatedly referred to Youkilis' shot off "the toolshed in centerfield." Youkilis, later made famous in the book Moneyball as the "Greek God of Walks," was named the game's MVP and the rest, as they say, is history.

Sports Around Town

As explained in greater detail below, Wilmington, or the "Port City," has unsuccessfully hosted two minor-league baseball teams in recent years, in addition to the city's current team, the Wilmington Sharks of the CPL. The other major spectator-sports operation in town is the University of North Carolina-Wilmington, which features Division I competition in sports including baseball and basketball, but not football. The Seahawks basketball teams have had great success in recent years, even reaching the NCAA Tournament in 2002, 2003, and 2006.

Wilmington's most notable native sons are former NFL star quarterbacks Roman Gabriel and Sonny Jurgenson, both of whom played for New Hanover High School in the football stadium adjacent to Buck Hardee Field.

BROOKS FIELD

Leading Off

Opened: 1994

Capacity: 3,000

Dimensions: 340L, 360LC, 380C, 360RC, 340R

Current Team: UNC-Wilmington Seahawks (NCAA Division I, Colonial Athletic Conference)

Previous Teams: Port City Roosters, Southern League (1995-1996),
Wilmington Waves, South Atlantic League (2001)

ESSENTIALS

Address: Riegel Road off of Price Drive, Wilmington
Website: UNCWsports.com
Phone: 910/910-962-7536 or 800/808-UNCW
Ticket Prices: $5 Adult, 12 and under free

Soaring with the Seahawks

Home of the University of North Carolina-Wilmington's Seahawks, this facility boasts a high-quality playing surface, Triple-A-caliber lighting, and a raised concrete grandstand with a section of club seats at ground level. These club seats were among the improvements made by the Mudcats ownership during Brooks Field's two-year stint as a Double-A facility. A host of other improvements, including permanent bleachers, a picnic deck, and dugout upgrades were the legacy of the ill-fated Wilmington Waves.

The field is named after William J. Brooks, the former head coach and athletic director at the school. The Seahawks compete in the Colonial Athletic Conference, which has ranked as high as fourth in the Division I end-of-season RPI rankings in recent years.

Brooks Field is an excellent college facility, and with a concrete grandstand and three-story press box building, it's easy to see why minor-league teams have been attracted to playing here. It looks like a minor-league park, although one of 1980s vintage. Parking can be a challenge, as it is on most campuses, and you have to wind your way through a few turns and stoplights along the way. And watch the speed bumps; they'll tear out your rear axle if you're not expecting them.

Unfortunately, this is a two-team town where it's never possible to see both clubs play during the same trip, since the college season and the CPL season do not overlap. If you're in Wilmington, though, Brooks Field is worth a visit, if simply for its unusual history.

Brooks Field at the University of North Carolina-Wilmington. *Photo courtesy of the University of North Carolina-Wilmington.*

For schedule information, visit **www.uncwil.edu/athletics/Baseball.htm**.

Godwin Field

Opened: 1949

Previous Teams: Wilmington Pirates, 1949-1950 (Tobacco State League)

On the Seaport, Where the Pirates Roamed

This ballpark once hosted the Wilmington Pirates, members of the Class-D Tobacco State League during the 1949 and 1950 season. The Pirates had previously played at the Legion Stadium complex. Today, the park hosts some men's adult baseball and is managed by the city's recreation department. Located on S. 41st Street off of Shipyard Boulevard, the ballpark has a basic cinderblock grandstand seating approximately 400. There's no roof, but a small press box sits atop the grandstand, and the seating bowl is entered via a tunnel. This facility was considered, although briefly, when the CPL was getting started. It was deemed to have inadequate lighting, and the outfield distances are very short. There's not much to it, but it's a neat little park, and so close to Legion Stadium that it's worth checking out before a game.

Wilmington Attractions

BATTLESHIP NORTH CAROLINA

In addition to its roles as the official North Carolina memorial to World War II and an authentically restored battleship, the attraction is a museum with a large and diverse collection of artifacts. The battleship tour begins in the Visitors Center with an orientation film taking you through the wartime history of the ship, with a few exhibits on view before you go onboard. Portions of nine decks are open where you can enter gun turrets, inspect the bridge, view officer's and crew's quarters, sick bay, engine room, and more.

Battleship North Carolina
#1 Battleship Rd.
910/251-5797
battleshipnc.com

FORT FISHER AQUARIUM

The Fort Fisher Aquarium includes indoor and outdoor exhibits, auditorium, classrooms, meeting rooms, and a gift shop. In addition, there are daily programs featuring live animals, marine life videos, and special activities. Located along U.S. 421 just south of Kure Beach, N.C.

North Carolina Aquarium at Fort Fischer
900 Loggerhead Rd.
Kure Beach, NC
910/458-8257 or 866/301-3476
ncaquariums.com

HISTORIC DOWNTOWN WILMINGTON

The historic area is situated right across the water at the mouth of the river opposite the Battleship North Carolina. This is the area where *Dawson's Creek* (where it stood in for a fictitious Massachusetts coastal town) and *One Tree Hill* television series were filmed. Serving as the cultural center for the region, downtown Wilmington houses major arts and cultural facilities, such as Thalian Hall Center for the Performing Arts, along with many private art galleries. An attractive riverfront park functions as a focal point for downtown activities, serving as a popular gathering place for daily lunches and conversation breaks, as well as the main stage for outdoor entertainment events throughout the year.

ALONG THE CAPE FEAR SHORELINE: WRIGHTSVILLE, CAROLINA & KURE BEACHES

Situated closest to Wilmington is the first of two Cape Fear islands: Wrightsville Beach. A clean and uncluttered five-mile stretch of white sand and sparkling water invites a day of beachcombing, swimming, sunbathing, surfing, and pier or surf fishing. A little further down the coast you will find two Pleasure Island beach communities: the larger Carolina Beach and Kure Beach. home to Fort Fisher Aquarium. For more information about Cape Fear attractions, visit cape-fear.nc.us.

Lodging

In the middle of Wrightsville Beach, opening onto views of the ocean, this seven-story Blockade Runner Resort Hotel & Conference Center is far superior to the lackluster string of motels along Lumina Avenue. Guest rooms are comfortably and attractively furnished, and often have private patios. Normally a hurricane is a bad occurrence, but the East

Restaurant seems to have rebounded from recent hurricanes to become better than ever, luring the former sous chef of the Harvard Club in Manhattan, Thomas Sullivan. The SeaEscape beach bar offers drinks in a poolside setting, complete with beach volleyball and a new beachfront dining patio. Facilities include the restaurant, two bars and lounge, pool, exercise room, Jacuzzi, sauna, limited room service, massage, babysitting, nonsmoking rooms, and rooms for those with limited mobility.

Blockade Runner Resort Hotel & Conference Center
275 Waynick Blvd.
Wilmington, NC 28480
800/541-1161, 910/256-2251
blockade-runner.com

Built more than a century ago as a commercial building, the Wilmingtonian is more of a glorified B&B in which all the rooms are suites. Accommodations on the second and third floors have balconies. All suites contain kitchenettes. A small library is located near the front desk, and an intimate on-site pub offers beer and wine.

The Wilmingtonian
101 S. 2nd St.
Wilmington, NC 28401
800/525-0909, 910/343-1800
thewilmingtonian.com

You'll find a number of chain hotels Market Street near I-40, not very close to both the historic downtown and the ocean resorts. One alternative, the Jameson Inn, is a newer hotel convenient to the ballpark and downtown, yet typically available at a value price.

Jameson Inn
5120 Dunlea Ct.
Wilmington, NC 28405
910/452-5660
jamesoninns.com

 **Directions**

To Buck Hardee Field From the West:

Take I-40 East to Wilmington. As you get into Wilmington, I-40 ends and the road becomes South College Road. Continue south, bear right on Shipyard Blvd. just before the Hardees (follow sign for "State Port"). Turn right onto Carolina Beach Road at the McDonald's. Turn right onto Stadium Drive; Buck Hardee Field is on the right just beyond the football facility, Legion Stadium.

To Brooks Field Via I-40:

I-40 becomes US 132/S. College Road once the Interstate ends. Continue traveling south on College Road approximately 3 miles. Turn left onto Randall Drive at the traffic light. You are now on the UNCW campus. Take your first right onto Wagoner Drive. When Wagoner Drive ends, turn left onto Hurst Drive. Turn left at the traffic light onto Hamilton Drive. Travel approximately ¼ mile and turn right onto Riegel Road. Brooks Field is approximately ¼ mile on right.

To Godwin Field Via I-40:

Take I-40 East to Wilmington. As you get into Wilmington, I-40 ends and the road becomes South College Road. Continue south, bear right on Shipyard Blvd. just before the Hardee's (follow sign for "State Port"). Continue on Shipyard Blvd., then turn right onto S. 41st St. until you see the ballpark on your right.

GREENVILLE

Greenville is best known as the home of East Carolina University, and a renovated Clark-LeClair Stadium is one of North Carolina's college-baseball showcases after an $11 million renovation. Combine a Pirates game with a visit to a quaint WPA-era ballpark formerly housing Class D ball: Guy Smith Stadium.

CHAPTER 25

Clark-LeClair Stadium

Leading Off

Opened: 1971; renovated 2005

Capacity: 5,000

Dimensions: 320L, 390C, 320R

Current Team: East Carolina University Pirates (NCAA Division I, Conference USA)

Elite Ballpark for the NCAA Elite

Fans of the ECU Pirates proudly point out that they finally have a facility worthy of their program's recent accomplishments. After all, this is a program with a string of seven straight NCAA appearances between 1999 and 2005 (with a return in 2007) playing in a conference ranking in the top half dozen in the country. Since 1998, the Pirates have captured back-to-back Colonial Athletic Conference championships, a championship in Conference USA (which they joined in 2001), and advanced to two NCAA Super Regional appearances since 2000.

The current ballpark, with a concrete and brick grandstand seating 3,000 people, was a sorely needed upgrade. Clark-LeClair was built on the same site as the Pirates' former home, Harrington Field, and utilizes the same playing field. Harrington consisted of a 2,000-seat collection of aluminum bleachers with minimal amenities, including a single tiny concessions stand, two small ticket windows, and not a seat back in sight.

The fundraising campaign to finance this facility was launched years ago, and the promise of a new stadium had been dangled before recruits who are long gone. But, in a very broad-based effort that included over 150 donors who contributed $10,000 or more (including homebuilder Bill Clark's donation of $1.5 million), the ECU athletic department was able to raise $11 million, and the end product has proved worth the wait.

The stadium is named in part for Clark, while the other stadium namesake is former Pirate head coach Keith LeClair, who died July 17, 2006 after a heroic five-

year battle with ALS, better known as Lou Gehrig's disease. As head coach from 1997 to 2002, LeClair was instrumental in promoting the new facility off the field, and he initiated an era of success unprecedented in ECU's NCAA history. Fittingly, the new stadium was inaugurated March 4, 2005 with the opening game of the second annual Keith LeClair Classic, where ECU defeated Michigan, 2-1.

The centerpiece of the new facility is the state-of-the-art press box with separate booths for two radio broadcasters, TV, and writers, as well as stadium operations. A hospitality suite for fans and donors is known as the Pirate Club. Other amenities include the full array of indoor and outdoor batting cages, coaches' offices, and a spacious clubhouse and players lounge. The reworked playing surface features Celebration Bermuda infield turf over a clay base with crushed-brick warning track. A new lighting system meets specification for televised night baseball.

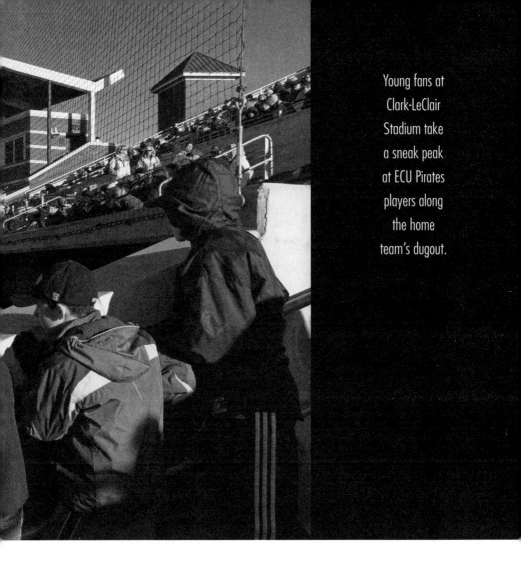

Young fans at Clark-LeClair Stadium take a sneak peak at ECU Pirates players along the home team's dugout.

The new ballpark has several unique architectural elements, including a break between the center section of the grandstand and the third-base side seats that brings to mind the notch in Cincinnati's Great American Ball Park. The gap will feel familiar to regulars of the old ballpark.

The re-creation of the outfield spectator areas was a sensitive issue, and the Pirates seem to have made most of their fans happy with the end product. Like all college baseball venues in North Carolina, you couldn't buy a beer here. But at Harrington Field, you were able to drink a beer. For most fans, this was the only redeeming feature of the former facility. The tailgating area amongst the trees beyond the left and center field fence was nicknamed "The Jungle," in honor of the greenery and the savage treatment offered up to visiting outfielders and relief pitchers. Here, fans paid to park and then watch the game in what was technically only a parking area located behind the left-field fence. Much like a drive-in movie, you could bring in as many people and as much food and drink as you cared to load into the car.

Despite the fears of many Jungle regulars, this feature was retained, although in a somewhat kinder, gentler version. The pine trees are gone, but there's a new grass berm that runs all the way around the outfield with some new oak trees planted around the perimeter. It will take awhile before these trees provide enough cover to justify calling this area "The Jungle," but the berm is a definite upgrade. Previously, you had to stand on tiptoes or scrounge up a crate to see any of the game if you weren't standing right up against the fence.

Most importantly to Jungle regulars, the policy on alcohol has remained basically unchanged; you can tailgate in the parking area behind the Jungle, but a white fence separates the parking from the backside of the berm, and no alcohol is allowed beyond that point. Certainly the atmosphere is a little different, as the cover of the old pine trees and a small makeshift seating area with the Jolly Roger flying above it had given the Jungle a kind of renegade atmosphere. But the new Jungle is certainly more comfortable and can accommodate many more people, and to the great relief of the Pirate faithful, the all-important element of adult refreshment is still allowed.

The exterior design of Clark-LeClair Stadium is imposing and unique.

Wide concourses and impressive amenities are featured at Clark-LeClair.

The fans are responding to this great new facility. Announced attendance has topped 5,000 three times, including one game in May 2007 when a crowd of 5,076 watched the Pirates drop a 5-1 game to in-state rival UNC.

You should come to this ballpark with a big appetite. The main concession stand is nearly as impressive as the rest of the facility, featuring more than a dozen reasonably priced items. At the low end, you can choose between sunflower seeds and blow pops for only 50 cents, or go top-line with the newly added Philly cheese steak at $6. Fry bread at $4 is a popular item, and the generous portion of tasty thick-cut fries is a bargain at just $2.

It was no secret that part of the rationale for constructing a first-class ballpark at ECU was to help fulfill Coach LeClair's oft-stated goal of reaching the College World Series in Omaha. ECU claimed the NAIA national championship in 1961 and has achieved a winning record in 54 of its 56 seasons. Despite playing in a very tough conference with a grueling travel schedule and the perceived lack of respect from their ACC neighbors, ECU's proud baseball history combined with this fine new facility will undoubtedly bring many NCAA Regionals to Clark-LeClair. This is a program still doggedly pursuing Coach LeClair's dream: Omaha.

⚾ **Insider's Tip**

The sight lines in this ballpark are excellent, but the sun can pose problems at certain times of the day. The earliest plans for the stadium renovation included a reorientation of the entire facility that would have put home plate in what is now the left-field corner. In the end, though, it was more cost-effective to keep home plate in the same spot. With the current configuration, the scoreboard didn't have to be moved and it wasn't necessary to completely rebuild and regrade the playing field. The result of this is that the late-day sun down the left-field line can present problems for the spectators on the first-base side of the grandstand. This factor, combined with the layout of the locker rooms, players lounge, and coaches offices underneath the grandstand, led the Pirates to abandon the first-base dugout that they had normally used in the old park for the third-base side. You'll want to do the same.

Unless, of course, you decide to visit The Jungle, which I highly recommend. Pull into the entrance closest to the left-field corner of the ballpark and turn left. Pay the general admission price ($6 adult, $3 12-and-under) to park, bring your cooler and your picnic basket, and enjoy baseball the way it was meant to be enjoyed — with a cold beer. Now, if only we could do something about those aluminum bats....

Author's Note

While the Pirates had great success in baseball, including an NAIA national championship, their recent history marks the program's high-water mark. The string of seven straight NCAA Tournament appearances (eight total) and two Super Regional appearances in that span included a record-breaking season in 2004. The Pirate squad that year featured seven players who would go on to sign professional contracts, including Greg Bunn.

Perhaps no player from the LeClair era better epitomized the Pirate program better than Bunn. A Raleigh native, Bunn was overlooked by the ACC teams in his backyard. Like many of his teammates, he went to ECU with something to prove. After excelling as ECU's closer, he became the Pirates' Friday night starter in his junior year. Bunn earned Conference USA Pitcher of the Year honors while leading his team to the school's first 50-win season and was drafted in the fifth round by the then-Montreal Expos on the day he pitched ECU into a Super Regional.

He's also notable, to me at least, because he also happens to be my wife's little brother. I had the pleasure of watching him play in Greenville a number of times, although Harrington Field was certainly not a pleasure. I was also in the ballpark on nights when he completely baffled high-school hitters with his curveball, including the game where he struck out 15 straight batters in an American Legion game. His father, Earl Bunn, was also a pitcher of some note who still holds nearly all the single-season and career records at Division III Methodist College in Fayetteville, North Carolina. A 6-1 righthander, Bunn currently pitches in the Washington Nationals minor-league system and is a fine uncle to his nephews Sam and Ty.

Sports Around Town

There are really only two games in town, and both are purple and gold. ECU's most successful program is certainly baseball, but Greenville loves its football too. Check out Dowdy-Ficklen Stadium, just a stone's throw from Clark-LeClair. After a major expansion project in 1998-99 the football Pirates' home reached a capacity of 43,000. That may not seem like much compared with the Big House in Ann Arbor or Neyland Stadium in Knoxville, but for a town of less than 70,000 people it's a pretty big deal.

The football program has seen some great days, and the most significant to their fan base are the wins against the North Carolina ACC teams, which feature prominently in any write-up of the school's athletic history. Former Coach Steve Logan ran a wide-open offense that produced Jacksonville Jaguars quarterback David Garrard, but a few disappointing seasons cost Logan his job. After hitting rock bottom under John Thompson, Skip Holtz (Lou's boy) seems to have righted the Pirate ship, guiding ECU to a winning season and a bowl appearance in just his second year.

GUY SMITH STADIUM

Leading Off

Opened: 1939

Capacity: 1,200

Former Teams: Greenville Greenies, 1939-1941, 1946-1949 (Coastal Plain League); Greenville Robins, 1950-1951 (Coastal Plain League)

Echoes of Class D Ball at Guy Smith Stadium

While there hasn't been a minor-league team in Guy Smith Stadium in decades, one only needs to sit in the cozy brick grandstand to imagine the sights and sounds of a Class D game in 1939, the year the park opened. Built as a WPA project for the Greenville Greenies of the Class D Coastal Plain League, not much has changed in this ballyard. There is wooden bench seating with back and arm rests throughout the grandstand. With a capacity of approximately 1,200 and small concessions stands and locker rooms tucked up underneath, this park would require some additional seating and fan amenities to be suitable for any type of higher-level baseball. But it's beautifully maintained and, if you're a ballpark nut, you won't want to miss it.

Greenville is a baseball town, as evidenced by ECU's new ballpark. Pitt County Community College has a baseball program that is quickly gaining stature. Greenville Rose High School is a powerhouse in North Carolina prep baseball, and the local Little League team made it to the Little League World Series just a few years back.

Despite the popularity of baseball in Eastern North Carolina in general and Greenville in particular, professional baseball departed the city after the 1951 Coastal Plain League season and has never returned. Professional baseball was first played in Greenville in 1928 and 1929 when the Greenville Tobacconists were members of the Eastern Carolina League, but the remainder of Greenville's professional baseball history was spent in the Coastal Plain League.

Exterior view of Guy Smith Stadium. Photo courtesy of Dennis Bastien.

In recent years, attempts to bring collegiate summer baseball to Guy Smith Stadium have proved unsuccessful. There was also an effort to place a team in Guy Smith by the new independent South Coast League, but with Greenville's commitment to their Babe Ruth youth baseball program, this has not worked out. For the serious baseball, this is unfortunate.

Lodging

Greenville is set apart from the main population centers in the middle of North Carolina, while still a journey if you're heading east for the ocean beaches. If you plan to stay a night, you'll usually find a nice room at a good value. Here are some options.

City Hotel & Bistro
203 W. Greenville Blvd.
Greenville, NC 27834
252/355-8300
cityhotelandbistro.com

Wingate by Wyndham -- Greenville
3212 S. Memorial Dr.
Greenville, NC 27834
252/355-4283
wingateinns.com

 **Directions**

To Clark-LeClair Stadium From the Triangle:

Take U.S. 64 from Raleigh heading east. Take U.S. 264 in Zebulon and head east past Wilson and into Greenville. Take U.S. 264 to Allen Road and turn right. Allen Road turns into Greenville Boulevard. Take Greenville Boulevard to Charles Boulevard and take a left (the ECU message board is on the corner). Take Charles Boulevard one block and locate parking wherever open lots are available on either side of Charles (the ballpark is located on the right).

To Guy Smith Stadium:

When entering Greenville, 264 East becomes Stantonsburg Road. Immediately after Pitt County Memorial Hospital, turn right on Moye Boulevard and continue through the intersection with Route 13. The ballpark will be on your left in a large complex known as Guy Smith Park.

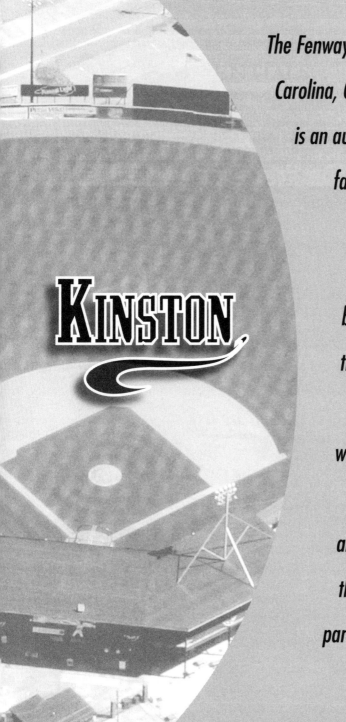

The Fenway Park of North Carolina, Grainger Stadium is an authentic, old-time facility sporting well-planned renovations, bringing fans all the conveniences of a new park without sacrificing the character and atmosphere that make old parks so special.

CHAPTER 26

GRAINGER STADIUM

Leading Off

Opened: 1949

Capacity: 4,100

Dimensions: 335L, 390C, 335R

Current Team: Kinston Indians, Carolina League (1987-present)

Former Teams: Kinston Eagles, 1949-52 (Coastal Plain League); Kinston
Eagles, 1956-73 (Carolina League); Kinston Expos, 1974 (Carolina
League); Kinston Eagles, 1978-81 (Carolina League);
Kinston Blue Jays, 1982-85 (Carolina
League); Kinston Eagles, 1986
(Carolina League)

ESSENTIALS

Address: 400 Grainger Av., Kinston
Website: kinstonindians.com
Phone Number: 252/527-9111 or 800/334-5467
Ticket Prices: Box $7; Reserved $6; Reserved Seniors, Student, Military $3;
General Admission $5; Children 5 and under, free

Authenticity, Enthusiasm Make for a Solid Draw in Kinston

Grainger Stadium is the Fenway of North Carolina ballparks. It's an authentic, old-time facility sporting well-planned renovations, bringing fans all the conveniences of a new park without sacrificing the character and atmosphere that make the old parks so special. In return, the Kinston fans consistently support their hometown team with solid attendance and a rare level of enthusiasm for the game itself.

The Indians have had their high Class-A affiliate in Kinston since 1987 when future Cleveland manager Mike Hargrove guided the first edition of the K-Tribe, and the fans of Kinston have been enjoying winning clubs ever since. The Kinston Indians have qualified for the postseason so regularly that a season without a playoff berth is considered a failure in this flat, sandy part of North Carolina.

During that time, a parade of future big-league stars passed through Kinston, including Jim Thome, Manny Ramirez, Richie Sexson, Bartolo Colon, Julian Tavarez, Charles Nagy, C.C. Sabathia, Albert Belle, and more. This success has been in marked contrast to Kinston's struggles in the 1970s and early 1980s, when the city went several years without baseball and later fielded two nonaffiliated teams. Kinston also spent a year with the Expos that left local fans wondering if they wouldn't have been better off without a team.

Much of the business success of the Kinston Indians over the last 15 years can be traced to the arrival of a new general manager, North Johnson, in 1986. After stints with the Lynn (Mass.) team in the Eastern League and Lynchburg in the Carolina

League, Johnson took over the nonaffiliated Kinston Eagles prior to the 1986 season and watched as the team struggled to a 60-76 record. He also watched as the team's finances staggered under the weight of paying player salaries and a variety of other expenses normally covered by a major-league parent.

That experience, combined with Kinston's remote location and small size, made it clear to Johnson that if the franchise could secure a major-league affiliation they would do everything in their power to keep the parent club happy. Indeed, Kinston management is legendary for going to great lengths in looking after the coaches and players Cleveland has provided. Indians officials have said privately that this approach is what keeps them coming back year after year.

After a 17-year run, Johnson departed Kinston following the 2003 season to take the helm of the Rancho Cucamonga Quakes in the California League, where he won that league's Executive of the Year award in just his second season. Johnson returned to the Carolina League as GM of the Myrtle Beach Pelicans in 2007. The team has retained its focus on keeping the parent club happy under General Manager Shari Massengill, who worked for Johnson for many years. Cleveland, in turn, keeps sending Kinston winning teams.

You can't think of going to a Kinston Indians game without thinking of barbecue…or Bojangles chicken. Ideally, you'll be in town long enough to eat a couple of meals. If not, you'll just have to eat twice.

Grainger Stadium is easily seen from Highway 70 Business, just east of the middle of downtown. (Look for the scrolling marquee with the Bojangles ad on it.) The big parking lot between the ballpark and Business 70 used to be a row of modest homes; they were demolished during the last major ballpark renovation. This set of improvements included a new plaza and concessions stand down the right-field line, as well as expanded restrooms and a great new playground. This was the second major overhaul the park had seen in recent years. The first round of work, completed in 1992, added a new team office and clubhouse building down the left-field line, as well as a spacious new concourse, wrought-iron fencing and gates, a walk-in souvenir stand, and expanded concessions.

⚾ Insider's Tip

You must try some Bojangles chicken if you've not had the pleasure. "Bo's" is very juicy fried chicken with a Cajun seasoning that you can also get sprinkled on your fries. With some Texas Pete's hot sauce added for good measure, it's a little bit of heaven. And at the ballpark, unlike in the restaurants, you can eat your Bo's with beer. The biscuits and sandwiches taste just as good, but aren't quite as messy and fun to eat.

The reason Bojangles is on the menu at Grainger Stadium year after year: The team's primary owner, Cam McRae, is a restaurant tycoon who owns all the Bojangles Chicken and Biscuit restaurants east of I-95 in North Carolina. If you don't get a chance to eat Bojangles at the game, or if you're a purist and just have to have a hot dog, stop by the Bojangles just west of the ballpark on Highway 70. It's always spotless and, as the hometown restaurant of the chain's local franchisee, it often has new items prior to rollout elsewhere in the region.

When you walk up the gentle ramp into the center of the grandstand, you'll see a sparkling emerald playing surface outlined by a cinderblock outfield wall running ever so slightly downhill from left to right. Ads are painted directly onto the wall, making this one of the only parks in the country still using an actual sign painter for much of the outfield advertising.

The grandstand features exposed steel girders supporting a roof covering almost the entire grandstand. The seating bowl is split by a walkway, with a dozen rows of dark green chairback seats above and four rows of box seats below. These are genuine boxes, each marked off from its neighbor by pipe railings and sporting a small engraved plastic sign bearing the name of the ticket holder. Outfitted with plain metal folding chairs, these boxes seem somehow unfinished at first glance, but it's clear that fans enjoy the flexibility of arranging the chairs as they need them, as well as the extra leg and elbow room partially filled boxes allow.

Unfortunately, you won't be able to buy one of these box seats, as they are all sold as season tickets, mostly to local companies. But the reserved seats in the grandstand offer a wonderful, comfortable view of the game. These reserved seats are all new as of 2003. It was late in the 2002 season when a sizable chunk of concrete fell from the underside of the grandstand, narrowly missing a fan. As the park's owner, the City of Kinston faced the prospect of condemning the park and potentially losing professional baseball. To their credit, city officials acted quickly to replace the concrete in the entire seating bowl, retaining the original steel work and roof. When the park reopened in the spring of 2003, the only sign of the work was the newness of the concrete, particularly on the field side of the grandstand where the large swaths of unpainted concrete are at odds with the aged charm of the rest of the facility.

Like Birmingham's Rickwood Field, Grainger Stadium's roof houses two of the park's light towers. The bullpens are down the lines in foul territory.

If you go, definitely have a cold beer — there are lots of places to get one. The food is excellent and varied, but the Bojangles chicken is the highlight (*see Insider's Tip*).

A wide variety of souvenirs is available in a walk-in gift shop just to the third-base side, on the back of the grandstand. This is also a nice place to get a little air conditioning on a steamy summer night.

The playground is all the way down the first-base line, well protected by netting. There's plenty of space for Mom and Dad to sit and watch the game while keeping one eye on the rugrats. This playground is part of the last round of renovations, with a new raised plaza area featuring a full, modern cement-block concessions stand. This space replaced an aging wooden stand and a sea of picnic tables; fans stood on them to get a glimpse of the game.

Kinston is a must-see for any baseball fan traveling to North Carolina. With the ballpark construction boom that has seen new or rebuilt facilities throughout the state, Grainger Stadium, Winston-Salem's Ernie Shore Field, and Burlington

Overhead view of Grainger Stadium in Kinston. *Photo courtesy of the Kinston Indians.*

Athletic Stadium are the only ballparks built prior to 1992 currently hosting professional baseball in North Carolina. With Winston-Salem's Ernie Shore Field going by the wayside in 2009, that will leave Grainger Stadium as the only true Carolina League ballpark left in the Carolina League.

Insider's Tip

You may want to designate a driver at Grainger Stadium; it's one of the few ballparks anywhere that sells beer in a pitcher. The price is good, and you get to keep the pitchers. They make a great souvenir, printed with the K-Tribe's "rawhide" logo on one side and Budweiser on the other.

You may also want to be aware that Thirsty Thursdays in Kinston draw a ton of Marines from Camp Lejeune. There also are lots of students from East Carolina University in nearby Greenville. The atmosphere's friendly, but you may want to leave your protest signs at home.

Sports Around Town

Minor-league baseball is sports in this town. Kinston did produce UNC Tar Heel standout Jerry Stackhouse, who left Chapel Hill after his sophomore year and was the third player selected in the NBA draft in 1995. He's played for the Philadelphia 76ers, the Washington Wizards, the Detroit Pistons, and the Dallas Mavericks.

Stackhouse aside, baseball has been the game in Kinston since the city's first entry into minor-league baseball all the way back in 1908. Through stints in the Virginia League, the (old Class D) Coastal Plain League, and the current run in the Carolina League, minor-league baseball has been a big deal to the people in Kinston.

In addition to the many great Indians players listed in this chapter, there have been some truly notable players even on some of Kinston's worst teams. Ron Blomberg (1968) went on to become the first designated hitter in Major League history, and Jay Schroeder spent the 1982 season in Kinston before quitting to become an NFL quarterback with the Los Angeles Raiders and the Washington Redskins. Other notables include Ron Guidry (1972), Tippy Martinez (1972), Jesse Barfield (1978), Fred McGriff (1982), Cecil Fielder (1984), and Glenallen Hill (1984). With this level of talent streaming through Kinston, it's no wonder that the fans here actually focus on the game, rather than the promotions and contests.

SPORTS AROUND TOWN EXTRA

Stack is a big name, but in certain circles, Jaime Pressly's is much bigger. A former Playboy Playmate who grew up in Kinston, Pressly now stars as Joy Turner in the hit broadcast TV series *My Name is Earl*. Pressly was also rumored to have been romantically linked with current Cleveland Indians star Grady Sizemore when he was an Indians farmhand playing in Kinston.

Local Attractions

I've often combined a game in Kinston with a trip to the beach at North Carolina's "Crystal Coast." Emerald Isle boasts beautiful and unspoiled beaches, while Beaufort offers a charming downtown right on the water. If your schedule allows, it's only about an hour and half drive once you're in Kinston, and its well worth the trip. For more information on the Crystal Coast area, see **crystalcoastnc.org.**

There are some interesting things to do if you stay in Kinston, as well.

Among Kinston's most notable attractions is a state-owned historic site, CSS Neuse Historic Site and Governor Richard Caswell Memorial. This is the burial plot for North Carolina's first elected governor (that's Caswell) and the remains of the Confederate ironclad gunboat (that's the Neuse), scuttled in April 1865 by Confederate troops to prevent approaching Union forces from capturing the newly completed war vessel.

CSS Neuse Historic Site and Governor Richard Caswell Memorial
2612 W. Vernon Av. (Highway 70 Business)
252/522-2091
visitkinston.com/historic.html

Enter the world of the late-1800s firefighter at Caswell No. 1 Fire Station Museum. The Fire Station was built in 1895 after a disastrous fire destroyed much of the downtown Kinston area. A 1922 American LaFrance Pumper is the focus of the museum, along with a collection of helmets, nozzles, ladders, fire extinguishers, and other memorabilia spanning a 100-year period.

Caswell No. 1 Fire Station Museum
118 S. Queen St.
252/527-1566 or 252/522-4676

While it may seem strange to see a store listed as an attraction, this massive Neuse Sports Shop is a major landmark in the Kinston area. Catering to the local sportsman as well as the traveler on their way to the beach, this is the only sporting-goods store in the state where you can try out that new rod and reel right in the store.

Neuse Sports Shop
US 70 East Bypass
Phone: 252/527-5058
nssnc.com

If you like the smell of burning rubber (and, gosh, who doesn't?), you'll want to get over to the Kinston Drag Strip. Enough said.

Highway 11 South, Kinston (Track)
2869 Hull Rd. (Office)
252/527-4337
kdsmotorsports.com

Local Lodging

Hampton Inn
1382 Hwy. 258 S.
Kinston, NC 28501
252/523-1400
hilton.com

Holiday Inn Express Hotel & Suites
1156 Hill Farm Rd.
Kinston, NC 28504
252/252-559-8888
holiday-inn.com

Super 8 Motel
212 E. New Bern Rd. (Hwy. 70)
Kinston, NC 28501
800/800-8000
Super8.com

Dining

Wilbur's BBQ and King's BBQ offer visiting fans a chance to taste quintessential Eastern North Carolina BBQ. This is a vinegar-based pulled pork barbecue, served with hush puppies and two vegetables (don't tell the USDA, but in North Carolina, macaroni and cheese is a vegetable). You'll need to wash it all down with sweet tea. Don't order iced tea, it's just "tea," and it will be sweet. Order "unsweet" if you can't take a healthy dose of sugar.

King's Restaurant & Catering
405 E. New Bern Rd.
252/527-2101
kingsbbq.com

Wilbur's BBQ
4172 US Highway 70 E
Goldsboro
919/778-5218

King's Restaurant
910 W. Vernon Ave.
Phone: 252/527-1661
kingsbbq.com

For more info on these and other attractions and lodging, see **visitkinston.com**.

New Bern

Current Team: None

Former Teams: New Bern Truckers, North Carolina League (1902); New Bern, Eastern Carolina League (1908); New Bern Bears, Coastal Plain League (1934-1936); New Bern Bears, Coastal Plain League (1937-1941, 1946-1951)

Source of the Handy CPL Beer Truck — Just Not Here Anymore

New Bern has a charming, walkable little downtown that leads right up to the waterfront, and it's home to North Carolina's first capital building, as Tryon Palace served as the governor's mansion and as the colonial capital. New Bern was also once one of the cornerstone franchises in the old Coastal Plain League. The name Bears (bern is German for bear) was synonymous with baseball during that league's on-and-off history, and the name is now carried by the New Bern High School athletic teams.

What New Bern doesn't have as of 2008 is a baseball team. We've included them, nonetheless, out of respect for their significant place in the history of the old Coastal Plain League and, to a lesser degree, their more recent unsuccessful foray into the new Coastal Plain League. And, New Bern is a lovely town that is certainly worth a visit if you are in Kinston or someplace else "Down East" looking for a day trip.

Like the league itself, the New Bern Bears began as a semi-pro operation in 1934, mostly using college players on their summer vacation. After three seasons, the league's owners decided to join the National Association as a Class D minor league.

After five seasons of professional play, the Coastal Plain League (like most of the country's minor leagues) shut down operations as the United States entered World War II. While President Roosevelt encouraged the Major Leagues and all of professional baseball to continue operation for the sake of national morale, a shortage of able-bodied young men forced the suspension of play in many of the country's minor leagues.

The Coastal Plain League resumed operations again after the war, but after six more seasons of mixed results the second incarnation of the league shut down for good following the 1951 campaign.

New Bern has not hosted minor-league baseball since. But, in the meantime, the town has come full circle. They had a team for a few years in the new Coastal Plain League, a summer-collegiate circuit like the original CPL, but they're out of the game again.

The Bears' former home field, Kafer Park, still sees some baseball, but it was not a realistic option to host the CPL club. It's sandwiched onto a small lot, with odd dimensions and no room to build the type of grandstand or other support facilities that even a summer-collegiate team would warrant these days.

So, instead, the new CPL era in New Bern began with a team playing at New Bern High School some distance from the quaint downtown. This, of course, meant no beer sales. And, while many of the CPL's teams have had success with historical minor-league names, New Bern High had already laid claim to the nickname Bears. So, New Bern's ownership group, Sabrina and Steve Bengel, opted for a whole new identity as the River Rats.

And a whole new identity had seemed truly promising when New Bern first petitioned for an expansion franchise. There was talk of a local foundation financing a new multi-million-dollar ballpark near New Bern's redeveloped waterfront. Sadly, the new ballpark never materialized and, like the CPL's other teams that play in high-school or amateur facilities, this franchise struggled to match the level of business success achieved by clubs playing in minor league-style stadiums; at the end of the 2007 the Bengels threw in the towel.

This community would seem to stack up fairly well with some of the league's smaller cities, such as Edenton, and one can only hope the community comes to understand what a tremendous asset this team could be to the area's quality of life and tourism in a new downtown ballpark.

If you'd like to see what once was New Bern's "downtown" ballpark, old Kafer Park is pretty easy to find. Just start from the circle in front of the Tryon Palace and head straight north, away from the water, on George Street. Eventually, the ballfield will be on your left with a cemetery on your right.

If you're interested in seeing the more recent CPL park, you can head south from town for a few miles on US 17, and keep your eyes open for New Bern High School. You'll likely be disappointed, though, as this is simply a run-of-the-mill high school field. Your time would be better spent strolling around New Bern's downtown.

Author's Note

In addition to North Carolina's former colonial capital building and a beautiful waterfront, New Bern is home to Maola Dairy. During the CPL's expansion era in the late '90s, Maola supplied the CPL's teams with a key ingredient: beer coolers. To be more exact, surplus refrigerated truck bodies. When the league started up, most of the ballparks had not seen beer sales in many years, if ever. There certainly were no walk-in coolers or draft beer equipment in place. But, those of us in the league office felt that beer, and specifically draft beer, was a key to attracting fans and creating a credible minor-league atmosphere in our ballparks. So, we borrowed from Miles Wolff's bag of tricks and started buying old milk-truck bodies.

You see, the back end of a milk truck is in fact a free-standing refrigerator on wheels. Remove the wheels, and you've got a cut-rate draft beer cooler. Mounted on cinder blocks or a concrete slab, you could simply plug it in, run some taps through the side wall, build a tiki bar-style serving area in front, and you have a perfect little beer garden. This worked especially well in the cities like Wilson, where there was a great deal of concern about introducing beer sales to previously dry ballparks. The milk trucks let us create beer-serving areas separated from the main concessions and seating areas.

Getting these milk-truck bodies from New Bern to the ballparks wasn't always a simple process. It certainly was an adventure when I picked up a milk body headed to Florence, S.C. With a rented full-size pickup truck, I headed from Raleigh to New Bern, where the Maola folks sold me a milk body and were kind enough to load it onto a borrowed trailer. This should have been my first clue that trouble lay ahead: they used a crane to load it up.

The trailer I borrowed was designed for moving these types of boxes and consisted primarily of a pair of steel beams, two axles, and four wheels. The milk box had been loaded near the back of this nearly 30-foot-long trailer. As I started down the winding two-lane state roads along the North Carolina coast, the truck's transmission groaned, the box wobbled and bounced, and the trailer seemed to have its own ideas about which way it was headed.

By the time I reached the ballpark in Florence, my back ached, I was drenched in sweat, and I felt like I had run a marathon. Florence general manager David Sandler and I then began to debate how we were going to get the box off the trailer. This is when I realized why the people at the dairy had used a crane.

Using scrap wood and cinderblocks, we began the next step of this excruciating process. We destroyed two car jacks, rented two more, and began wrestling the box off the trailer, an inch at a time. Several hours later, when the trailer had been pulled free and we had both risked our lives several times scrambling under the box to place another timber or cinderblock, I faced the long drive back to Wilson and then Raleigh. I had promised to return the trailer that night.

By the next morning, the cooler box was at the ballpark, the good folks in Wilson had their trailer back in front of their shop, and the truck was back at the rental agency, too. I, though, counted myself lucky to have emerged unscathed, and promptly got out of the trucking business for good.

But if you go to the CPL ballparks in Gastonia, Wilson, Wilmington, Florence, or Fayetteville, you can still see a milk-box beer cooler in use. Or, if history is your thing, check out the cooler in Burlington, the granddaddy of them all. That truck cooler has been quenching the thirst of fans at the Burlington Athletic Stadium for nearly 20 years, but remember it was retired from the milk business first. Unlike the others, this one still has its wheels, although they are not visible. But, if you ask the staff to open the outer cooler door, you can still see the taillights.

Where to Eat

For a little something different, try the Cow Café: ice cream is made on the premises, and you'll find a host of cow-themed merchandise. There's a kids' play area, too.

Cow Café
319 Middle St.
252-672-9269

What to Do

TRYON PALACE HISTORIC SITE & GARDEN

This elegant Georgian-style mansion was both home to the British colonial Governor William Tryon as well as the capital of the Colony of North Carolina. Tryon Palace looks as it did in the 18th century and is furnished with an outstanding collection of antiques and art. The grounds are home to a breathtaking botanical garden, and guides in period costume provide historical context and craft demonstrations.

Tryon Palace Historic Site & Garden
610 Pollock St.
252/514-4900
tryonpalace.org

BIRTHPLACE OF PEPSI

Caleb Bradham invented "Brad's Drink" in his pharmacy on this spot.
This carbonated beverage was later renamed Pepsi Cola. Enjoy a cold
soda at the re-created fountain and browse an extensive selection
of souvenirs.

Birthplace of Pepsi
256 Middle St.
252/636-5898
pepsistore.com

Lodging

SHERATON NEW BERN HOTEL & MARINA

This 170-room full service hotel is the signature piece to New Bern's
waterfront redevelopment. With views of the marina on one side and the
historic downtown on the other, you can't go wrong.

Sheraton New Bern Hotel & Marina
100 Middle St.
New Bern, NC 28560
252/638-3585
starwoodhotels.com

HARMONY HOUSE INN

If a bed and breakfast is more your taste, try downtown's largest inn,
with 10 rooms. Located just a couple blocks from the Tryon Palace and
the waterfront, this inn also offers wireless internet in all rooms and a
charming historic place to rest up for another day of baseball.

Harmony House Inn
215 Pollock St.
New Bern, NC 28560
252/636-3810
harmonyhouseinn.com

 **Directions**

From East and West:

Take Route 64 to Route 220 North. Exit at Presnell Street and turn left (westbound) onto Presnell. Take next left onto McCrary Street and follow approximately two miles. Ballpark will be on your right.

From Goldsboro and the West:

Take U.S. 70 East to U.S. Route 70 Business (Vernon Avenue), then take a left on East Street.

From New Bern and the East:

Take U.S. 70 West to Highway 58, where you'll hang a right. Take a right onto Vernon Avenue, then a left on East Street.

From Jacksonville and the South:

Take Highway 258 North and then go right on Business NC-11 (Vernon Avenue). Hang a left on East Street.

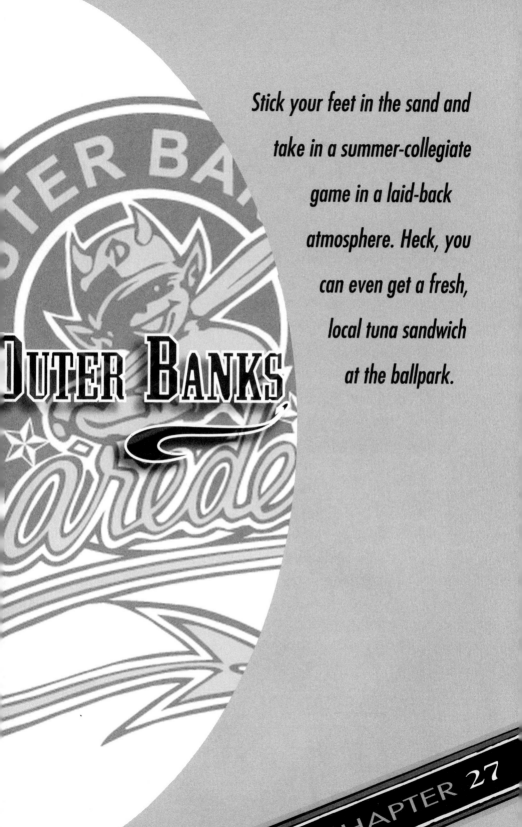

Stick your feet in the sand and take in a summer-collegiate game in a laid-back atmosphere. Heck, you can even get a fresh, local tuna sandwich at the ballpark.

CHAPTER 27

FIRST FLIGHT BASEBALL COMPLEX

Leading Off

Capacity: 1,200

Dimensions: 355L, 368LC, 385C, 368RC, 355R

Current Team: Outer Banks Daredevils, Coastal Plain League (2006-present)

ESSENTIALS

Address: 111 Veterans Drive, Kill Devil Hills
Website: obxdaredevils.com
Phone Number: 252/202-1842 or 252/482-0903

What's a Family Vacation Without Some Baseball?

The Outer Banks Daredevils were born as a charter member of the summer-collegiate Coastal Plain League in 1997. While it was veteran sports executive Blake Cullen who was the team's first owner, it was Warren Spivey who gave the team life.

Shut down after an inaugural year marked by poor attendance and light sponsorship support, the Daredevils were reborn under Spivey, a construction equipment and port-a-potty supplier from Virginia Beach. Warren owned a beach house in the town of Duck on the Outer Banks and, probably not coincidentally, had a son playing college baseball at Virginia Wesleyan. Money was no object for Warren, a blue-collar guy who had built his businesses up to a level where he once said that he couldn't bring himself to sell them, because "they just bring in so much money."

For Warren, the Daredevils were a hobby and a passion, and the bottom line took a backseat to providing his kids first-class travel and accommodations, manning the grill, and riding the umpires. He passed away in 2006 at age 66 after battling cancer for several years, and those of us from the CPL family who had come to appreciate Warren's passion and love for his team were deeply saddened.

The future for baseball in the Outer Banks was thrown into question as Warren's health problems worsened. Without Warren's support and deep pockets, it seemed that the Daredevils might close up shop for the second time in 10 years. But local civic booster Marcus Felton stepped forward to purchase the team in the fall of 2005 and helped ensure its continued presence on the Outer Banks. Felton has lived on the Outer Banks for nearly 25 years, heavily involved in local youth baseball. He is also a past president of the local chamber of commerce and runs a very successful septic pumping business serving the Outer Banks and Ocracoke Island.

The team had played at Coy Tillet Field at Manteo High School until 2006. That field had been upgraded to host a major youth tournament prior to the team's arrival. Tillet Field boasted high-quality lights, a professional-quality playing surface, about 3,000 seats in two big sets of bleachers flanking the field, and a two-story press box and concessions building. It was unmistakable as a high-school field, but it was one heck of a high-school field. (Those wishing to visit Tillet Field need only follow the simplest ballpark directions in history; take 64 East, turn left at the sign for Manteo High School.)

The team now plays at First Flight Baseball Complex in Kill Devil Hills, which seats about 1,200 (including lawn chairs). The team's long-term plans include a new facility with a small covered grandstand, but their current home field also houses the First Flight High School baseball team and is located on the school's campus. This means, of course, there are no beer sales. (A moment of silence, please....)

Bordered by sand dunes, FFBC is nonetheless a refreshing and unusual venue for summer-collegiate baseball with an atmosphere reminiscent of the Cape Cod League, but with a Carolina flavor. You can bury your feet in the sand and take in the game. Folding chairs are recommended as bleacher seating is limited and, as of yet, there are no fixed-back seats available. The concessions range from fruit smoothies to all-beef hot dogs to a sandwich made from fresh, local tuna caught off Oregon Inlet charter boats. Like Coy Tillet Field, this park is unmistakable as a high-school field, but given the surroundings, it's nonetheless a tremendously pleasant place to watch a game and is more accessible to the bulk of the beach visitors than the facility in Manteo.

After the game, enjoy the laid-back local lifestyle. The Outer Banks have fantastic restaurants. The normal vacation day consists of spending the day at the beach, then wrapping up the day with a lavish meal and drinks. For a relaxed atmosphere, try the Black Pelican in Kitty Hawk or the fresh local steamed or raw varieties of seafood at Goombay's Grill & Raw Bar in Kill Devil Hills. If you're looking for some nightlife, hit the late-night action at Kelly's Restaurant & Tavern in Nags Head. The Jolly Roger in Kill Devil Hills is the place to catch breakfast the morning after, with $1.99 two-egg breakfast specials.

This is certainly not the finest ballpark in the state, and the Outer Banks are well off the beaten path. But the remote location is part of the area's charm, and if you are looking to take a beach vacation as part of your baseball trip, the easy-going, family-friendly Outer Banks might just be perfect.

First Flight Baseball Complex hosts the Dare Devils and the local high school team.
Photo courtesy of the Outer Banks Dare Devils.

Lodging

Affordable lodging can be found at the Holiday Inn Express in Kitty Hawk. If you are looking for oceanfront accommodations, try the Best Western Ocean Reef or Ramada Plaza, both located in Nags Head. Other local attractions in Manteo include the North Carolina Aquarium, Lost Colony Outdoor drama, and Elizabethan Gardens; and nearby you'll find the scenic beauty of the Cape Hatteras National Seashore and the iconic historic lighthouses that have been visible symbols of the Outer Banks for over 160 years. Offshore charter fishing trips for tuna, sailfish and blue marlin, and saltwater surf fishing are also popular activities.

Outer Banks Attractions

Although the beaches are the leading destination for many of the millions of Outer Banks visitors every summer, several other worthy attractions draw people away from the ocean views.

THE LOST COLONY

Written by Pulitzer Prize-winning playwright Paul Green, the production tells the story of the English colonists — men, women, and children who came to the New World in search of a better life, struggled to make a home, and then vanished without a trace. The Lost Colony is an American original dating to 1937 with a total attendance of more than 4 million over the years. The Lost Colony also produces other seasonal events, including a children's theater and a Broadway musical.

Located at the Waterside Theatre in Fort Raleigh National Historic Site on Roanoke Island, the production runs from early June to mid-August.

The Lost Colony
Fort Raleigh National Historic Site on Roanoke Island
866/468-7630
thelostcolony.org

NORTH CAROLINA AQUARIUM ON ROANOKE ISLAND
The North Carolina Aquarium on Roanoke Island presents the aquatic environments of coastal Carolina through its theme, "Water of The Outer Banks." The aquarium's variety of exhibits features coastal freshwater river otters, turtles, and American alligators, as well as saltwater habitats from grass flats to Gulf Stream waters. Watch as fish and sharks cruise by the 35-foot long viewing window of the 285,000-gallon "Graveyard of the Atlantic" tank. History buffs will marvel at the one-third-scale replica of the USS Monitor.

Located just off of Highway 64/264 on Airport Road on the north end of Roanoke Island, the Aquarium is open daily year-round.

North Carolina Aquarium on Roanoke Island
252/473-3494
ncaquariums.com

THE ELIZABETHAN GARDENS
Flower-bordered walkways, antique garden statuary, and majestic trees greet visitors at this 16th-century pleasure garden created by The Garden Club of North Carolina as a living memorial to the lost colonists. Highlights include the thatched gazebo, a Shakespearean herb garden, and formal sunken gardens. Possibly the most underappreciated attraction on the Outer Banks, these impeccable gardens are a serene change of pace that can be appreciated by all.

The Elizabethan Gardens
1411 National Park Dr.
252/473-3234
elizabethangardens.org

Lodging and Dining
Recommendations for lodging and dining are mentioned higher up in this chapter. Given the extent of tourism in the Outer Banks area, your choices are good and many. An especially good resource for visitors is **outerbanks.org**.

 **Directions**

From the South:

Take US-64 East to Manns Harbor/Manteo. Cross the Manns Harbor Bridge to stop light. The road becomes the 158 bypass. Stay on bypass for 10 miles. Turn left onto Colington Road (Dairy Queen on right). At first light, turn left onto Veterans Drive. Bear right at circle and go to end of street. The ballpark will be on your left.

From the West:

Take I-95 to Hwy. 58 East to Bowers Hill to I-64 toward Virginia Beach. Take Exit 158 (Nags Head). Cross over Wright Brothers Memorial Bridge and go approximately eight miles. Turn right on Colington Road. At first light, turn left onto Veterans Drive. Follow from above.

From North:

Take I-64 through the Hampton Roads Tunnel. Take Hwy. 158 East exit and follow 158 to the Outer Banks, crossing over Wright Brothers Memorial Bridge. Continue from above.

APPENDIX
North Carolina Division I College Baseball

Appalachian State University
City: Boone
Nickname: Mountaineers
Head Coach: Chris Pollard
Website: *GoASU.com*
Conference: Southern
Phone: 828/262-2845
Home Field: Don Beaver Field at Jim and Bettie Smith Stadium
Location: West of the Newland Drive / Stadium Drive intersection

Campbell University
City: Buies Creek
Nickname: Camels
Head Coach: Chip Smith
Website: *GoCamels.com*
Conference: Atlantic Sun
Phone: 910/814-4367
Home Field: Taylor Field
Location: East of Main Street and north of Howard Drive on NC-1531

University of North Carolina at Charlotte
City: Charlotte
Nickname: 49ers
Head Coach: Loren Hibbs
Website: *Charlotte49ers.com*
Conference: Atlantic 10
Phone: 704/687-6312
Home Field: Tom & Lib Phillips Field at Robert and Mariam Hayes Stadium
Location: Just east of Phillips Road, northwest of Cameron Boulevard

Davidson College
City: Davidson
Nickname: Wildcats
Head Coach: Dick Cooke
Website: *DavidsonWildcats.com*
Conference: Southern
Phone: 704/894-2123
Home Field: Wilson Stadium
Location: 202 Martin Court Drive

Duke University
City: Durham
Nickname: Blue Devils
Head Coach: Sean McNally
Website: *GoDuke.com*
Conference: Atlantic Coast
Phone: 919/684-8708
Home Field: Jack Coombs Field
Location: Along Whitford Drive, east of Science Drive

East Carolina University
City: Greenville
Nickname: Pirates
Head Coach: Billy Godwin
Website: *ECUPirates.com*
Conference: C-USA
Phone: 252/328-4523
Home Field: Clark-LeClair Stadium
Location: Just east of S. Charles Street (NC 43), north of Greenville Boulevard (U.S. 264)

Elon University
City: Elon
Nickname: Phoenix
Head Coach: Mike Kennedy
Website: *ElonPhoenix.com*
Conference: Southern
Phone: 336/278-6741
Home Field: Latham Park
Location: East of N. Williamson Avenue and north of Phoenix Drive

High Point University
Nickname: Panthers
City: High Point
Head Coach: Sal Bando Jr.
Website: *HighPointPanthers.com*
Conference: Big South
Phone: 336/841-4605
Home Field: Coy O. Williard Sr. Stadium
Location: Just east of W. College Drive, south of Lexington Avenue

University of North Carolina
City: Chapel Hill
Nickname: Tar Heels
Head Coach: Mike Fox
Website: *TarHeelBlue.com*
Conference: Atlantic Coast
Phone: 919/962-0084
Home Field: Boshamer Stadium
Location: Along Ridge Road, just east of Stadium Drive

University of North Carolina Asheville
City: Asheville
Nickname: Bulldogs
Head Coach: Willie Stewart
Website: *UNCABulldogs.com*
Conference: Big South
Phone: 828/251-6931
Home Field: Greenwood Baseball Field
Location: Southwest of the Division Street / Campus Drive parking areas

University of North Carolina Greensboro
City: Greensboro
Nickname: Spartans
Head Coach: Mike Gaski
Website: *UNCGSpartans.com*
Conference: Southern
Phone: 336/334-5615
Home Field: UNCG Baseball Stadium
Location: Northwest corner of Kenilworth Street and Theta Street

University of North Carolina Wilmington
City: Wilmington
Nickname: Seahawks
Head Coach: Mark Scalf
Website: *UNCWsports.com*
Conference: Colonial Athletic
Phone: 910/962-4099
Home Field: Brooks Field
Location: Along Riegel Road between Hamilton Drive and Walton Drive

North Carolina A&T State University
City: Greensboro
Nickname: Aggies
Head Coach: Keith Shumate
Website: *NCATAggies.com*
Conference: Mid-Eastern Athletic
Phone: 336/334-7141
Home Field: War Memorial Stadium
Location: Along Yanceyville Street, north of E. Lindsay Street.

North Carolina State University
City: Raleigh
Nickname: Wolfpack
Head Coach: Elliot Avent
Website: *GoPack.com*
Conference: Atlantic Coast
Phone: 919/515-1182
Home Field: Doak Field
Location: Along W. Dunn Avenue, north of Sullivan Drive

Western Carolina University
City: Cullowhee
Nickname: Catamounts
Head Coach: Bobby Moranda
Website: *CatamountSports.com*
Phone: 828/227-2339
Home Field: Childress Field at Hennon Stadium
Location: Along Forest Hills Road, northeast of NC 107

Photo Credits

SECTION 1: Charlotte & Westward

1954 Asheville Tourists – Photo courtesy of the Asheville Tourists *p. 5, 15*

Tourists 1968 program – Image courtesy of the Notre Dame Rare Books collection *p. 8*

Downtown Asheville crowd – Photo courtesy of the *Winston-Salem Citizen-Times p. 10-11*

Eddie Murray in 1975 – Photo courtesy of Miles Wolff *p. 12*

McCormick Field entrance – Photo courtesy of Miles Wolff *p. 12*

Biltmore House – Photo by E.M. Ball, courtesy of the U.S. Army *p. 17*

Crockett Park firefighter – Photo by Mark B. Sluder / *Charlotte Observer*, courtesy of the Robinson-Spangler Carolina Room, Public Library of Charlotte & Mecklenburg County *p. 27, 32*

Crockett Park aerial after the fire - Photo by Mark B. Sluder / *Charlotte Observer;* courtesy of the Robinson-Spangler Carolina Room, Public Library of Charlotte & Mecklenburg County *p. 28*

Frances Crockett on the mound – Photo courtesy of the Charlotte Knights *p. 34*

Crockett Park night game – Photo courtesy of University of North Carolina Charlotte – Sumner Collection *p. 36*

Hayes Stadium grandstand – Photo courtesy of University of North Carolina Charlotte Athletic Department *p. 40*

Hornets 1909 program – Image courtesy of the Notre Dame Rare Books collection *p. 41*

Tony Oliva swinging – *Charlotte Observer* photo courtesy of the Robinson-Spangler Carolina Room, Public Library of Charlotte & Mecklenburg County *p. 42*

Hornets 1963 program – Image courtesy of the Notre Dame Rare Books Collection *p. 43*

1991 Gastonia Rangers program – Image courtesy of the Notre Dame Rare Books collection *p. 53*

Dale Earnhardt Jr. at Kannapolis – Photo courtesy of the Kannapolis Intimadators *p. 73*

Don Pagett Salisbury score card – Image courtesy of the Notre Dame Rare Books collection *p. 78, 80*

Newman Park infield – Photo courtesy of Dennis Bastien *p. 78*

Newman Park exterior – Photo courtesy of Dennis Bastien *p. 80*

Two Owls ballplayers – Photo courtesy of the Forest City Owls *p. 83*

Smoky Burgess memorabilia – Exhibited at the North Carolina Baseball Museum in Wilson *p. 84*

1910 Forest City ball club – Photo courtesy of the Forest City Owls *p. 86*

1949 Rutherford County Owls – Photo courtesy of the Forest City Owls *p. 88*

SECTION 2: Greensboro-Piedmont

Greensboro War Memorial Stadium from overhead – Photo courtesy of the Greensboro Grasshoppers *p. 102*

Greensboro War Memorial Stadium grandstand – Photo courtesy of the Greensboro Grasshoppers *p. 104*

Burlington Athletic Stadium overhead – Photo courtesy of the Burlington Royals *p. 126*

Latham Park infield and grandstand – Photo courtesy of Elon University p. *137, 140*

THE MOVIE

SECTION 3: Raleigh-Durham-Triangle

JACK MCKEON

Jack McKeon in Greensboro – Photos courtesy of Elon University *p. 283, 284*

SECTION 4: Down East & The Coast

Catfish Hunter display – Exhibited at Carolina Baseball Museum in Wilson *p. 301, 309*
Hicks Field infield – Photo courtesy of Edenton Steamers Baseball *p. 302*
Hicks Field panoramic – Photo courtesy of Edenton Steamers Baseball *p. 304-305*
Dusk at Hicks Field – Photo by Bill Miller *p. 305*
Youngsters and Steamers on the field – Photo courtesy of Edenton Steamers Baseball
   p. 306
Alex Pascual batting – Photo courtesy of Edenton Steamers Baseball *p. 307*
Historic Hicks Field scoreboard – Photo courtesy of Edenton Steamers Baseball *p. 308*
Brooks Field – Photo courtesy of UNC-Wilmington Sharks *p. 313, 320*
Action at Buck Hardee Field – Photo courtesy of the Wilmington Sharks *p. 314*
1995 Roosters program – Image courtesy of the Notre Dame Rare Books collection *p. 316*
Brooks Field under the lights - Photo courtesy of UNC Wilmington *p. 322-323*
Grainger Stadium overhead view – Photo courtesy of the Kinston Indians
   p. 343, 348-349
Grainger Stadium field level – Photo courtesy of the Kinston Indians *p. 344*
First Flight Baseball Complex – Photo courtesy of the Outer Banks Daredevils *p. 362*
Daredevils sign on fence – Photo courtesy of the Outer Banks Daredevils *p. 364*

All other photos from **BallparkDigest.com**.

About the Author

Mark Cryan spent four years as the General Manager of the Burlington Indians, the Cleveland Indians' affiliate in the rookie-level Appalachian League. During his time with the team, community and charity efforts were enhanced, and the club was honored with the 2004 Freitas Award from Baseball America magazine for long-term franchise excellence.

Mark currently works as Athletic Director for the Burlington Recreation & Parks Department, serves as an adjunct professor at Elon University, and teaches on-line for the University of California Davis Extension. His earlier sports management experience includes stints with the Raleigh IceCaps hockey team, and in baseball the Fayetteville Generals and origination of the summer collegiate Coastal Plain League.

A graduate of Hamilton College in upstate New York, Mark holds an MBA from North Carolina Central University in Durham.

Index